ABRAHAM LINCOLN
AND THE BIBLE

ABRAHAM LINCOLN AND THE BIBLE

A COMPLETE COMPENDIUM

GORDON LEIDNER

Southern Illinois University Press
Carbondale

Southern Illinois University Press
www.siupress.com

26 25 24 23   5 4 3 2

Library of Congress Cataloging-in-Publication Data
Names: Leidner, Gordon, 1954– author.
Title: Abraham Lincoln and the Bible : a complete compendium / Gordon Leidner.
Identifiers: LCCN 2022044204 (print) | LCCN 2022044205 (ebook) | ISBN 9780809339006 (paperback) | ISBN 9780809339013 (ebook)
Subjects: LCSH: Lincoln, Abraham, 1809-1865—Religion. | Presidents—Religious life—United States. | United States—Politics and government—Civil War, 1861-1865. | BISAC: BIOGRAPHY & AUTOBIOGRAPHY / Presidents & Heads of State | RELIGION / Biblical Reference / Quotations
Classification: LCC E457.2 L449 2023 (print) | LCC E457.2 (ebook) | DDC 973.7092—dc23/eng/20221028
LC record available at https://lccn.loc.gov/2022044204
LC ebook record available at https://lccn.loc.gov/2022044205

Printed on recycled paper ♻

Southern Illinois University System

For my heroes, my sons.

Daniel Philip Leidner, Michael Ryan Leidner,

and

←　❋　→

Jason Michael Leidner

1985–2020

←　　→

And he said to him, "You shall love the Lord your God with all your heart and with all your soul and with all your mind. This is the great and first commandment. And a second is like it: You shall love your neighbor as yourself." —Matthew 22:37–39

Jason, you loved well.

CONTENTS

Acknowledgments   ix

Introduction   1

1. Annals of the Poor: Origins of Lincoln's Calvinist Roots   9

2. The Mind Impelled: New Life in New Salem   21

3. He Will Do for Me Yet: Quoting the Bible for Cause   29

4. Drawing the Sword: Building Lincoln's Biblical Foundation
   against Slavery   43

5. A House Divided: Debating Slavery as a Moral Evil   56

6. A Humbled Instrument: Rise to the Presidency   81

7. The Fiery Trial: Transforming the Purpose of the War   94

8. To Highly Resolve: The Tide of War Changes   108

9. The Will of God: Seeking God's Purpose for America   118

10. The Judgments of the Lord: Lincoln's Sermon for America, the
    Second Inaugural Address   132

Conclusion   140

Appendix: Lincoln's Use of the Bible in the *Collected Works*   149

Notes   203

Bibliography   225

Index   235

Gallery of illustrations beginning on page 71

ACKNOWLEDGMENTS

A number of friends and colleagues have contributed generously of their time and knowledge in helping to bring this book to completion. I would like to express my special thanks to the following people.

Michael Burlingame, Jonathan W. White, and Bill Harris, fellow board members of the Abraham Lincoln Institute, for their mentorship and encouragement in my various writing projects over the course of the last twenty years.

James Cornelius, executive editor of the *Journal of the Abraham Lincoln Association*, who was the first to suggest that my mass of research notes be organized into book form rather than a journal article.

My good friends Michael (Buck) Black, Glenn Hickman, and Leo Vadala who carefully read the manuscript and suggested invaluable improvements and clarifications. Each of these men have been pastors or elders in Christian churches, and are well versed in not only the Bible, but the distinctives of Reformed theology.

Southern Illinois University Press executive editor Sylvia Rodrigue, who enthusiastically embraced the project and patiently molded the work into a book I trust will be useful to scholars, students, and the general public who seek to better understand America's greatest president. Also, my thanks to editorial, design, and production manager Linda Jorgensen Buhman, project editor Khara Lukancic, marketing manager Chelsey J. Harris, copyeditor Lisa Marty, and editorial assistant Sarah Jilek for their care, skill, and absolute professionalism in all things.

Library technical assistants Roberta Fairburn and Meghan Harmon of the Abraham Lincoln Presidential Library and Museum in Springfield, Illinois, for their relentless pursuit of the elusive Lincoln-related images.

Stacy Humphreys, chief of interpretation and resource management of the Abraham Lincoln Birthplace National Historical Park, in Hodgenville, Kentucky, for her cheerful cooperation in all things related to the Thomas Lincoln family Bible.

And most of all to the love of my life, my beautiful wife, Jean. As with everything else of value I've ever accomplished, she has been my ardent cheerleader, supporter, and adviser. In this work, she was often successful in helping me find two-thirds of Mark Twain's keys to good writing, i.e., "the exact word" and "the clarity of statement." But Twain's third key, "a touch of good grammar for picturesqueness" required both Jean's skills *and* the power of the talented editorial staff at SIU Press.

ABRAHAM LINCOLN
AND THE BIBLE

INTRODUCTION

But where shall wisdom be found? And where is the place
of understanding?

—Job 28:12.

President Abraham Lincoln walked solemnly through the private corridor that led from his office to the family living quarters in the White House. The war news was weighing heavily upon him. Union general Joseph Hooker and the Army of the Potomac had recently suffered a defeat at the Battle of Chancellorsville, Virginia, and the president was grieving deeply for the thirty thousand casualties exacted on the two armies. He had been to the hospitals many times during the war to visit both the Union and Confederate wounded. He had personally witnessed their agony, wept at their bedsides, and held the hands of dying men.

The war had been going on for over two years now, and it seemed there was no end in sight. Lincoln had been unable to find a Union commander who could defeat Confederate general Robert E. Lee in Virginia, and now the War Department told him that the Confederates might invade Maryland again. Even the war in the West was progressing slowly, and the powerful Union army under General U. S. Grant seemed stymied. The campaign to take the last Confederate stronghold on the Mississippi River, Vicksburg, had dragged on for months. Grant's army was bogged down in a siege of that city, and no one knew how long the siege would last or how many thousands of casualties would result.

Lincoln walked into the family quarters, where Mary stood in the middle of the room with her friend and seamstress Mrs. Elizabeth Keckley, who was fitting a dress on the First Lady. As soon as they saw him, they knew he was discouraged. He walked slowly to the sofa and threw himself on it in a dejected manner, "like a tired child," Mrs. Keckley later recalled, and covered his face with his huge, powerful hands.

According to Mrs. Keckley's remembrance of that day, Mrs. Lincoln, observing her husband's troubled look, asked: "Where have you been, Father?"

"To the War Department," was reportedly Lincoln's brief, almost sullen answer.

"Any news?" Mrs. Lincoln asked.

"Yes, plenty of news, but no good news," was Lincoln's reply. "It is dark, dark everywhere."

Lincoln reached for a small Bible from a stand near the head of the sofa, Keckley remembered, and began reading.

The Lincolns had several Bibles in the White House, each in a convenient place so that they could be easily reached by the president. He liked to read the Bible every day when he could, especially before breakfast or at lunchtime. The Bibles in the living quarters were kept for his devotions, and the one he kept in his office was for quick reference when he was writing letters or important documents.

Sixteen-year-old Julia Taft, who babysat the Lincoln boys and her brothers in the White House, had often observed Lincoln reading the Bible in the family living quarters. She noted that he always read it in a relaxed manner, with one leg crossed over the other, absorbed in it as if he was "enjoying a good book." Mrs. Keckley was also familiar with this habit of the president, and was not surprised that Lincoln became quickly engaged in his Bible reading.[1]

Mrs. Keckley relates what happened next:

> A quarter of an hour passed, and on glancing at the sofa the face of the President seemed more cheerful. The dejected look was gone, and the countenance was lighted up with new resolution and hope. The change was so marked that I could not but wonder at it, and wonder led to the desire to know what book of the Bible afforded so much comfort to the reader.
>
> Making the search for a missing article an excuse, I walked gently around the sofa, and looking into the open book, I discovered that Mr. Lincoln was reading that divine comforter, Job. He read with Christian eagerness, and the courage and hope that he derived from the inspired pages made him a new man.[2]

Lincoln's most significant achievements are widely recognized. He successfully led the nation through the Civil War, which prevented the breakup of the Union and another possible failure of democratic government on Earth. He also transformed the purpose of the Civil War from one with the single objective of preserving the republic to one with the additional goal of abolishing slavery. This transformation was especially significant because at the inception of the great American conflict, most of the northern people went to war for the exclusive purpose of preserving the Union rather than eliminating slavery.[3]

Today, although a number of leadership theories can be applied to Lincoln, he is frequently identified as a transformational leader. Transformational leaders are unique in their ability to earn the trust, loyalty, and respect of followers and raise their morality level—inspiring them to reach a higher moral plane and make personal sacrifices to benefit the larger group or society. It was primarily because of his ability to inspire the people of the northern states into pursuing the higher purpose of abolishing slavery that Lincoln is often described as a transformational leader.[4]

How did Lincoln accomplish this great inspirational feat? Even though leadership had been discussed by individuals such as Plato, Sun Tzu, and Machiavelli over the course of history, the academic field of leadership studies was not developed until the early twentieth century. Although Lincoln was an avid student of all things—he even checked out a book on military strategy from the Library of Congress during the war—books that addressed the subject of leadership would have been difficult for him to find.[5]

Charles Francis Adams, son of one American president and grandson of another, acknowledged Lincoln's limitations. Adams was Lincoln's ambassador to Great Britain during the Civil War, and when he first met Lincoln in 1861, he feared that the sixteenth president would be incapable of dealing with the national crisis. Recalling those days twelve years later, Adams said, "I must . . . affirm, without hesitation that, in the history of our government down to this hour, no experiment so rash has ever been made as that of elevating to the head of affairs a man with so little previous preparation for his task as Mr. Lincoln."[6]

Herewith is an intriguing question. How could this self-educated, untrained, inexperienced small-town lawyer from the Illinois prairie attain the astounding results of winning the most desperately fought war in American history, preserving national unity and democratic government, and abolishing the powerful institution of American slavery?[7]

According to three men that knew Lincoln well, it was not because he depended on strategic counsel. His old friend Supreme Court justice David Davis "asked him [Lincoln] once about his Cabinet: he said he never Consulted his Cabinet. He said they all disagreed so much he would not ask them—he depended on himself—always." One of Lincoln's secretaries, John Hay, said that Lincoln ruled his cabinet with "tyrannous authority," and "the most important things he [Lincoln] decides & there is no cavil." Lincoln's close friend Leonard Swett said that "he [Lincoln] would listen to everybody; he would hear everybody; but he rarely, if ever, asked for opinions. . . . As a politician and as president, he arrived at all his conclusions from his own reflections, and when his opinion was once formed, he never doubted that it was right."[8]

Swett mentions Lincoln's reflections. What did Lincoln "reflect" on? What was the source of the wisdom and strength that guided and sustained him through multitudes of military battles, leadership decisions, and political conflicts?

To formulate and review all the possible answers to the question of how Lincoln became a great leader is beyond the scope of any single book. But Lincoln scholar Rev. William E. Barton, who in 1925 published the book that is today acknowledged as the most balanced investigation into Lincoln's religious beliefs, said "he [Lincoln] read the Bible, honored it, quoted it freely, and it became so much a part of him as visibly and permanently to give shape to his literary style and to his habits of thought." Lincoln scholar Earl Schwartz observed that "Lincoln's legacy, far more than any other president, has, over time, become inextricably bound up with the words and themes of the Bible." Many scholars attest to the fact that the Bible had a significant influence on Lincoln, and based on my research into the *Collected Works of Abraham Lincoln* (Roy Basler, ed., nine volumes, with supplement), I have determined that he quoted the Bible more than any other book, including his other favorite, *The Works of William Shakespeare.*[9]

Lincoln scholar Ronald C. White correctly states that the Bible's influence in nineteenth-century America was of extraordinary significance and cannot be over-emphasized. Consequently, in this work I will focus on Lincoln and the Bible. In each chapter of the biography, I will take into consideration the following questions as we discuss each phase of his life: How was he using the Bible?, What did he say about the Bible and God?, and How was the Bible informing his leadership?[10]

Since there are no documented quotations of the Bible from Lincoln until he moved to Springfield, which is covered in chapter 3, in the first and second chapters I will rely primarily on anecdotal information from those who knew him. In the remaining chapters I will use Lincoln's own words to answer these questions.

In the conclusion I will briefly discuss Lincoln's personal faith in his presidential years. However, I will not attempt to answer the question of whether Lincoln was a Christian. I will instead follow Lincoln's suggestion from his 1846 *Handbill Replying to Religious Infidelity,* and "[Leave] the higher matter of eternal consequences between him and his Maker." The debate as to whether Lincoln was a Christian is a rock on which the ships of many historians have foundered over the course of the last one and a half centuries.[11]

The competing claims about his personal piety, originating with Lincoln's contemporaries and proliferated by scholars today, are always interesting, but inevitably inconclusive. With the exception of a brief but necessary discussion in chapter 2 of what some of his colleagues said about this subject, and two anecdotes from his best friend Joshua Speed in the conclusion, we will let Lincoln's words speak for themselves when it comes to his personal religious beliefs.

In this book Lincoln's words are, with a few noted exceptions, drawn from the *Collected Works of Abraham Lincoln*. Lincoln's statements of a religious nature that are not from the *Collected Works* (hereafter referred to as *CW*) are identified in the biography's endnotes as "non-*CW*" sourced.

Lincoln quoted or alluded to scripture from sixteen books of the New Testament and sixteen from the Old Testament. Slightly less than one half of the scriptures Lincoln used were from the New Testament. The New Testament books Lincoln quoted most often in the *CW* are the gospels: Matthew, Mark, Luke, and John. The most frequently quoted Old Testament books are Genesis, Psalms, Exodus, and Job. He used all five books of the Pentateuch. Although he rarely quoted the historical books that lie between the Pentateuch and Job, or the major and minor prophets, non-*CW* sources reveal that he was nevertheless familiar with these books, also.

I have often been asked whether Lincoln read the entire Bible. Although no one knows for certain, taking into consideration his ravenous appetite for reading and the fact that the Bible was often one of the few books available to him, it is quite likely he did. Regardless, Lincoln undoubtedly read much more of the Bible than he quoted in the *CW*. It is reasonable to assume that the scripture used in the *CW* is indicative of the books of the Bible that Lincoln was the most familiar with.

HOW THE BOOK IS ORGANIZED

Biography

The biography explores Lincoln's life through the lens of the Bible—how he used it, what he said about it and God, and how his leadership was informed by it. Each statement from the *CW* that includes a direct quote of scripture is underlined and the associated Bible passage is specified immediately afterward within brackets. If Lincoln's quoted material is a paraphrase or allusion to scripture, the succeeding note in brackets starts with "allusion to" the implied Bible passage. If the scripture is from more than one book in the Bible, as is frequently the case when scripture from the synoptic gospels is quoted, I credit as the source that book of the Bible whose text most closely matches

Lincoln's statement. All scriptures used by Lincoln in the *CW*, plus alternate or supplemental scriptural references, are documented in the appendix. Since Lincoln used the King James Bible, this translation is always used and quoted. All quoted material will retain original spellings and punctuation, without the addition of sic for misspellings.

A few Bible scholars have criticized Lincoln's way of quoting the Bible, saying that he did not always use scripture in a manner consistent with its original intent. As an example, in his second inaugural address Lincoln employed the scripture, <u>Woe unto the world because of offences! for it must needs be that offences come; but woe to that man by whom the offence cometh!</u> [Matthew 18:7] in a manner that does not measure up to modern exegesis of that passage. Today, Bible scholars point out that the Greek word for "offences," as well as the context indicate that Lincoln should have used a more severe example of the notion of sin than the one he did—which had to do with those who tempt little children. However, Lincoln was not a Bible scholar—he read few, if any, books about theology—but was instead a man who had read the Bible a great deal and drawn his own conclusions. Taking into consideration the fact that he attended primitive frontier churches when a youth, he did not hear much in the way of erudite exposition of biblical text until he was under the pastoral care of Rev. James Smith at the First Presbyterian Church in Springfield, Illinois, and Rev. Phineas D. Gurley at the New York Avenue Presbyterian Church in Washington. Consequently, when he found a scripture in his King James Bible that he thought was a pertinent illustration of the point he wanted to make, he simply used it—and his audience understood what he meant.[12]

Many Lincoln scholars have elaborated on his various purposes for quoting the Bible. I have my own interpretations, and when I believe it is necessary for clarifying his intentions, I will point out when I think Lincoln is using a specific scripture for moral argument, expression of his personal faith, political allegory or metaphor, theological illustration, or exhibitive purpose (oratorical style, rhetorical emphasis, humor, sarcasm, etc.).[13]

Approximately one third of the nonsecular uses of scripture (see below) in the appendix were employed by Lincoln for the purpose of supporting moral arguments. These moral arguments were primarily either against the evil of slavery, in support of the rights of Black people, or in support of the temperance movement. His most persistent use of scripture in a public forum began with his attack on the Kansas-Nebraska Act in 1854, continued through his debates with Stephen A. Douglas in 1858, and pressed on into his follow-up attacks on slavery in 1859. Between his temperance address in 1843 and the passage of the Kansas-Nebraska Act in 1853, Lincoln made the fewest public references to the

Bible. This is because during that era he made no significant political effort in support of a moral cause.[14]

Appendix

Lincoln quoted or alluded to the Bible 201 times in the *CW*, all of which are tabulated in the appendix.

The appendix includes 167 instances of scripture quoted or alluded to by Lincoln from the *CW* that he used in a nonsecular manner for expression of his personal faith, moral argument, political allegory, theological illustration, or exhibitive purposes. It also includes thirty-four *CW*-sourced scripture quoted by Lincoln in his 1858 "First Lecture on Discoveries and Inventions." This lecture was presented by Lincoln for the secular purpose of documenting what the Bible reveals about the timeline of when various inventions and discoveries were made.

The 167 nonsecular references to the Bible in the appendix include either *direct quotes from the Bible*: such as "<u>A house divided against itself cannot stand</u>" (Mark 3:25); *strong allusions, usually to specific scripture*: "But in the right <u>to eat the bread, without leave of anybody else, which his own hand earns</u>, he is my equal" (allusion to Psalm 128:2); and *less definite allusions, usually to multiple scriptures*: "Meanwhile we must work earnestly <u>in the best light He gives us</u>" (allusion to Job 29:3, Psalm 119:105, and 2 Samuel 22:29).

The appendix does not include biblical language or phrases that were only two or three words long *and* questionable as to whether Lincoln was using them in a conscious reference to the Bible. For instance, the phrase "and this, too, *shall pass away*," is not included even though "shall pass away" can be found in different books of the Bible such as Jeremiah 8:13 and Matthew 24:35. It is not included because the context in which Lincoln used the phrase in *CW* 3.481–482 indicated he may have taken it from one of the ancient eastern fables instead of scripture.

To assemble the appendix, I began with what other scholars had documented in previous works and then added over fifty additional instances of scripture from the *CW* that had not been previously identified as biblical references. Preeminent among these are Lincoln's ten references in the *CW* to Psalm 128:2 ("For thou shalt eat the labour of thine hands"). Although Psalm 128:2 is different from the often quoted "in the sweat of thy face shalt thou eat bread" from Genesis 3:19, Lincoln used them interchangeably. Other examples from the list of unrecognized scriptures are simply Bible passages that had been previously identified but that were not fully documented. Foremost among these are *CW*'s thirteen uses of the "house divided" scripture (Mark 3:25). Philip Ostergard, in his book *The Inspired Wisdom of Abraham Lincoln*, itemized many scriptural passages Lincoln used, but documented only a single instance of the "house divided" (in *CW* 1:315) and simply said it was the "first of many uses." In this book I document every instance from the *CW*. Most of the remaining unrecognized scriptures are brief allusions to the Bible that Lincoln made in letters or speeches that, although easily overlooked today, were useful for Lincoln's quick political allegories or exhibitive illustrations.[15]

Biblical Language and Phrases

In addition to Lincoln's 201 uses of scripture, he also employed biblical language—those instances when he talked *about* God and the Bible or invoked God's name but did not quote scripture. This use of language occurred hundreds of times in the *CW*, and I incorporate many of these expressions into the biography to illustrate Lincoln's thoughts about God and the Bible. But since they are not scripture, they are not included in the appendix.[16]

Of course, there are sometimes gray areas between the less definite allusions and biblical language or phrases. There are also scripture that have similar intent as statements made by Lincoln (such as Psalm 32:8 for his famous second inaugural statement of "As God gives us to see the right"), but in my opinion are missing the convincing word(s) necessary to include them in the appendix. No doubt some readers may think more should have been included as quotable scripture, and some less. I can only say that I have used my best judgment.

It is my hope that *Abraham Lincoln and the Bible: A Complete Compendium* will serve as a sound introduction to the study of Lincoln's use of the Bible and will facilitate more thorough investigations into Lincoln's leadership and how he was personally transformed by his lifelong study of scripture.

1. ANNALS OF THE POOR

ORIGINS OF LINCOLN'S CALVINIST ROOTS

For I know the thoughts that I think toward you, saith
the Lord, thoughts of peace, and not of evil, to give you
an expected end.

—Jeremiah 29:11

Time What an emty vaper
tis and days how swift they are swift as an indian arr[ow] *[Meter]*
fly on like a shooting star the presant moment Just [is here]
then slides away in h[as]te that we [can] never say they['re ours]
but [only say] th[ey]'re past[1]

Thes verses come from the first page of the *Collected Works of Abraham
Lincoln*. They were written in his copy book when he was fifteen years old and are
therefore the earliest of the future president's known writings. They are taken
from the first two stanzas of an old Isaac Watts hymn entitled "The Shortness
of Life and the Goodness of God."[2]

The first three stanzas of Watts's hymn display a similar spirit to the poem
"Mortality" by Scotsman William Knox, who—from the age of thirty-seven
onward—Lincoln would claim as his favorite. Rather than comparing the exact
words of each poem here, in the table below we will consider their continuity
of thought.[3]

William Knox's entire poem reflects the basic theme that life is short, and
death is sure. Volumes have been written about Lincoln's melancholia in adulthood, his infatuation with death, and the reasons he called Knox's work his
favorite poem. But it has gone largely unobserved that his melancholia was
manifest from the very first page of his school copy book.[4]

The Shortness of Life and the Goodness of God	Mortality
By Isaac Watts	*By William Knox*
Time! what an empty vapour 'tis!	Oh, why should the spirit of mortal be proud?
And days how swift they are!	Like a swift-fleeting meteor, a fast-flying cloud,
Swift as an Indian arrow flies	A flash of the lightning, a break of the wave,
Or like a shooting star.	He passes from life to his rest in the grave.
[The present moments just appear,	The leaves of the oak and the willow shall fade,
Then slide away in haste,	Be scattered around, and together be laid;
That we can never say, "They're here,"	And the young and the old, and the low and the high
But only say, "They're past."]	Shall moulder to dust, and together shall lie
[Our life is ever on the wing,	The infant a mother attended and loved,
And death is ever nigh;	The mother that infant's affection who proved,
The moment when our lives begin	The husband that mother and infant who blest
We all begin to die.]	Each, all, are away to their dwelling of rest.

The depth of his melancholia is made even clearer by the fact that Lincoln chose to copy only the first two stanzas of Watts's hymn, and ignored the denouement, which begins with the fourth verse. It is here that Watts soars from despair to the message of Christian hope. In verses four to seven Watts supplies the answers to life's deepest questions. "Yet, mighty God" provides for us; his sovereign mercy "finds us food"; he points out the road that "leads our souls above"; his mercy "never knows a bound," and at last—after we have closed our eyes—in heaven we will praise him, "till time and nature dies."[5]

Why did fifteen-year-old Abraham Lincoln focus only on the first verses of the Watts hymn, a song based on the Bible that he had probably heard sung all the way through dozens of times at the Little Pigeon Creek Baptist Church? Abe's mother had taught him to revere the Bible as the word of the Lord, and one of her dying requests to her nine-year-old son was that he would "reverence and worship God." But by the time he scrawled these verses six years later, he had become more of a jester than a worshiper. After church services, he would stand on a stump to mimic the preacher and repeat the sermon, virtually word for word, to the children who sat on the ground around him and did "the Crying."[6]

Abe's ability to repeat the sermon word for word is not only a demonstration of his exceptionally powerful memory, but also an indication that he had listened carefully. According to Abe's cousin Dennis Hanks, Nancy Lincoln had raised her children on the Bible, repeating the Bible stories to them "when very young," helping them to "study it & the stories in it and all that was morally & affectionate in it," and then taught them to read using the Bible. Dennis would later recall that Abraham was "much moved by the stories." But Abe's jocoseness at the age of fifteen leads us to ask the question: What would become of the biblical faith of this boy who had stood by his mother's side six years prior, in their one room cabin, and watched helplessly as she died a horrible, retching death?[7]

The answer to this question is a long one, and begins with his parents, Thomas and Nancy Hanks Lincoln.

Abraham Lincoln's father, Thomas, was born in Virginia on January 6, 1778. Thomas moved to Kentucky in 1782 with his parents, Abraham and Berhsheba, two sisters, and two brothers. Like every preceding Lincoln ancestor since the family immigrated to America in 1637, Thomas's father was a man of respectable means who had a reputation for integrity and public service. Unfortunately, father Abraham was killed by Indians in May of 1786, and if it were not for the straight shooting of Thomas's oldest brother Mordecai, eight-year-old Thomas would have been killed or captured, too.[8]

By the rule of primogeniture Mordecai Lincoln inherited most of his father's estate when he came of age, so when Thomas and his brother Josiah grew up, they had to "fend for themselves." But Thomas did not fear hard work, and through manual labor and, perhaps, the help of his brother Mordecai, he purchased in 1802 a 238-acre farm on Mill Creek near Elizabethtown, Kentucky. At this time Thomas was described as "honest," "quiet, and good-natured," and "truthful, conscientious, and religious."[9]

Nancy Hanks's life had been a hard one, too. She was born in 1784 to Lucy Hanks of Richmond County, Virginia. According to Lincoln's law partner William H. Herndon, Abraham Lincoln told him Nancy's father was "a well-bred

Virginia farmer or planter," and she was illegitimate. Nancy was raised by her grandparents in Kentucky until the age of nine, when she was sent to live with her mother and stepfather. Apparently, she did not get along well with her immediate family, and at the age of twelve went to live with her Aunt Elizabeth and her aunt's husband, Thomas Sparrow.[10]

Elizabeth and Thomas Sparrow cared deeply for Nancy and provided her with a stable home life. While living with them Nancy learned to read and became an excellent seamstress. Elizabeth and Thomas were evidently people of Christian faith. Two of their sons would later become preachers and Nancy developed a reputation as a religious young woman who loved to read the Bible. Although she was never formally adopted by her aunt and uncle, Nancy called herself Nancy Sparrow, and s referred to Elizabeth and Thomas as "mother and father."[11]

Later, Nancy worked as a seamstress in the Beechland, Kentucky, home of her friend Polly Ewing Berry. Polly was married to Richard Berry Jr., who was a friend of Thomas Lincoln. A romance between Nancy and Thomas developed, and they were married by Rev. Jesse Head on June 12, 1806, in the Berry home. At the time of their marriage Thomas was twenty-eight years old and Nancy was twenty-two.[12]

The newly married couple moved into a log cabin that Thomas had built in Elizabethtown. Thomas worked as a carpenter and at odd jobs such as constable and guard of county prisoners, and Nancy probably continued to employ her sewing skills at least until their first child, Sarah, was born on February 10, 1807. Nancy was characterized as "calm and imperturbable, with little formal education but much good judgment and even shrewdness." She seemed "more inclined toward spiritual concerns than material ones, showed appreciation for acts of small kindness, exuded affection and generosity [that was] tinged with melancholy." In his mature years, Lincoln described his mother as an "intellectual."[13]

In 1808 Thomas and Nancy, who was pregnant with their second child, moved from Elizabethtown to "Sinking Spring Farm," a 300-acre tract on Nolin Creek, two miles southwest of Hodgenville, Kentucky. Shortly before sunrise on February 12, 1809, Abraham Lincoln was born.[14]

← ❄ →

There is disagreement among historians as to when Thomas and Nancy first joined a church. A few sources say that shortly after marrying "they were united with one of the churches of Baptized Licking Locust Association of Regular Baptists in Kentucky." The Licking Locust Association was founded by David

Barrow, and represented one of the earliest Kentucky churches that supported the abolition of slavery, known as "emancipationist" churches. Most sources, however, do not associate the Lincolns with any church until they began attending the emancipationist church formed by William Downs called Little Mount Separate Baptist Church. It is not certain when they began attending Little Mount, but it was sometime after that church split away over the issue of slavery in 1808 from South Fork Baptist Church of Elizabethtown.[15]

Little Mount Separate Baptist Church was located about three miles east of Hodgenville. Per nineteenth-century Baptist historian J. H. Spencer, the primary difference between Regular Baptists and Separate Baptists, both of whom were Calvinist, was that the latter group refused to accept any sort of creed that would dictate their beliefs, especially about predestination. Although members of Little Mount agreed with the Philadelphia Confession of Faith, (a Calvinist creed that was commonly accepted by frontier churches—including the more numerous "Regular" Baptist churches), because of their insistence on independence they refused to formally accept it. Few of the preachers had much in the way of formal education, because Separate Baptist churches valued God's call to preach over schooling, and believed that a spontaneous utterance was more suggestive of the leading of the Holy Spirit than a prepared sermon.[16]

In 1811 Thomas was subjected to a lawsuit over the title to his land and moved his family to a thirty-acre farm he leased along Knob Creek, about seven miles east of Hodgenville. It is here that Abraham's education began, with his mother reading the Bible to him and Sarah when they were very young, and then using the Bible to teach them to read as they got older. According to Lincoln scholar Joshua Wolf Shenk, "After he learned to read, [Abraham] had access to only two books: The Bible and John Bunyan's Pilgrim's Progress." There were no children's books or nursery rhymes in the Lincoln home.[17]

In 1860, journalist John Locke Scripps sought Lincoln's help when he was writing a campaign biography of the president-elect. Lincoln was reluctant to provide much background on his youth, saying only that his life could be described as "the short and simple annals of the poor," as in Gray's elegy. Nevertheless, Scripps was able to squeeze the following out of Lincoln about his mother:[18]

> It was her [Nancy Lincoln's] custom on the Sabbath when there was no religious worship in the neighborhood—a thing of frequent occurrence—to employ a portion of the day in reading the Scriptures aloud to her family. After Abraham and his sister had learned to read, they shared by turns in this duty of Sunday reading. This practice, continued faithfully for a number of years, could not fail to produce

certain effects. Among other things, its tendency was to impart an
accurate acquaintance with Bible history and Bible teachings; and it
must also have been largely instrumental in developing the religious
element in the character of the younger members of the family . . .
There are few men in public life so familiar with the Scriptures as
Mr. Lincoln.[19]

As an adult, Lincoln told a friend that "the Bible stories, and the interest and
love he acquired in reading the Bible through this teaching of his mother, had
been the strongest and most influential experience in his life" and that "even
yet, when he read certain verses which he had in early boyhood committed to
memory by hearing [his mother] repeat them as she went about her household
tasks, the tones of his mother's voice would come to him and he would seem to
hear her speak those verses again."[20]

Life on Knob Creek farm included at least two important milestones for
the Lincolns. First was the tragic death of their third child, infant Thomas
Lincoln, Jr., in 1812. Second was Thomas Lincoln's baptism by Rev. William
Downs in Knob Creek and his formal joining of the Little Mount Church in
1816. Evidently Thomas was not bothered by the fact that the man who baptized
him had previously been admonished by his church for drinking. According
to nineteenth-century historian J. H. Spencer, Downs had at least once "been
summoned before the church to answer the charge of being intoxicated."[21]

Tired of land title problems in Kentucky, in December of 1816 Thomas and
Nancy packed up their meager belongings and moved their children to the
Little Pigeon Creek region in the new state of Indiana, fifteen miles north of
the Ohio River in what is now called Spencer County. Their first winter was a
harsh one. They lived in relative isolation, and since winter weather precluded
the construction of a proper cabin, they had to initially make do with a three-
sided shelter and an open campfire in front.

When warm weather arrived in the spring of 1817, Thomas and Nancy were
able to become better acquainted with their neighbors. The Little Pigeon community consisted of about twenty families, a general store, and a grain mill.
The Lincolns began meeting with members of a local church that had been
organized by Thomas Downs, whose brother William Downs had baptized
Thomas in Kentucky. Known as Little Pigeon Creek Baptist, it was a Calvinist
church that was composed of about fifteen families. Thomas and Nancy joined
in fellowship with them, but being Separate Baptists of good conscience, they
did not formally join the Little Pigeon Church—which was Regular Baptist.[22]

Of course, one of the most important tasks the Lincoln family had before them in the spring was the building of a better cabin and the clearing of land. Eight-year-old Abraham was given an ax so that he could help his father cut down trees, clear brush, and split logs. As the weeks went by, they built a cabin, cleared their land, sowed their first crop, and put up fences. Things were looking brighter by the fall, when Nancy's aunt and uncle, Elizabeth and Thomas Sparrow, and her eighteen-year-old cousin Dennis moved into their neighborhood.

In addition to building their cabin and fencing crops, the Lincoln family's weekdays were preoccupied with farming, hunting, and preparing meals. Although they were far from wealthy, they were grateful for what they had been given, and at supper Thomas Lincoln's blessing was always the simple "Fit and prepare us for humble service for Christ's sake, amen." At the end of their long day they would relax and entertain themselves. This usually involved visiting with neighbors, reading whatever books they had borrowed, or telling stories around the fire. Abe and Sarah took turns, along with Nancy, reading the Bible aloud. On Sundays they went to neighbors' houses for church service because Little Pigeon Church did not yet have a building.[23]

All went well for the Lincoln and Sparrow families from the winter of 1817 through the summer of the following year, but late September of 1818 brought disaster. Nancy's aunt and uncle were poisoned with what would later be called "milk sickness." Known today as tremetol vomiting, it was contracted by drinking the milk from cows that had eaten a poisonous plant known as "snake root." Their symptoms rapidly progressed from weakness to pains, muscle stiffness, vomiting, severe constipation, and coma. Although Nancy cared for her surrogate parents as well as she could, doctors were scarce in the Indiana wilderness, and little could be done. Within a week both Elizabeth and Thomas were dead.[24]

As terrible as this was, the family had little time for grieving, because Nancy immediately contracted milk sickness too. According to Dennis Hanks "she struggled on day by day," but Nancy was soon exhausted and within the week faced the fact that she, too, was going to die. Finally, she called the children to her bedside, told them she was not going to live, and encouraged them to be "good and kind to their father, to one another, and to the world." She also expressed her sincere hope that they would "reverence and worship God." On October 5, 1818, thirty-four-year-old Nancy Lincoln passed over.[25]

The Lincoln family and Dennis were shattered by their loss. Nancy was, in Dennis's words, "a good Christian woman . . . known for kindness, tenderness, charity and love to the world." No preacher was in the neighborhood to conduct a funeral service, so Thomas, his son, and Dennis built Nancy a simple wooden coffin from whipsawed pine logs and buried her near their cabin. Dennis moved in with the Lincoln family and shared the loft with Abe.[26]

Life became extremely difficult for the survivors, especially for eleven-year-old Sarah, who now carried the load of cooking and household chores. Missing her mother, she would often sit by the fire and cry. Dennis and Abe tried to cheer her up, doing little kindnesses like bringing her a baby raccoon and a turtle. But Abraham would later say that the Bible his mother had taught him to read was the greatest comfort he and his sister had after she was gone. Life dragged on like this for about a year.[27]

Finally, Thomas developed a plan to help his family. He thought of a woman he had grown up with in Kentucky by the name of Sarah Bush Johnston. Sarah had married a man named Daniel Johnston the same year that Thomas married Nancy, but Sarah's husband died three years ago, leaving her a widow with three young children. In the winter of 1819, Thomas left his son, daughter, and Dennis to journey to Elizabethtown, Kentucky, to seek Sarah Bush Johnston's hand in marriage. He and Sarah were married "straight off" on December 2, 1819, and Thomas soon loaded Sarah, her children, and her household belongings into a wagon and fetched them all home to Indiana.[28]

Sarah, whom Thomas called "Sally," must have had quite a shock when she arrived at her new home. The cabin had a dirt floor and needed basic repairs. The children looked "wild—ragged and dirty." Undaunted, she quickly took charge of her new family. She scrubbed and clothed Abe and Sarah, making them look "more human." She ordered Thomas and Dennis to repair the roof and door of their cabin, install a window, and put in a floor made of wood planking.[29]

Although she had received no education, Sally Lincoln encouraged the children to pursue theirs. In Kentucky Abe and Sarah had attended two brief sessions of school—typically held during the winter months—under the tutelage of Zechariah Riney in 1815 and Caleb Hazel in 1816. In Indiana they had attended three sessions of school after Nancy died—with teachers Andrew Crawford, Azel Dorsey, and James Swaney. According to Abe's classmates, in Indiana Abe studied arithmetic and spelling, but not grammar or geography. As students they read primarily the Bible, *Pilgrim's Progress*, *Robinson Crusoe*, and hymn books.[30]

Since Sally Lincoln did not read at all, and Thomas read very poorly, it was primarily Abe and his sister Sarah who used the family Bible—not only for family devotions but, as mentioned previously, as a schoolbook. In the local country schools, the school masters frequently used the Bible to exercise the young scholars in their reading lessons.

Scripture was incorporated into virtually everything they read, including Abraham's textbooks such as the Thomas Dilworth speller, which had lessons taken from the Psalms and Proverbs. As an example, Psalm 19:9 in the King James Bible (which Lincoln would quote one day in his second inaugural address), says, "The judgments of the Lord are true and righteous altogether." Dilworth closely paraphrased this as "The judgments of the Lord are always righteous and true."[31]

Abe was immersed in the tenets of Calvinist (also called Reformed) theology, even in the schoolbooks he studied. According to Abe's Indiana neighbor Elizabeth Crawford, the schoolbook from which "Abe learned his school orations, Speeches, and pieces to recite" was the *Kentucky Preceptor*, which is full of statements about the providence of God.[32]

The Little Pigeon Creek Church Community was the axis about which the Lincoln family rotated. Although the Lincolns were not officially members, in 1822, Thomas and his thirteen-year-old son helped the Little Pigeon Creek congregation build a church about a mile from the Lincoln cabin. The Lincolns fulfilled their responsibilities as if they were official members, which in 1823 finally became true. Thomas joined the Little Pigeon Church "by letter" on June 7, 1823, and Sally, who may not have been a member of a church in Kentucky, joined "by experience" the same day. Thomas's letter was from his previous church, Little Mount in Kentucky.[33]

Unfortunately, little information about Little Pigeon Creek Baptist Church services survives. The church minutes deal primarily with the monthly business meetings and inquiries into "the peace of the church" rather than church liturgy, what was preached, the administration of sacraments, or habits of worship and prayer. We do know that the Lincolns used Dupuy's and Watts's song books, and among the most popular of the hymns at Little Mount were, "Am I a Soldier of the Cross" (written by Watts), and "Come Thou Fount of Every Blessing" (Robinson).[34]

Dennis Hanks said that Abe "Never would Sing any Religious Songs it apered to Me that it Did Not souit him." Dennis continued, "But for a Man to preach a Sermond he would Listin to with great Attention." Although we do not have any details on what exactly was preached at Little Pigeon Church, an idea of how wilderness Baptists generally preached comes from Thomas Ford, a governor of the state of Illinois, who published an early history of that state in 1854:[35] "Sometimes their sermons turned upon matters of controversy; unlearned arguments on the subject of free grace, baptism, free-will, election, faith, good works, justification, sanctification, and the final perseverance of the saints.... These, with the love of God to sinful man, the sufferings of the Saviour, the dangerous apathy of sinners, and exhortations to repentance, furnished themes for the most vehement and passionate declamations."[36]

Lincoln historian John F. Cady notes that at about half of the Little Pigeon church's monthly business meetings, complaints would be raised about either public offenses by members or personal disagreements between congregants. The church would routinely function as a court and if necessary, set up special committees to investigate complaints. Biblical guidelines outlined in Matthew 18:15–17 had to be followed before matters were brought before the church, and it was considered disgraceful for Christian brethren to take matters to law. Honesty, sobriety, and sexual morality were "sturdily insisted upon."[37]

The Lincolns' church was a part of the Little Pigeon Association, which consisted of about a dozen churches within a radius of fifteen or twenty miles. Once a year, messengers of these churches would meet at Little Pigeon Church for two or three days for the purpose of mutual encouragement, fellowship, and the discussion of general polity.

The minutes of the Little Pigeon Association give an idea of a number of the issues the regional churches wrestled with, and what Abe would have heard the adults discuss. The biggest issue that vexed the association had to do with whether the churches should countenance the new system of missionary benevolences that the New England Baptist churches were sponsoring. This question arose in 1823, when Abe would have been fourteen, and continued as a perennial issue until at least 1828. Some historians have remarked that the antimission spirit of the frontier churches in the early nineteenth century was indicative of a Calvinism that would have "out-Calvined Calvin."[38]

Baptist historian William Warren Sweet, in his classic *Religion on the American Frontier,* said that the antimission Baptists were ultra-Calvinistic in doctrine (the modern term is Hyper-Calvinistic) and believed that God would bring His elect to repentance and redemption without the need of missionary activity.[39]

Nineteenth-century historian B. H. Carroll calls out Daniel Parker, John Taylor, and Alexander Campbell as the primary proponents of antimissionism in the Indiana-Kentucky-Tennessee region. Church leaders such as these men would visit small churches, which typically had annual church budgets of about fifteen dollars, and declaim that the influential eastern Baptist churches should not be supported because they were motivated by greed rather than Christ's Great Commission.[40]

John Cady believes that Daniel Parker may have been the most extreme opponent of the missionary program in the Illinois-Indiana-Kentucky region, and fifteen-year-old Abraham would have undoubtedly heard the mission controversy. Abe's stepmother said that "Abe, when old folks were at our house, was a silent & attentive observer—never speaking or asking questions till they were gone and then he must understand Every thing—even to the smallest thing—minutely & Exactly." I agree with Cady when he states that the young Abraham Lincoln would have been repelled by Parker's hypocritical efforts to instill dissension among church members about their fulfillment of Jesus's Great Commission.[41]

← ❀ →

Although most of Abe's days were occupied with farming, he considered farm work tedious and boring, and would often escape into the pages of a book during breaks from the plow or scythe. Many friends and relatives attest to this and recall that "he read everything he could lay his hands on."[42]

This lack of interest in farm work created a strain between Abe and his father. Dennis Hanks said Thomas would occasionally have to "slash him for neglecting his work by reading." Another relative said that "Thos. Lincoln never showed by his actions that he thought much of his son Abraham when a Boy. He treated him rather unkind than otherwise. [Thomas] Always appeared to think much more of his stepson John D Johnston than he did of his own Son Abraham."[43]

The fact that Thomas not only used Abe to work on his own farm, but also hired him out to work for other farmers did not help his son's attitude. Abe's father had the right to keep his son's wages until he was twenty-one, but the ruthless way he exploited this practice led Abe to later say that "he used to be a slave." In his late teens Abe increasingly looked for opportunities to get out from under his father's supervision and stay away from home. When his sister Sarah married Aaron Grigsby in the summer of 1826, seventeen-year-old Abe spent a great deal of time at their home. At nineteen he helped a neighbor guide a flatboat all the way to New Orleans to sell farm goods, and later (unsuccessfully) sought work on a steamboat.[44]

Tragically, in January of 1828, Abe's sister, Sarah, died giving birth to her first child. The Grigsby family did not send for a doctor soon enough, and when the doctor finally arrived, he was drunk and could not help. Upon hearing the news of this heartbreaking event, Abe "sat down on a log and hid his face in his hands while the tears rolled down through his long bony fingers." With Sarah gone, his ties to the family were strained even further.[45]

By the time he was twenty, Abe had not only lost his mother and sister, but in a sense, he had lost his father too. Yet there was one bright spot in his familial relationships—his stepmother. He would later say that no one could have loved a mother better than he loved her, and she thought highly of him as well. In her old age she would recall that Abe was "the best boy I ever saw. . ." "He was kind to Everybody and Everything."[46]

Although Sarah was an affectionate stepmother, it is unlikely that she had much of a positive influence on her stepson's spiritual life. She could not read the Bible, and she "was particularly identified as a 'hardshell Baptist,'" meaning she was against missionary work. In her old age she was asked about Abe's Bible reading and religious beliefs, and she replied that he "read the Bible some, though not as much as said: he sought more congenial books—suitable for his age," and that he "had no particular religion—didn't think of that question at that time, if he ever did—He never talked about it." It is difficult to conceive of the devout Nancy Hanks Lincoln, had she lived, ever making such an apathetic statement about her son's religious faith.[47]

When he reached manhood at age twenty-one, Abe could have left his father without admonition, but Thomas had one last job for his son to do. After receiving a letter from John Hanks reporting that the soil in Illinois was better for farming, and the additional incentive of a fresh outbreak of milk sickness in Indiana, Thomas decided to move his family to the Prairie State.[48]

Abe, his parents, five additional adult relatives and five children packed their belongings onto oxcarts and moved to Decatur in north-central Illinois. Abe spent the entire summer doing farm work for his father and others, and by the fall of 1831 they were well prepared for normal winter weather. Unfortunately, the winter of 1831–32 would be one of the worst on record, and at its end, Thomas Lincoln decided he wanted to move his family back to Indiana.[49]

But Thomas's son decided he would not go with them. In the spring of 1831, twenty-two-year-old Abraham Lincoln bid farewell to his family and packed his meager belongings into an old canoe. He pushed out into the current of the Sangamon River and headed toward the pioneer village of New Salem, Illinois, where he had been promised a job as store clerk. If he reflected on his life as he paddled westward, there can be little doubt that Abe was glad to be getting out from under his father's authority.

Farm work for him had been drudgery, and he felt that he had been treated like an enslaved person. His schooling had been sporadic, and if it had not been for the Bible he would not have had a single comprehensive resource for his education. With the love and loss of his mother and sister, he had seen a sovereign God give and take away. Finally, although he had not yet figured out the chasm between what he had learned of the Bible's teachings and the behavior of some people who read it, he knew one thing. He was determined to rise above his circumstances.

2. THE MIND IMPELLED

NEW LIFE IN NEW SALEM

... and the ear of the wise seeketh knowledge.

–Proverbs 18:15

When Lincoln first arrived in New Salem in 1831, resident William Butler described him as "as ruff a specimen of humanity as could be found." Another New Salem resident, James Short agreed that the newcomer's appearance was bucolic. Short observed that when he first saw Lincoln, he was coarsely dressed, wearing pants that "failed to make the connection with either coat or socks."[1]

Nevertheless, when the six foot four-inch Lincoln arrived in New Salem, he was at the peak of his physical strength and stature. New Salem resident Caleb Carmen admitted "his Appearance was very od," but "after all this bad Apperance i Soon found [him] to be a very inteligent young man."[2]

Lincoln was still a jester, and one townsman, Royal A. Clary, recalled that he "was humorous—witty & good natured & that geniality drew him into our notice So quick." People soon discovered that he was not only humorous and intelligent, but kind and generous, with a genuine interest in helping those in need. Caleb Carman observed that Lincoln was "very good Kind and courteous to children & women," and the ladies of the town all liked him. Lincoln quickly made friends in New Salem.[3]

Although resident Denton Offut had offered Lincoln a job as store clerk, the prospective tradesman had neither stock to sell nor a building to sell it in when Lincoln first arrived in town. New Salem's newest citizen was forced to find room, board, and employment while he waited for his "gassy—windy—brain rattling" employer to get organized. But finding work was easy, and he picked up odd jobs from local merchants and farmers. Room and board were not a problem, either, because he "worked for his board" and lived with various residents such as Mentor Graham and J. Rowan Herndon.[4]

The local schoolmaster, Mentor Graham, was immediately impressed with Lincoln because he was kind and considerate to his customers and always dealt honestly with them. Another resident, Robert B. Rutledge, attested to Lincoln's character, saying, "People relied implicitly upon his honesty, integrity, and impartiality." It was in New Salem that Lincoln developed what would become his lifelong sobriquet "Honest Abe."[5]

People also noticed that Lincoln loved to read—just about everything. Rowan Herndon, whom Lincoln first lodged with when he moved to New Salem, said Lincoln "wusd the Bible" frequently. Lincoln also enjoyed poetry, Shakespeare, mathematics, history, science, philosophy, biographies, and humor. It wasn't simply that Lincoln read a lot, but he diligently studied his subjects. No longer restricted by a father who confined him to farm work, Lincoln always had a book under his arm. It was not unusual to see him walking down the street in New Salem reading an open book as he went along, or lying on his back under a tree with his feet propped against a tree trunk, book in hand.[6]

Lincoln and Mentor Graham became close friends, and the old school master was thrilled to assist his eager "student." Graham helped Lincoln tackle several subjects he had never studied, including grammar. He also recalled that "in New Salem he [Lincoln] devoted more time to reading the Scripture, books on science and comments on law and to the acquisition of Knowledge of men & things than any man I ever knew."[7]

Within a few months Denton Offutt's store finally opened, but in a few more months it folded. Offutt, whom resident James Short described as "not much of a business man," had attempted to establish a third general store in a town that could only support two. Lincoln was soon back to the odd jobs he had done over the summer, plus clerking part-time at the oldest establishment in New Salem, Samuel Hill's store.[8]

Several citizens recognized Lincoln's underlying talents and encouraged him to run for the lower house of the Illinois state legislature. Although he was concerned about his lack of schooling, Lincoln decided to heed their advice and run for the legislature in the spring of 1832. But the Black Hawk War erupted, and Lincoln's political campaign was put on hold when he picked up a rifle to serve in the militia. Chief Black Hawk and his band of Sauk and Meskwaki (Fox) tribes had decided to reclaim their ancestral lands in Illinois and crossed over the Mississippi River from the Iowa Indian Territory in April 1832.[9]

To Lincoln's surprise, the company of volunteers that he joined, which included a group of local toughs that Lincoln had befriended known as the Clary's Grove Boys, elected him their captain. Lincoln was pleased by this honor, saying over twenty-five years later that "no other success ever gave him so much unalloyed satisfaction." Although the Sangamon volunteers did a lot of searching, they never found their enemy. The closest they came to shedding blood was when an old drunken Pottawatomie Indian scout stumbled into camp. Believing he was a spy, several of Lincoln's men decided to kill him. But Lincoln stood in their way, and told them that if they wanted to harm him it would have to be done over "his dead body." The old Indian left camp unharmed. Within three months the war was over, and the Sangamon boys came home.[10]

Upon return, Lincoln had only ten days to campaign before election day. He began making speeches, and on March 9, 1832, published a political handbill. This handbill contains the first reference to the Bible made by Lincoln in the *CW*. He presented his political platform, which included—among many other endeavors—a desire for improvement of roads and navigable streams. Always conscientious about his own lack of formal education, he included the following on this subject:

> Upon the subject of education, not presuming to dictate any plan or system respecting it, I can only say that I view it as the most important subject which we as a people can be engaged in. That every man may receive at least, a moderate education, and thereby be enabled to read the histories of his own and other countries, by which he may duly appreciate the value of our free institutions, . . . to say nothing of the advantages and satisfaction to be derived from all being able to read the Scriptures and other works, both of a religious and moral nature, for themselves.[11]

This was Lincoln's first public acknowledgment of the Bible's importance. Considering that his own father could barely read the Bible, the acknowledgment of the importance of reading the scriptures was not merely lip service for Lincoln. Lincoln knew that for many people the Bible was the only book they owned.

The election took place on August 6, 1832. Despite winning 277 of the 300 votes cast in his home precinct of New Salem, Lincoln lost due to his lack of notoriety in other precincts. Nevertheless, he was undeterred. A friend, Judge Matheny, told him he was "sowing seeds of success," and that next year "he would win."[12]

Meanwhile, Lincoln continued to look for a more suitable job. He became co-owner of another general store in New Salem, but it also failed. He was appointed postmaster in New Salem, and in 1833 started dabbling in law. He obtained an old law book that contained legal forms and began drawing up contracts and other legal documents for people, gratis. He frequently attended the court of the local justice of the peace, Bowling Green, who encouraged Lincoln to make extemporaneous comments during hearings. Lincoln would later tell New Salem resident A. Y. Ellis that "he owed more to Mr. Green for his advancement than any other Man."[13]

In 1833 Lincoln developed a romantic interest in Ann Rutledge, the twenty-year-old daughter of James Rutledge, proprietor of New Salem's inn and tavern. Mentor Graham described Lincoln's first love interest as "Amiable—Kind—tolerably good Schollar . . . beloved by everybody." Ann and Lincoln had similar temperaments and interests, and many residents noticed their increasing attentiveness to one another. Lincoln also took notice of a young lady named Mary Owens, who was in town for a month to visit relatives, but he preferred Ann's company.[14]

By the summer of 1833, Lincoln's personal finances were running low. He earned a meager salary as postmaster, and debts from his failed business forced him to take every odd job he could find, which included clerking in Samuel Hill's general store. Finally an opportunity for more cerebral work presented itself when the surveyors of Sangamon County hired him as an assistant surveyor. Lincoln acquired a compass and chain, studied two surveying books, borrowed a horse from a friend, and in January 1834 recorded his first survey.[15]

In 1834 Lincoln ran for the state legislature again, and his prospects were significantly improved over what they had been in his first political campaign. Since then his jobs as soldier, surveyor, store proprietor, and postmaster had won him many friends—Whig and Democrat alike.

Two of the men that Lincoln lodged with in New Salem, Mentor Graham and J. Rowan Herndon, testified that Lincoln read the Bible "frequently" while living with them. Lincoln biographer William E. Barton agreed that Lincoln read the Bible while he was in New Salem, but adds that he also read other books that criticized the Bible, such as C. F. Volney's *Ruins* and Thomas Paine's *Age of Reason*. It was during this time that Lincoln's reputation as a religious skeptic began.[16]

His reputation as a skeptic has persisted primarily due to the research done in the late 1860s by William H. Herndon, who interviewed several of New Salem's surviving residents and/or their children. Herndon uncovered several stories, the most significant one being a recollection about Lincoln's bringing an essay he had written to Samuel Hill's store that was critical of the Bible. Lincoln intended to discuss it with friends, but the details of his criticisms went up in smoke when his employer Samuel Hill threw the document into a fire.

Although respected Lincoln scholar Douglas Wilson has concluded that the evidence for Lincoln's little book on infidelity is "very strong," other Lincoln scholars disagree. Joseph Fornieri and Stewart Winger believe that a solid case can be made that the book Samuel Hill burned might have instead been an essay Lincoln wrote in support of universal salvation based on 1 Corinthians 15:22 ("For as in Adam all die, even so in Christ shall all be made alive"). Mentor Graham claimed to have read this essay, and said that "in the point of perspicacity and plainness of reasoning [he] never read one to surpass it."[17]

Of course, either an essay critical of the Bible or one in support of universalism would have resulted in the Baptist preachers of that day condemning Lincoln as an infidel. Rev. William E. Barton, who had himself taught school in the mountains of Kentucky in 1881, said that most Baptist preachers of Lincoln's day would have "classified" him "as an infidel" for believing that the earth was round.[18]

Regardless of what Lincoln's evolving religious opinions were in New Salem, he continued to read the Bible while he lived there. Even if the books he read by authors like Paine and Volney caused him to doubt the Bible's veracity and supported his branding as a skeptic or "infidel," much of the oral testimony we have today of his religious beliefs in New Salem leans more toward universalism and predestinarianism than atheism. It is fair to say that no one knows for certain the "precise nature" of Lincoln's arguments about the Bible when he talked with friends in New Salem, and later Springfield. What is important is that even if he was a skeptic of the Bible as a young man, his beliefs changed significantly as he grew older.[19]

Lincoln's canvas for the legislature in 1834 was successful and he won the August 4 election. Lincoln's first session as an Illinois state legislator would not start until December 1, so he had plenty of time to earn extra money by clerking at Samuel Hill's store.

As it turns out, Hill had more than clerking for Lincoln to do in August. For months, Sam had been feuding with Peter Cartwright, a famous Methodist circuit rider. Cartwright liked to mix politics with religion, and in 1832 he had been one of the Democratic candidates who beat young Abraham Lincoln in the latter's first political campaign. Hill's store in New Salem was sometimes a gathering place for the local men to discuss politics, and Cartwright, who disliked Hill, "began to abuse the proprietor publicly in front of his own store. He [Cartwright] would come and sit for hours and laugh and talk about Hill, while Hill stayed indoors."[20]

Hill had neither the wit nor the debating skills needed to effectively refute Cartwright's barbs, but his young clerk did. Lincoln had met Cartwright four years prior, when he was still helping his parents establish their farm near De-catur. Lincoln heard Cartwright making a campaign speech and openly chal-lenged some of the political points he was making. According to one witness, Lincoln "beat him [Cartwright] in the argument."[21]

Hill asked Lincoln to "ghost write" a political jab at Cartwright and have it published in a local paper. Lincoln, happy to accommodate his employer as well as take Cartwright down a peg, gladly obliged. Lincoln still disdained preachers like Cartwright who he believed were narcissistic and overbearing with their followers. This disdain may have originated from his youthful ob-servations of the preacher Daniel Parker in southern Indiana, who had bullied many of the Baptist churches in the Little Pigeon Association into opposing missionary work. The following is an excerpt of what was published in the *Beard-stown Chronicle* on September 7 as a letter to the editor from Samuel Hill, alias Abraham Lincoln:

> I believe the people in this country are in some degree priest ridden. I also believe, and if I am not badly mistaken "all informed observers" will concur in the belief that Peter Cartwright bestrides, more than any four men in the northwestern part of the State.
>
> He [Cartwright] has one of the largest and best improved farms in Sangamon county, with other property in proportion. And how has he got it? Only by the contributions he has been able to levy upon and collect from a priest ridden church. It will not do to say he has earned it "by the sweat of his brow" [Genesis 3:19], for although he may sometimes labor, all know that he spends the greater part of his time in preaching and electioneering.
>
> And then to hear him in electioneering times publicly boasting of mustering his militia, (alluding to the Methodist Church) and marching and counter-marching them in favor of, or against this or that candidate—why, this is not only hard riding, but it is riding clear off the track, stumps, logs and blackjack brush, notwithstanding. For a church or community to be priest ridden by a man who will take their money and treat them kindly in return is bad enough in all conscience; but to be ridden by one who is continually exposing them to ridicule by making a public boast of his power to hoodwink them, is insufferable.[22]

Cartwright made no direct response to either Hill or Lincoln yet did not "turn the other cheek." Lincoln would hear again from the Rev. Peter Cartwright.

← ❈ →

In the fall of 1834 Lincoln began a more serious study of the law, and began borrowing books from his mentor, Whig Party leader and friend John Todd Stuart. One of the books that Lincoln studied so earnestly was William Blackstone's *Commentaries on the Laws of England,* a classic law book often read by aspiring lawyers. Although a ponderous read, Lincoln devoured it. Joseph Fornieri has observed that Lincoln believed in a natural law interpretation of morality, and that he thought laws created by humans should be scrutinized against both reason and the Bible.[23]

Lincoln took a stagecoach to Vandalia in early December to begin his political career in the Ninth General Assembly of the Illinois state legislature. He learned quickly under the mentorship of John Todd Stuart, who taught him the basics of writing bills and maneuvering them through the legislature. Lincoln faithfully attended the Assembly's sessions, promoted the New Salem/ Springfield communities, and supported internal improvements.

After an uneventful session, Lincoln returned home to New Salem in mid-February 1835. There he continued working at his surveying and clerking jobs, and studying lawbooks supplied by John Todd Stuart. His friendship with Ann Rutledge quickly resumed and they spent a lot of time reading poetry and studying grammar together. Tragically, in the late summer of 1835, a wave of typhoid hit the town of New Salem, and, in August, Ann came down with the deadly sickness. Neighbor John Jones said, "It was very evident that [Lincoln] was much distressed." Lincoln walked out to the Rutledge cabin and visited her as often as he could, but Ann grew steadily worse and died on August 25. Lincoln was heartbroken and fell into a state of deep depression.[24]

Lincoln's friend Mentor Graham, who was a member of the Baptist church about a mile from town, tried to comfort his friend. According to Graham, Lincoln "told Me that he felt like Committing Suicide often, but I told him God [had a] higher purpose [for his life]—He told me he thought so somehow—couldn't tell how—He said that my remarks and others had often done him good." Many of Lincoln's friends feared he was "mentally deranged," and fearing suicide, they "kept watch and ward" over him.[25]

Lincoln referred to his bouts of depression as "the hypo," which was short for hypochondriasis. His tendency to melancholy and depression would be an impediment to Lincoln for most of his life. Lincoln slowly recovered from this sad chapter in his life, just as he had when he lost his sister and mother. There is no record of Lincoln seeking solace in the Bible during this time of grief.[26]

In the summer of 1836 Lincoln once again turned his attention to politics. On June 13, 1836, he published in the *Sangamo Journal* a cavalier announcement of his candidacy for a second term in the state legislature. Unlike his 1832 political announcement, Lincoln discussed neither the details of his political positions nor the importance of "the Scriptures."

In late summer Lincoln's prospects began to improve when he won reelection to the legislature, and was admitted to the Illinois bar. His second term in the legislature would not start until December, so he spent the remainder of the fall surveying, continuing his law studies, and beginning a rather tepid courtship with his previous acquaintance, Mary Owens.

Initially Mary was glad to receive Lincoln's attentions, but he displayed little enthusiasm for the courtship, and it did not take her long to conclude that Lincoln was "deficient in those little links which make up the chain of woman's happiness." When Lincoln left for Vandalia in early December to take his seat in the lower house of the state legislature, the letters he wrote her from Vandalia never mentioned love but were instead, in his words, "dry and stupid."[27]

Lincoln's duties in the tenth session of the Illinois state legislature were more numerous than they had been in the ninth, and his most noteworthy accomplishment came on March 3, 1837, when he filed a formal written protest in the assembly that stated, "The institution of slavery is founded on both injustice and bad policy." In this antislavery statement, which was co-signed by one other legislator, Lincoln also criticized abolitionists, arguing that "the promulgation of abolition doctrines tends rather to increase than to abate its [slavery's] evils." He also addressed the issue of slavery in the nation's capital, writing that "the Congress of the United States has the power, under the constitution, to abolish slavery in the District of Columbia; but that power ought not to be exercised unless at the request of the people of said District." Even though it was a modest statement against slavery, it nevertheless demonstrated political courage. Although Illinois was a free state, most of the residents were supportive of the South's right to own enslaved persons.[28]

The tenth session ended, and Lincoln moved from New Salem to Springfield on April 15, 1837. John Todd Stuart had made him junior partner in his Springfield law firm, and Lincoln wanted to immediately begin what he called his "experiment as a lawyer." His years in New Salem had been very profitable, and while there he had acquired dozens, if not hundreds, of friends. Lincoln was truly reaping the fruit of "doing unto others as you would have them do unto you" (Matthew 7:12).[29]

3. HE WILL DO FOR ME YET

QUOTING THE BIBLE FOR CAUSE

For the vision is yet for an appointed time, but at the end
it shall speak, and not lie: though it tarry, wait for it.
—Habakkuk 2:3

On May 7, 1837, three weeks after moving from New Salem to Springfield, Lincoln wrote another of his uninspiring letters to Mary Owens, and this one showed no indication that his interest in her was increasing. Referring to his social life in Springfield, he reported that "I've never been to church yet, nor probably shall not be soon. I stay away because I am conscious I should not know how to behave myself." Mary Owens had finally had enough of Lincoln's unromantic missives. She never responded to this letter.[1]

In Springfield, Lincoln shared a room with a man about his age named Joshua Speed, living above Speed's general store. They lived in Speed's apartment for four years, encouraging one another in their vocational pursuits, politics, and their mutual interest in the opposite sex. Speed had a melancholy temperament like Lincoln and they became life-long best friends. Speed would one day offer valuable insight into Lincoln's religious beliefs.

Lincoln continued reading the Bible in his early months in Springfield. This is evidenced by his first definitive use of the Bible, namely, inserting several scriptural allusions into a political speech known today as his Lyceum Address. He presented this address entitled "The Perpetuation of our Political Institutions" on January 27, 1838, in Springfield.

The purpose of the Lyceum forums was to allow young men to practice oratory skills. In addition to the Bible, his arguments in this address reveal the influence of Blackstone's *Commentaries* on his beliefs about civil vs. natural law. Lincoln offered a meticulously prepared argument that employed several scriptures, starting with a simple exhibitive illustration, "In the great journal of things happening <u>under the sun</u>, [Ecclesiastes 1:9], we, the American people, find our account running, under date of the nineteenth century of the Christian era."[2]

He followed up his introduction with a brief description of the blessings that America had received and, after alluding to future dangers for the American people, he proposed the following, which would become one of his most frequently quoted statements: "At what point then is the approach of danger to be expected? I answer, if it ever reach us, it must spring up amongst us. It cannot come from abroad. If destruction be our lot, we must ourselves be its <u>author and finisher</u> [Hebrews 12:2]. As a nation of freemen, we must live through all time, or die by suicide."[3]

The national "suicide" Lincoln feared was a disregard for the rule of law, as evidenced by two instances of mob violence Lincoln had heard of in the St. Louis area. The first instance was when a mob committed the horrific crime of chaining a young free Black man named Frank McIntosh to a tree and incinerating him. The second was a result of several mob actions against the abolitionist Elijah Parish Lovejoy. After mobs had destroyed three of Lovejoy's printing presses, trying to stop his antislavery publication, he moved to the Illinois town of Alton across the Mississippi River. Lovejoy was then killed on November 7, 1837, by another mob when he tried to protect his fourth printing press.

Lincoln condemned the mob actions and then presented an unsophisticated solution to the violence—simply proposing that people respect the law. But Lincoln's voice was a lonely one crying in the wilderness. According to Lovejoy's biographer Paul Simon, no other legislator in Missouri or Illinois condemned the mob violence in St. Louis and Alton.[4]

After offering a seemingly incongruous warning about the future rise of a despotic American "Caesar," Lincoln said the solution to the dangers America faced was for the people to resist passion and employ "cold, calculating unimpassioned reason" to "furnish all the materials for our future support and defence." Lincoln ended his speech with the sentiment that by returning to obedience of the law, the "proud fabric of freedom" would survive, just "as truly has been said of the only greater institution [the church]," and the "<u>the gates of hell shall not prevail against it</u>" [Matthew 16:18].[5]

The Lyceum Address is one of the most scrutinized of Lincoln's speeches, primarily because some scholars think that it includes subliminal messages by Lincoln that are useful for analyzing his psyche and predicting his future. However, other scholars more realistically state that, rather than some sort of prophecy, it was simply an opportunity for the young speaker to show off his nascent speaking skills.[6]

Two years would pass before Lincoln would use the Bible in another written communication. In a December 1839 speech to the state legislature, about the subtreasury, he warned his audience of the dangers of trusting men with public funds. The speech has significance because it was his first reference to Christ, using Jesus and Judas Iscariot to illustrate the good and evil sides of man's nature. He stated that "the Saviour of the world chose twelve disciples, and even one of that small number [Judas Iscariot], selected by superhuman wisdom, turned out a traitor and a devil [John 6:70]. And, it may not be improper here to add, that Judas carried the bag [John 12:6]—was the Sub-Treasurer of the Saviour and his disciples."[7]

About this time, Lincoln met the future love of his life, his law partner's twenty-year-old blue-eyed cousin, Mary Todd. In October of 1839 Mary had moved to Springfield from Kentucky to live with her sister and brother-in-law, Elizabeth and Ninian Edwards. Mary was witty, sophisticated, and, unlike most women of her day, extremely interested in politics. An unapologetic Whig, she boldly announced to her suitors that the man she married would one day be president of the United States.

Somewhat coquettish, Mary had many suitors. The Edwards home was a popular social center and was frequented by many of the town's young bachelors, including Whig legislator Abraham Lincoln and Democratic legislator Stephen A. Douglas. Lincoln and Douglas, who had recently crossed swords for the first time in the lower house of the Illinois state legislature, were soon rivals for the attentions of Mary. Although Douglas's pursuit of Mary was short-lived, his diverse contests with Lincoln were just beginning. In the coming years they would oppose each other hundreds of times—in the courtroom over legal argument, and on the stump over politics.

Lincoln was captivated by Mary, and a serious romance ensued. According to Mary's sister Elizabeth Edwards, it was comical to watch the young couple when they were together. They would sit on the sofa in the Edwards's parlor, and while Mary breathlessly chattered on, rapidly switching from subject to subject, Lincoln would sit in silence with a mesmerized look on his face. Mary and Lincoln became engaged in 1840—the same year he won his fourth term in the state legislature. But their relationship hit rough water in the latter months of the year, and on the first of January 1841, Lincoln broke off their engagement. The fact that he had disappointed Mary threw Lincoln into another serious bout of "the hypo."[8]

Still depressed, in the late summer of 1841 Lincoln made a trip from Springfield to Farmington, Kentucky, to visit his best friend, Joshua F. Speed. Speed had moved to Kentucky in early 1841 to take over the management of his father's estate. Lincoln spent six weeks with the Speed family, and his hosts took it upon themselves to try to cheer him up. Joshua's mother, Lucy Speed, presented Lincoln with an Oxford edition of the King James Bible, and encouraged him to read it. Lucy's decision to give Lincoln a Bible indicates that he may not have had one of his own at that time.[9]

Shortly after Lincoln returned to Illinois from Farmington, he wrote to Joshua's sister Mary, and revealed that he still had questions about the Bible when he said, "Tell your mother that I have not got her 'present' [the Oxford Bible] with me; but that I intend to read it regularly when I return home. I doubt not that it is really, as she says, the best cure for the 'Blues' could one but take it according to the truth." His statement "could one but take it according to the truth" indicates Lincoln might still have been harboring doubts about the Bible as the divinely inspired word of God.[10]

Five months later, in early February 1842, Lincoln's skeptical friend Joshua Speed wrote Lincoln a letter, expressing his concern that Fanny Henning—the woman he was falling in love with—might die. On February 3 Lincoln wrote Speed a surprising response in which he admitted not only his belief in God, but also faith that the Almighty was intervening in Speed's situation. He tried to encourage his friend's love for Fanny, yet brace him for her potential death, and give him hope that if Fanny did pass away, her Methodist faith might be to her benefit:

> I almost feel a presentiment that the Almighty has sent your present affliction expressly for that object [to banish doubts about his love for Fanny Henning]. . . . The death scenes of those we love, are surely painful enough; but these we are prepared to, and expect to see. They happen to all, and all know they must happen. Painful as they are, they are not an unlooked-for-sorrow. Should she, as you fear, be destined to an early grave, it is indeed, a great consolation to know that she is so well prepared to meet it. Her religion, which you once disliked so much, I will venture you now prize most highly.[11]

It is noteworthy Lincoln told Speed that he must "now prize" Fanny's religion "most highly" since her life was in danger. Even if Speed did not prize it, it was evident that Lincoln did. Lincoln was undoubtedly sincere, because he would never have offered disingenuous hope to his best friend in as grave a matter as this. This letter prompts the question, "Why was Lincoln praising Fanny's religious faith?" As will be seen in the next speech he makes, Lincoln was aware of the evangelistic/revivalist movement by the Methodists and New School Presbyterians. Instead of wondering whether God had predestined them for heaven as most Calvinists did, the evangelicals believed they could change their lives through the renouncement of sin and acceptance of Christ. Was Lincoln suggesting that it might be possible for Speed to change and see Fanny again in heaven if she died?[12]

Joseph Fornieri correctly observes that the letters to Speed indicate that a residual biblical faith from Lincoln's youth was still "coexisting" with his reservations about religion. Speed would later say that Lincoln had been a skeptic when they lived together in Springfield. But in these candid letters to his closest friend, Lincoln demonstrated that his biblical faith was growing stronger and becoming more conventional. What is more, in his letter to Speed, Lincoln was using the Bible to make a serious effort to encourage his skeptical friend and give him hope. Lincoln was interpreting the events in Speed's life (as well as his own) in deference to God's providential design. Stewart Winger also notes the significance of the Speed letters, and observes it was at this time Lincoln began using the sort of biblical language that he would later become famous for.[13]

Lincoln's next speech on February 22 was practically a sermon, where he encouraged his listeners to imitate Christ. Lincoln addressed an organization known as the Washington Temperance Society. The Washingtonians, a national organization composed mainly of reformed alcoholics, had formed a much more effective temperance strategy than had previously been active in the United States. Their approach was to encourage recovering alcoholics to pursue an active spiritual life, similar to the approach followed in today's Alcoholics Anonymous. Lincoln saw temperance as a worthwhile moral cause, and welcomed the opportunity to speak to former alcoholics and their supporters. Since the temperance society met at the Second Presbyterian Church in Springfield, this favorable venue (and Lucy Speed's Bible, which he had told her he planned to read "regularly") emboldened and enabled Lincoln to make extensive use of scripture in this speech. It was his first in-depth use of the Bible for the support of a moral cause, and in it he quoted or alluded to eight separate Bible verses— more than any other speech except the second inaugural address.[14]

In the temperance address, Lincoln condemned the ways of preachers, lawyers, and hired agents in their self-righteous efforts to fight "the demon of intemperance" by means of "too much denunciation" and not enough "entreaty and persuasion." While Lincoln condemned the errant ways of the preachers and lawyers, he praised the methods of the Washingtonians:

They adopt a more enlarged philanthropy. *They* go for present as well as future good. *They* labor for all now living, as well as all hereafter to live. *They* teach hope to all—-despair to none. As applying to their cause, they deny the doctrine of <u>unpardonable sin</u> [allusion to Luke 12:10]. As in Christianity it is taught, so in this they teach, that "While the lamp holds out to burn, / The vilest sinner may return" [taken from Isaac Watts Hymn 88, book 1]. And, what is matter of the most profound gratulation, they, by experiment upon experiment, and example upon example, prove the maxim to be no less true in the one case than in the other. On every hand we behold those, who but yesterday, were the chief of sinners, now the chief apostles of the cause.[15]

Most of Lincoln's scripture references in this speech are exhibitive uses of the Bible such as his praise of the Washingtonians, who "<u>out of the abundance of their hearts</u>" [Luke 6:45], their tongues give utterance"; or, of the reformed alcoholic as "one, who has long been known as a victim of intemperance, '<u>bursts the fetters</u> that have bound him' [Mark 5:4], and appears before his neighbors "<u>clothed, and in his right mind</u>" [Luke 8:35]. Also, he speaks of the Washingtonians' cause as being "suddenly transformed from a cold abstract theory, to a living, breathing, active, and powerful chieftain, '<u>going forth conquering and to conquer</u>'" [Revelation 6:2].[16]

But in addition to the five exhibitive allusions above plus two others not included here, Lincoln uses the Bible more theologically through a reference to Christ when he attacks those who had been condemning the alcoholic: "If they believe, as they profess, that Omnipotence condescended to <u>take on himself the form of sinful man</u>, and, as such, to die an <u>ignominious death</u> for their sakes [allusion to Philippians 2:7-8], surely they will not refuse submission to the infinitely lesser condescension, for the temporal, and perhaps eternal salvation, of a large, erring, and unfortunate class of their own fellow creatures."[17]

Stewart Winger points out that in this speech Lincoln was using the language of "conversion experience," where one could simply "choose this day whom one would serve" that was more typical of nineteenth-century Methodism and New School Presbyterianism than the Calvinism of the mature Lincoln. From his acknowledgment of Christ's "ignominious death" for "sinful man" in this speech, it is evident that by this time in his life Lincoln understood the gospel message of Christ's atoning sacrifice.[18]

Lincoln soon learned not only that Fanny Henning's health had improved, but that she and Speed were married. Lincoln again quoted the Bible when on February 25 he sent his congratulations to Speed, which began with "Yours of the 16th Inst. announcing that Miss Fanny and you 'are <u>no longer twain, but one flesh</u>' [Mark 10:8], reached me this morning."[19]

In a subsequent letter to Speed dated July 4, Lincoln again demonstrated his belief that life events were guided by providence. Noteworthy here is that Lincoln referred to himself as "superstitious" when he talked about God. This might be evidence that Lincoln was working through his own confusion over the issues of superstition, fatalism, evangelism, Calvinism, and providence. Or, it may have simply been Lincoln's careful way of quoting the Bible to his skeptical friend. Lincoln wrote: "I always was superstitious; and as part of my superstition, I believe God made me one of the instruments of bringing your Fanny and you together, which union, I have no doubt He had fore-ordained. Whatever he designs, he will do for me yet. '<u>Stand still and see the salvation of the Lord</u>' [Exodus 14:13 and 2 Chronicles 20:17] is my text just now."[20]

This July 4 letter adds more evidence that Lincoln's biblical faith was evolving. In his statement that he was always "superstitious" he spoke of a providential God who "foreordains" human events. These events could be quite diverse, from a union in marriage to "the salvation of the Lord." Stewart Winger points out that the scripture "stand still and see the salvation of the Lord" would have been typically used by Hyper-Calvinists.[21]

Some scholars have described Lincoln as simply a fatalist. This might have been true before he moved to Springfield, but by 1842 he had clearly gone beyond simple "fatalism." Scholars such as Joseph Fornieri, Ronald C. White, and David Hein argue persuasively that by 1842 Lincoln's position had changed from simple fatalism to a belief in a providential God who used people and events for beneficent purpose. We will later see their position reinforced in an 1847 statement by Lincoln regarding his former belief in "the doctrine of necessity." In this July 4 letter Lincoln for the first time sees himself as a beneficent "instrument" of God for providential good. The belief in himself as an instrument of the Almighty would later be a theme of Lincoln's in the 1860s.[22]

Joshua Speed must have been quite surprised at his friend's newfound faith. But as two men with melancholic personalities, Speed and Lincoln had been through a great deal together, and genuinely welcomed one another's counsel. In Lincoln's statement that he (Lincoln) should "<u>stand still and see the salvation of the Lord</u>" [Exodus 14:13] Lincoln may have been expressing his hope that God would help him in his own relationship with the opposite sex. Taking his letters to Speed into account, it is easy to agree with Stewart Winger, who concludes that by 1842 his [Lincoln's] respect for religion was "obviously sincere."[23]

Lincoln's patient waiting on the Lord soon paid dividends. On November 4, 1842, the thirty-three-year-old bachelor was wed to the twenty-three-year-old woman who had been determined to marry a future president of the United States. Mary was a good match for Lincoln intellectually and politically, but their temperaments could not have been more dissimilar. Her mood swings and short temper would cause many problems for her melancholic husband over the course of their marriage. But Lincoln had given Mary a ring engraved with the words "Love is eternal" [allusion to 1 Corinthians 13:8] and he was committed to their marriage covenant.[24]

Despite Mary's temper, and the fact that she had grown up with enslaved people as household servants, she did not insist on a pampered life. As newlyweds they lived in a small apartment at the Globe tavern until a few months after their son Robert Todd was born on August 1, 1843. After this they moved into a small, rented house for a few months, and then bought a one and a half story house at Eighth and Jackson Streets in Springfield.

When they were first married, Mary regularly attended the Episcopal Church, but Lincoln, still unsure of how to behave himself, rarely accompanied her. Although Lincoln had still not joined a church, he continued to read the Bible. He also developed an amicable relationship with several Springfield pastors.

Historian Richard Carwardine has observed that by the middle 1800s, most Protestant evangelical men in America were deeply involved in politics. Taking this into consideration, Lincoln's lack of church membership may have had an adverse effect on his political aspirations. This is manifest in early 1843 when he attempted to attain the Whig Party's nomination for the House of Representatives in the 7th congressional district. He lost to his friend Edward Baker. Writing to a friend about this on March 26, he said:[25]

> There was . . . the strangest combination of church influence against me. Baker is a Campbellite, and therefore as I suppose, with few acceptions got all that church. My wife has some relatives in the Presbyterian and some in the Episcopal Churches, and therefore, whereever it would tell, I was set down as either the one or the other, whilst it was every where contended that no christian ought to go for me, because I belonged to no church, was suspected of being a deist, and had talked about fighting a duel.[26]

Lincoln was continuing in the footsteps of his father, who had always been reluctant to join a community church too quickly. It is significant that despite the advantages of doing so, Lincoln did not believe in joining a church simply for political benefit.[27]

From 1837–1844 Lincoln had been the junior partner of two legal firms, but in the fall of 1844 he decided to start his own law practice, and hired a young lawyer named William H. Herndon as junior partner. Like Lincoln, Herndon was a solid Whig in politics, and the junior partner had a great deal of political influence with the young men of Springfield.

Lincoln continued to occasionally use scripture in political communications. In an October 3, 1845, letter to political associate Williamson Durley, Lincoln used two New Testament scriptures for a political analogy. These were "[We are not] to do evil that good may come" [allusion to Romans 3:8], and "An evil [man] cannot bring forth good fruit" [allusion to Luke 6:44–45].[28]

The Lincolns were in an extremely busy phase of life, and it was about to get even busier. On March 10, 1846, Mary had another baby boy, whom they named Edward Baker after Lincoln's friend and political rival. Eddy, a sickly child, presented Mary additional difficulties besides the challenges of three-year-old Robert and a husband who was often absent because of his law practice. To make matters worse for Mary, Lincoln was soon on the hustings again. In the summer of 1846, he ran for Congress against his old New Salem antagonist, Rev. Peter Cartwright.

Cartwright played hardball Jacksonian politics, and in an apparent effort to "get even" with Lincoln for the ghostwriting the young store clerk did for Samuel Hill back in 1834, Cartwright began what Lincoln called a "whispering campaign." In his canvas, Cartwright supposedly complained that Lincoln had never joined a church, and started the rumor that Lincoln was an infidel. Infidelity was a serious charge in nineteenth-century American politics, and on July 31, 1846, Lincoln published a campaign circular in defense of his religious beliefs. It was an extremely revealing document, with a decidedly Calvinistic tone:

> A charge having got into circulation in some of the neighborhoods of this District, in substance that I am an open scoffer at Christianity, I have by the advice of some friends concluded to notice the subject in this form. That I am not a member of any Christian Church, is true; *but I have never denied the truth of the Scriptures* [italics added]; and I have never spoken with intentional disrespect of religion in general, or of any denomination of Christians in particular. It is true that in early life I was inclined to believe in what I understand is called the "Doctrine of Necessity," that is, that the human mind is impelled to action, or held in rest by some power, over which the mind itself has no control; and I have sometimes (with one, two or three, but never

publicly) tried to maintain this opinion in argument. The habit of arguing thus however, I have, entirely left off for more than five years [about the time he got his Bible from Mary Speed]. And I add here, I have always understood this same opinion to be held by several of the Christian denominations. The foregoing, is the whole truth, briefly stated, in relation to myself, upon this subject.[29]

I do not think I could myself, be brought to support a man for office, whom I knew to be an open enemy of, and scoffer at, religion. Leaving the higher matter of eternal consequences, between him and his Maker, I still do not think any man has the right thus to insult the feelings, and injure the morals, of the community in which he may live. If, then, I was guilty of such conduct, I should blame no man who should condemn me for it; but I do blame those, whoever they may be, who falsely put such a charge in circulation against me.[30]

In this printed handbill, Lincoln felt strongly enough about the charge that he had "denied the truth of the Scriptures" to state publicly, in writing, that this was not true. He admitted to having previously argued in favor of the fatalistic "Doctrine of Necessity," where the human mind is compelled by "some power" to obedience of action without free will. But since that time, he changed from questioning the existence of "some power" to his later position of "standing still" to "see the salvation of the Lord." Although he did not refute that his thoughts were unconventional, he took exception to the rumor that he had publicly and irreverently attacked scripture.[31]

← ❈ →

Lincoln easily defeated Cartwright for the Illinois 7th district on August 3, 1846, but the 30th Congress of the United States would not convene until December 6, 1847. Lincoln made no further use of the Bible in speeches or writings from the time of his campaign circular in 1846 until a few days before the Lincoln family departed for Washington in early December 1847. On December 1, Lincoln wrote a note to himself, something the *CW* often refers to as a "fragment," for use in a future speech about the protective tariffs and labor. In this fragment he referred to Genesis 3:19, "in the sweat of thy face shalt thou eat bread," as being God's plan for each man to work for his own sustenance. The right to work and better one's self would become a major theme of Lincoln's life. Lincoln scholar Gabor Boritt called the equal opportunity to get ahead in life Lincoln's "central idea."[32]

Lincoln, Mary, and their two sons arrived in Washington in early December of 1847. The *CW* reveals that Lincoln made only three references to the Bible in his entire two years in Congress. Once in a mid-January 1848 speech in the House of Representatives, another in a May 1848 letter to Rev. John M. Peck, and a third in a letter to William H. Herndon in which he made an exhibitive reference to the gallows of Haman from the book of Esther.

In his speech to Congress, Lincoln condemned President Polk for (Lincoln believed) unjustly starting the Mexican War. He stated that "the principal motive" for the president's decision to provoke the war "was to divert public attention from the surrender of 'Fifty-four, forty, or fight' to Great Britain, on the Oregon boundary question." Lincoln said Polk must feel that the blood spilled in the war was "like the blood of Abel, . . . crying to Heaven against him" [allusion to Genesis 4:10].[33]

In his May 1848 letter to Peck, a Baptist minister, Lincoln's tone is one of extreme frustration with this preacher who was supporting the war against Mexico. Lincoln believed that a victory in the war against Mexico would enable the Polk administration to expand slavery into territories taken from America's weaker neighbor. In his rebuke to Peck, he used Christ's Golden Rule, "Whatsoever ye would that men should do to you, do ye even so to them" [Matthew 7:12].[34]

The *CW* reveals that for the rest of 1848, Lincoln made only two indirect allusions to the Bible. One was in a fragment written about his admiration of Niagara Falls. Lincoln marveled that it had been flowing constantly since biblical times, as far back as Christ's crucifixion and even when Adam "first came from the hand of his Maker." The second was when he admonished his stepbrother, who had said he would "almost give his place in heaven for $70 or $80." Lincoln scolded his stepbrother by saying he valued his "place in Heaven very cheaply."[35]

Other than his application for a patent and a failed effort to write a bill that would end slavery in the nation's capital, Lincoln's term in Congress was quite unremarkable. In March of 1849, after his term in Congress was over, Lincoln returned to Illinois, put his political career on hold, and decided to pursue law "more assiduously than before." This meant not only a return to the courtroom and his law office, but also to the 8th Judicial Circuit for several months out of the year. His sole reference to the Bible in mid-1849 was when he sought a patronage job from the new presidential administration. He asked a political associate to see if he could help secure the commission of the General Land Office of Illinois for him: "Will you please write old Zach . . . as pretty a letter for me as you think the truth will permit? Time is important. What you do, do quickly" [John 13:27].[36]

On the judicial circuit, Lincoln continued his assiduous reading habits, carrying various books with him such as the Bible, Euclid's geometry, and

Shakespeare. Euclid may seem like a strange subject for a middle-aged lawyer to study, but he did so to strengthen his skills for the presentation of logical arguments to juries.

On February 1, 1850, another tragic event disrupted Lincoln's life when his second son, Eddy, died from "consumption" (tuberculosis). Lincoln and Mary were overwhelmed with grief. The lamenting parents had "Of such is the Kingdom of Heaven" [Matthew 19:14] engraved on Eddy's tombstone.[37]

The tragic loss of Eddy, whom his parents described as "tender-hearted," had a significant impact on Lincoln. Although he had avoided church for many years, Lincoln developed a friendship with Rev. James Smith of the First Presbyterian Church, the preacher who conducted Eddy's funeral. Like Lincoln, Smith had previously been a skeptic. But after Smith converted to Christianity, he wrote a book entitled *The Christian's Defense.* Lincoln read at least part of this book and according to his brother-in-law Ninian Edwards, Lincoln became "convinced of the truth of the Christian religion." According to William E. Barton, "He was deeply impressed by the argument of Dr. Smith in his *The Christian's Defense.* It was the first time he had heard the Christian apologetic rationally presented, and it made a lasting impression upon him without, however, fully satisfying him. He was, however, a much more religious man when he left Springfield than he was when he came to it, whether he knew it or not."[38]

After Mary switched her membership from the Episcopal Church to the First Presbyterian, Lincoln rented a pew there and began to attend occasionally. About a month after Eddy's death, Lincoln and Mary were cheered by the news that they were expecting another child.

On July 25, 1850, Lincoln quoted the Bible in his eulogy for former president Zachary Taylor. Referring to Taylor's humility, he quoted Christ's maxim that "he that humbleth himself will be exalted" (Matthew 23:12). Although Lincoln also quoted his favorite poem, *Mortality* by Knox, he made no allusions to heaven or afterlife in the eulogy.[39]

Lincoln and Mary had a special reason to rejoice on Christmas Day, 1850, because their third son William Wallace had been born four days before. Nicknamed "Willie," he would later be recognized as the son who most closely resembled his father, primarily because of his pleasant temperament and keen mind.

In 1851 the *CW* reveals only one occasion upon which Lincoln quoted the Bible. In this January 12 letter, written to his stepbrother John D. Johnston, Lincoln demonstrated a substantial knowledge of comforting scripture. Johnston had previously written to Lincoln to tell him his father was dying, and then, receiving no reply, wrote Lincoln again, wondering why he had not responded.

Johnston hoped that Lincoln would come to Charleston, Illinois, to see his father before he passed. In his January 12 return letter, Lincoln said his lack of response was not only because his wife was "sick a-bed," but also candidly admitted that even if that were not the case, he had thought that he "could write nothing which could do any good." Despite this, Lincoln then went on to present a comforting message he wanted Johnson to pass along to his father. He used scriptures from Proverbs, 2 Chronicles, and Luke in a manner that may have reflected his personal faith at the time. He wrote:

> I sincerely hope Father may yet recover his health; but at all events tell
> him to remember to call upon, and confide in, our great, and good,
> and merciful Maker; who will not turn away from him [2 Chronicles
> 30:9] in any extremity. He notes the fall of a sparrow [allusion to Luke
> 12:6], and numbers the hairs of our heads [allusion to Luke 12:7];
> and He will not forget the dying man, who puts his trust in Him
> [allusion to Proverbs 30:5]. Say to him that if we could meet now, it
> is doubtful whether it would not be more painful than pleasant; but
> that if it be his lot to go now, he will soon have a joyous [meeting]
> with many loved ones gone before; and where [the rest] of us, through
> the help of God, hope ere-long [to join] them.[40]

Lincoln's father, Thomas Lincoln, died January 17, 1851. Some of Lincoln's contemporaries criticized this letter from Lincoln to his father, saying that he was simply repeating sentiments that he thought were appropriate to say to a dying man, and that Lincoln himself did not believe what he said. An irate William H. Herndon responded to these criticisms, saying, "It has been said to me that Mr. Lincoln wrote the above letter to an old man simply to cheer him up on his last moments, and that the writer did not believe what he said. The question is, was Mr. Lincoln an honest and truthful man? If he was, he wrote that letter honestly, believing it." It is ironic that this same question could later be asked about some of Herndon's criticisms of Lincoln's faith when he was president.[41]

Although in the early 1850s Lincoln was focused primarily on his law practice, he was still interested in politics and actively supported the Whig Party. He also continued to make political speeches, and in mid-1852, he eulogized his "beau ideal of a statesman," Henry Clay.

In his analysis of this eulogy, Bible scholar Edwin D. Freed points out that Lincoln did not allude to any scriptures that would offer hope for heaven or life after death. Although the eulogy would have been an appropriate place for such observations, it is not surprising he omitted them. As has been pointed out many times by scholars, Lincoln "was not a theologian" or "a preacher," but was simply "a politician."[42]

A month or so after his eulogy of Clay, Lincoln, still a jester, made three lighthearted, passing allusions to scripture in a political speech he presented at the Springfield Scott club. No further use of the Bible is recorded in any public or private forum from the fall of 1852 to the fall of 1854.

The Lincolns' fourth son, Thomas (nicknamed Tad), was born on April 4, 1853. Lincoln recognized how challenging the care of three small children was for his wife, so he tried to spend more time at home. Thanks to the propagation of railway transportation in the 1850s, Lincoln's biannual travel on the circuit became easier, and he came home more frequently on the weekends.

Even though Lincoln's law practice was quite successful and yielded a comfortable income, his accomplishments in his law practice did not completely satisfy him. He believed that as a lawyer he would never be able to accomplish anything of lasting significance, and he had earlier expressed a desire to "be esteemed of my fellow men, by rendering myself worthy of their esteem." It was about this time that Lincoln said to Herndon, "How hard, oh, how hard it is to die and leave one's country no better than if one had never lived for it!"[43]

The ten-year period from 1841 to 1851 had been transformational for Lincoln's biblical faith. He started this decade as a fatalist and skeptic of the Bible who considered God to be some indifferent "power." However, in late 1841, during a period of deep depression, he began to diligently read the Bible, looking for a cure for "the blues." He soon began using the Bible to support moral arguments, beginning with his Temperance Address of 1842.[44]

By 1851 his faith was still unconventional, but having gone through significant life events that included deep depression and the loss of a son and his father, Lincoln was reading the Bible with newfound respect. For Lincoln, the Bible had gone from a book he used for catchy phrases and platitudes (such as his exhibitive quotes of the Bible in the Lyceum Address) to a book of purpose and promise, as evidenced in his letters such as the one to Joshua Speed where he talked about "the salvation of the Lord" in early 1842 and for encouragement to his dying father in early 1850.[45]

4. DRAWING THE SWORD

BUILDING LINCOLN'S BIBLICAL
FOUNDATION AGAINST SLAVERY

Lead me to the rock that is higher than I.

—Psalm 61:2

In the spring of 1854, while Lincoln was standing on an Illinois prairie, lamenting the fact that he might die before he could do something to benefit his country, his old nemesis Stephen A. Douglas was raising a ruckus in the nation's capital. Douglas, who had become one of the most powerful Democratic politicians in Washington, was chair of the Senate committee on the territories. Four years prior he had been a driving force in the acceptance of the Compromise of 1850, a bill that had defused the political confrontation between slave and free states on the status of territories acquired in the Mexican American War. At the age of thirty-nine, Douglas was already considered future presidential material.

Douglas was an unapologetic proponent of Manifest Destiny, and saw expansion into the western territories as a potential avenue for his rise to the presidency. He knew that a transcontinental railroad was the key to American civilization's expansion, and wanted it to start in Chicago, traverse some investment property he owned, and then continue a northern route to San Francisco. To attain his vision, Douglas needed to get additional political support, and he believed he knew where it could be found—the South.

He knew that the key to Southern support for just about anything was the slavery carrot. The Missouri Compromise of 1820 had precluded slavery everywhere in the western territories except for Missouri and the region below the latitude of 36 degrees, 30 minutes within the Louisiana Purchase territory. If Douglas could repeal the Missouri Compromise and open the rest of the western territories for the expansion of slavery, he knew he could get all the support he wanted from the South for his northern route across America. It took him three iterations of bill writing to accomplish this, but he finally obtained the South's support.[1]

Douglas realized that the repeal of the Missouri Compromise would raise a "hell of a storm" in the North, and to maintain his political base he would have to present a convincing argument as to why it should be done. He found this argument in the concept of popular sovereignty. Popular sovereignty would mean that the people in Nebraska, not Congress, would decide whether slavery should be allowed in their territory. What, Douglas asked, could be more democratic than to allow the residents of the territories to decide? He even thought he had a biblical foundation for this: that God "gave a choice" to Adam and Eve to decide between good and evil in the Garden of Eden. But Douglas's Bible knowledge was woefully inadequate, and Lincoln would soon make him pay for it.[2]

Douglas girded up his loins, so to speak, and pushed the Kansas-Nebraska Act through Congress. The bill repudiated the Missouri Compromise's imaginary border against slavery—36 degrees 30 minutes latitude—making it possible for all new territories to be organized with slavery if the residents voted for it. Democratic president Franklin Pierce signed the bill into law on May 30, 1854.

Douglas had no idea that the "storm" he had just created was of hurricane strength, and his own political career would soon be in jeopardy. As reports of Northern outrage and anger over the repeal of the Missouri Compromise multiplied over the coming weeks, he decided that before the summer was over, he would need to return to Illinois and show his constituents the error of their ways. Douglas was certain that he could bring people around to his way of thinking and gain their support for the Kansas-Nebraska bill.[3]

Lincoln was riding the lonely Eighth Judicial Circuit when he heard about the passage of the Kansas-Nebraska Act. Lincoln, who had always hated slavery, was outraged. His roommate on the circuit, Judge Theophilus Lyle Dickey, said that Lincoln stayed up all night contemplating this event. By morning, Lincoln's outrage had transformed to vision. "I tell you, Dickey," Lincoln purportedly said when Dickey awakened the next day, "this nation cannot exist half slave and half free!" The fight to prevent slavery's spread into the new territories became Lincoln's "cause."[4]

Douglas, as Illinois's senior senator, would soon go home to raise support for the Kansas-Nebraska Act and assist in the Democratic Party's efforts to win Illinois's junior Senate seat in the 1854 senatorial campaign. Lincoln decided he would run for the US Senate as a Whig candidate, and this campaign would give him a stage on which he could wage his moral fight with Douglas. He planned to be ready for it.

← ❈ →

In August Douglas traveled from Washington to Chicago and would later say that he could have made the trip by the light of "his own burning effigy" at night. The anger directed toward him had not subsided when he faced a fuming crowd of eight thousand in Chicago on September 1. When Douglas stood up on the platform and tried to speak, he could scarcely be heard among the cat calls, boos, swearing, and hisses of the enraged audience.[5] Douglas was shocked at the vehemence of their anger. But he was a fighter, and fearlessly made plans for a statewide campaign to defend his Kansas-Nebraska bill.

Over the coming weeks both Douglas and Lincoln spoke about the Kansas-Nebraska bill in various cities across Illinois. Douglas, nicknamed "the Little Giant," usually drew the crowd, and Lincoln would speak to the same audience after his opponent had finished. Over the course of several weeks, both Douglas and Lincoln refined their arguments. Douglas defended popular sovereignty as a great fundamental "principle of self-government," and Lincoln argued that it was no more than an obvious effort to spread slavery into the territories.

By early October 1854 Lincoln had perfected the speech that would serve as his foundational moral argument against slavery. Although initially presented to the public in a speech in Springfield, its most celebrated presentation was on October 16, 1854, in the state's second largest city, Peoria. In this three-hour-long speech Lincoln would use the Declaration of Independence, the Bible, and the Northwest Ordinance of 1787 to attack the Kansas Nebraska Act and condemn slavery as a moral evil.

Douglas offered his typical, combative arguments in favor of the Nebraska bill, and denied Lincoln's accusations that the repeal of Kansas-Nebraska and the appeal to popular sovereignty was a blatant attempt to spread slavery. Douglas claimed that he "didn't care" if slavery was "voted up or voted down" by the residents of the Nebraska territories. He was merely doing what the people wanted—attempting to organize the territory democratically and accommodating their demand that the Missouri Compromise's boundaries against slavery be repudiated.[6]

After Douglas finished, Lincoln began his Peoria speech by giving the audience a short lesson about the history of slavery in America, discussing the boundaries on slavery enforced by the Ordinance of 1787 and the Missouri Compromise of 1820. He praised the Missouri Compromise, saying that the slavery issue had remained dormant for over thirty years because of the limitations it placed on slavery in the new territories. He then launched into his argument that the repeal of the Missouri Compromise "is wrong, wrong in its direct effect, letting slavery into Kansas and Nebraska—and wrong in its prospective principle, allowing it to spread to every other part of the wide world where men can be found inclined to take it."

Then, speaking of the indifference Douglas had expressed regarding the spread of slavery into the new territories, Lincoln expanded his moral argument:

> This declared indifference, but as I must think, covert real zeal for the spread of slavery, I can not but hate. I hate it because of the monstrous injustice of slavery itself. I hate it because it deprives our republican example of its just influence in the world—enables the enemies of free institutions, with plausibility, to taunt us as hypocrites—causes the real friends of freedom to doubt our sincerity, and especially because it forces so many really good men amongst ourselves into an open war with the very fundamental principles of civil liberty—criticizing the Declaration of Independence, and insisting that there is no right principle of action but self-interest.[7]

It was in the speech at Peoria that Lincoln first began use of the Bible as justification for an attack on slavery. Lincoln realized that using the Bible in his cause was necessary because powerful proslavery advocates had already dismissed the Declaration of Independence as a viable authority against slavery. These attacks on the Declaration were not only coming from Stephen A. Douglas, but from prominent senators such as John Calhoun of South Carolina and John Pettit of Indiana. On the floor of the United States Senate, Pettit had infamously refuted the Declaration's declamation that the equality of men was a "self-evident truth," by instead calling it a "self-evident lie."[8]

In addition to the assault on the Declaration, Southern preachers were using the Bible increasingly to justify the continuation of slavery by pointing to scriptures such as those that instructed enslaved people to obey their masters. Lincoln believed that it was therefore essential to find effective biblical arguments to refute these claims. Consequently, at Peoria he began to draw upon his formidable knowledge of scripture for his moral arguments.[9]

Unlike abolitionists, Lincoln did not advocate for the immediate elimination of slavery in the South, but instead followed what he believed was the Founders' plan—to prevent the spread of slavery into new territories and thereby ensure an eventual death of the institution. In his first biblical allusion in this speech, Lincoln explained his reluctant acceptance of slavery's current existence in the Southern states by quoting Jesus's saying, "Sufficient unto the day is the evil thereof" [Matthew 6:34]. He admitted that "if all earthly power were given me, I should not know what to do as to the existing institution" in the Southern states. He said this, because he knew that many White people in the country, himself included, might support the idea of freeing enslaved people, but they were not interested in immediately making them their political and social equals.[10]

Next Lincoln launched a direct attack on Douglas's support of the Kansas Nebraska Act. Douglas had claimed that it was time to organize the Nebraska country into territorial government, that the public had demanded the repeal of the Missouri Compromise, and that popular sovereignty—allowing slavery to be voted on—was the "intrinsically right" thing to do.

Lincoln refused to accept any of these claims by Douglas, and denounced Douglas's efforts to dehumanize enslaved people:

> The doctrine of self-government is right—absolutely and eternally right—but it has no just application, as here attempted. Or perhaps I should say that whether it has such just application depends upon whether a negro *is not* or *is* a man. If he is not a man, why in that case, he who is a man may, as a matter of self-government, do just as he pleases with him. But if the negro is a man, is it not to that extent, a total destruction of self-government, to say that he too shall not govern himself? When the white man governs himself that is self-government; but when he governs himself, and also governs another man, that is more than self-government—that is despotism. If the negro is a man, why then my ancient faith teaches me that 'all men are created equal;' and that there can be no moral right in connection with one man's making a slave of another.[11]

Lincoln quoted the preamble of the Declaration—that all men are created equal—and referred to it as "our ancient faith." He "loved the sentiments of those old-time men." He refused to accept the Democrats' argument that Kansas-Nebraska was a great "Union-saving" measure and responded with a quote from Shakespeare's Hamlet that is itself an allusion to the Bible, saying that the Kansas-Nebraska Act "hath no relish of salvation in it."[12]

Lincoln then talked about the institution of slavery being founded upon man's selfishness, saying that "Slavery is founded in the selfishness of man's nature—opposition to it is [in] his love of justice. These principles are an eternal antagonism; and when brought into collision so fiercely, as slavery extension brings them, shocks, and throes, and convulsions must ceaselessly follow.

Repeal the Missouri compromise—repeal all compromises—repeal the decla-ration of independence—repeal all past history, you still can not repeal human nature." Then, using scripture from Christ's Sermon on the Plain, he said "It still will be the abundance of man's heart, that slavery extension is wrong; and <u>out of the abundance of his heart, his mouth</u> will continue <u>to speak</u>" [Luke 6:45].[13]

Lincoln invoked both the Declaration of Independence and the Bible to present a sharp contrast between the founders' original faith and the Demo-crats' new faith: "Little by little, but steadily as man's march to the grave, we have been giving up the OLD for the NEW faith. Near eighty years ago we began by declaring that all men are created equal; but now from that beginning we have run down to the other declaration, that for SOME men to enslave OTHERS is a 'sacred right of self-government.' These principles can not stand together. They are as opposite as <u>God and mammon</u>; and whoever <u>holds to the one, must despise the other</u>" [allusion to Matthew 6:24].[14]

Alluding to the washed robes of the saints in the book of Revelation, he stated that, in failing to combat slavery,

> our republican robe is soiled, and trailed in the dust. Let us repurify it. Let us turn and <u>wash it white, in the spirit, if not the blood</u>, of the Revolution [allusion to Revelation 7:14]. Let us turn slavery from its claims of "moral right," back upon its existing legal rights, and its arguments of "necessity." Let us return it to the position our fathers gave it; and there let it rest in peace. Let us re-adopt the Declara-tion of Independence, and with it, the practices, and policy, which harmonize with it. Let north and south—let all Americans—let all lovers of liberty everywhere—join in the great and good work. If we do this, we shall not only have saved the union; but we shall have so saved it, as to make, and to keep, it, forever worthy of the saving. We shall have so saved it, that the succeeding millions of free happy people, the world over, <u>shall rise up, and call us blessed</u>, to the latest generations [allusion to Proverbs 31:28].[15]

Before he ended his speech, Lincoln wanted to be sure to correct Douglas's erroneous claim that the Bible was the foundation for allowing people to choose whether they wanted slavery in Nebraska:

> In the course of my main argument, Judge Douglas interrupted me to say, that the principle [of] the Nebraska bill was very old; that it originated when God made man and placed good and evil before

him, allowing him to choose for himself, being responsible for the
choice he should make.... The facts of this proposition are not true
as stated. God did not place good and evil before man, telling him to
make his choice. On the contrary, he did tell him there was one tree,
of the fruit of which, he should not eat, upon pain of certain death
[allusion to Genesis 3:1–3]. I scarcely wish so strong a prohibition
against slavery in Nebraska.[16]

Lincoln observed that in Douglas's speech earlier that day, the Little Giant
tried to invoke the memory of Henry C. Clay and Daniel Webster against him.
Lincoln was a great admirer of those old time Whigs and had even proclaimed
that Clay was his "beau ideal of a statesman." Lincoln repudiated the idea that
Clay and Webster would have ever been against him on the Missouri Compromise, and then could not resist using the Bible to poke fun at his opponent,
who was having a hard time bringing his constituents back in line after Kansas-
Nebraska. Lincoln quipped: "The truth is that some support from Whigs is
now a necessity with the Judge, and for thus it is, that the names of Clay and
Webster are now invoked. His old friends have deserted him in such numbers
as to leave too few to live by. He came to his own, and his own received him
not [John 1:11], and Lo! He turns unto the Gentiles" [allusion to Acts 13:46].[17]

The Peoria speech was over, and with it Lincoln had not only transformed
the national argument against slavery from one that was primarily political or
economic to one that was moral, but he had also built a solid foundation for
his future ethical arguments against slavery. Lincoln's affirmation of the Black
man's humanity and natural rights emanating from the Declaration testified
to his aspirations for reaching a higher moral plane. Although he made use of
scripture and the Declaration of Independence for his polemic in Peoria, he
had not yet found his most powerful Biblical arguments against slavery. This
would not happen until he ran a second time for the U. S. Senate—against
Douglas in 1858.

A young journalist named Horace White, who was in the Peoria audiences
for both Douglas's and Lincoln's speeches, reflected on Lincoln's transformative manner: "His [Lincoln's] speaking went to the heart because it came from
the heart. I have heard celebrated orators who could start thunders of applause
without changing any man's opinion. Mr. Lincoln's eloquence was of the higher
type, which produced conviction in others because of the conviction of the
speaker himself. His listeners felt that he believed every word he said, and
that, like Martin Luther, he would go to the stake rather than abate one jot or
tittle of it."[18]

Within four months of the Peoria debate, Lincoln's first senatorial contest was over. On February 8, 1855, the Illinois legislature elected Democrat Lyman Trumbull to the Senate. Although this was a defeat for Lincoln, he was not completely discouraged with the result. Trumbull was an anti-Nebraska Democrat, and Lincoln knew that Stephen A. Douglas would have to defend his own Senate seat in 1858. Again, he planned to be ready.[19]

← ✸ →

With the Senate race over, Lincoln's platform for national moral argument was gone, and he made no further use of the Bible in 1855 except in a letter to Joshua Speed with another passing reference about the gallows of Haman from the book of Esther. Although his loss of the national stage was unfortunate, Lincoln's problem was that he was not certain what he should do about his political allegiances. Should he remain a Whig? Should he become a Republican? In the same letter to Speed, Lincoln expressed his quandary:[20]

> You enquire where I now stand. That is a disputed point. I think I am a whig; but others say there are no whigs, and that I am an abolitionist . . . I am not a Know-Nothing. That is certain. How could I be? How can any one who abhors the oppression of negroes, be in favor of degrading classes of white people? Our progress in degeneracy appears to me to be pretty rapid. As a nation, we began by declaring that "all men are created equal." We now practically read it "all men are created equal, except negroes." When the Know-Nothings get control, it will read "all men are created equal, except negroes, and foreigners, and catholics." When it comes to this I should prefer emigrating to some country where they make no pretence of loving liberty—-to Russia, for instance, where despotism can be taken pure, and without the base alloy of hypocracy.[21]

The Republican Party of Illinois officially organized in Bloomington on May 29, 1856, and shortly beforehand Lincoln joined their ranks. The party leaders recognized Lincoln's preeminence as a politician in the state, and he was called upon to present the keynote address. William H. Herndon declared this speech "the grand effort" of Lincoln's life up to that time. "Heretofore he had simply argued the slavery question on the grounds of policy—the statesman's grounds—never reaching the question of the radical and eternal right. Now he was newly baptized and freshly born; he had the fervor of a new convert; the smothered flame broke out; enthusiasm unusual to him blazed up; his eyes were aglow with an inspiration; he felt justice; his heart was alive to the right; his sympathies, remarkably deep for him, burst forth, and he stood before the throne of the eternal Right." Herndon admitted that at Bloomington he [Herndon] "attempted for about fifteen minutes . . . to take notes, but at the end of that time I threw pen and paper away and lived only in the inspiration of the hour." He was not alone. Many reporters were present, ready to transcribe the speech, but did not. Joseph Medill, editor of the Chicago *Tribune*, declared that it was the greatest speech he had ever heard. Like Herndon and everyone else, he laid down his pencil and lived in the moment. Today the fabled address in Bloomington is often referred to as Lincoln's "lost speech."[22]

Less than a month later the Republican Party held its first national convention in Philadelphia and picked the soldier-explorer John C. Frémont as its first presidential nominee. At the convention Lincoln was briefly considered as Frémont's vice-presidential running mate, receiving 110 votes. Although William L. Dayton of New Jersey was ultimately the one chosen, this was nevertheless an omen of Lincoln's increasing notoriety.

Lincoln's next important speech was at a Republican banquet in Chicago on December 10, 1856. At that event he observed that the Democratic Party was attempting to replace the idea of the equality of men with the idea of perpetuity of human slavery, and had begun talking instead of "State equality." Lincoln closed this speech by urging his listeners to support the concept of the equality of man, something he believed God himself favored: "Let us re-inaugurate the good old 'central ideas' of the Republic. We *can* do it. The human heart *is* with us—*God is with us* [italics added]. We shall again be able not to declare, that 'all States as States, are equal,' nor yet that 'all citizens as citizens are equal,' but to renew the broader, better declaration, including both these and much more, that 'all men are created equal.'"[23]

The latter half of 1855 and the entire year of 1856 were politically less busy for Lincoln, but this changed dramatically in early 1857. On March 6, 1857, the United Sates Supreme Court handed down its most infamous ruling—the Dred Scott decision. In the 7–2 vote, the court held that the US Constitution did not provide American citizenship for people of African descent, regardless of whether they were enslaved or free. Therefore, the rights and privileges it conferred upon American citizens could not apply to them. Chief Justice Roger Taney, who wrote the majority opinion, went even further to express his opinion that Black people had *no* rights that White people had to respect. Dred Scott not only outraged most of the North, it also inspired Abraham Lincoln to go back to the speaking circuit to declaim the Dred Scott decision and return to his moral arguments against slavery.[24]

Lincoln did not stop there. He theorized that the Dred Scott decision was merely the latest in a series of events that had been planned by Stephen A. Douglas, Roger Taney, James Buchanan, and Franklin Pierce to legalize slavery everywhere in the United States. Lincoln wanted to sound the alarm on this as well as renew his moral attack on the institution of slavery. His weapons of choice were, as usual, the Declaration of Independence and the Bible.

← ❄ →

Unfortunately, Lincoln discovered that the use of the Bible as a weapon against slavery could be problematic. As mentioned previously, many people, including Northern and Southern ministers of the gospel, believed that the Bible supported the institution of slavery. Famous theologians and preachers on both sides of the debate had argued this point for decades. Those who said that the Bible condoned slavery pointed to scripture such as "And he [God] said, cursed be Canaan; a servant of servants shall he be unto his brethren" [Genesis 9:25]; "Servants, obey in all things your masters according to the flesh" [Colossians 3:22]; "Servants, be obedient to them that are your masters according to the flesh, with fear and trembling, in singleness of your heart, as unto Christ" [Ephesians 6:5], and many others. According to biblical scholar Mark Noll, slavery proponents noticed the fact that although Jesus condemned many Old Testament practices such as polygamy and easy divorce, he never said anything against slaveholding.[25]

One of the North's most famous abolitionists of that day, William Lloyd Garrison, was not a minister of the Gospel, and therefore had no reservations about rejecting scripture as an indisputable revelation from God. Garrison proclaimed, "To say that everything in the Bible is to be believed, simply because it is found in that volume, is . . . absurd and pernicious." Statements such as Garrison's were counterproductive to the Northern ministers who wanted to use the Bible to make a case against slavery. Garrison's declamations allowed proslavery men such as Southern Methodist minister J. W. Tucker to tell a Confederate audience in 1862 that "your cause is the cause of God, the cause of Christ, of humanity. It is a conflict of truth with error—of the Bible with Northern infidelity—of pure Christianity with Northern fanaticism."[26]

Those Northern ministers who asserted the Bible did not condone slavery had a significantly greater challenge to exegetically support their position. Before they could enlist scripture such as the Golden Rule in support of their cause, they first had to compare the differences between the institution of slavery in the Bible to the institution as practiced in nineteenth-century America, to wit: In biblical times, slaves were considered valuable indentured servants and were not beaten or separated from their families; slaves in the Bible were not always condemned to slavery for their entire lives, as in America; and slavery in the Bible was not race-based like it was in America.

Just as he had once been frustrated with ministers' inadequate support of the temperance cause, Lincoln was exasperated with preachers who adduced that the Bible supported slavery. He also thought that most Northern ministers' rebuttals to the proslavery interpretation of the Bible were uninspired and ineffectual. Mark Noll agrees and calls their arguments "weak." He points out that antislavery pastors used scripture like Exodus 21:16, Leviticus 25, and the book of Philemon, but arguments based on these scriptures and "common sense" scripture such as the Golden Rule were usually refuted quickly by proslavery pastors with their more numerous proslavery scripture references.[27]

Lincoln, dissatisfied with the exegetics and hermeneutics offered by the theologians and ministers of his day, personally sought out scripture that would support his antislavery cause. In 1847 he had used God's curse of man recorded in Genesis, "In the sweat of thy face shalt thou eat bread, till thou return unto the ground; for out of it wast thou taken: for dust thou art, and unto dust shalt thou return" [Genesis 3:19] for a less significant purpose. But when he began his quest to use the Bible to support the rights of the slave, he interpreted this ancient curse of man to be a promise for the slave, saying that whatever bread the slave earned by his manual labor the slave—not the master or any other man—had the right to eat it. This was a significant first step. Lincoln's assertion was the straightforward argument that could appeal to anyone, Black or White, who had toiled the ground.[28]

Lincoln usually substituted for the Genesis 3:19 argument of earning bread by the sweat of one's face the analogous proclamation of Psalm 128:2. Lincoln first used Psalm 128 in Springfield on June 26, 1857, in a speech where he was talking about the injustice of slavery. In following up on what Stephen A. Douglas had said about the inequality of a Black woman compared to a White man such as Lincoln, Lincoln conceded that although she may not be equal in every way to him, "in her natural right to eat the bread she earns with her own hands [allusion to Psalm 128:2] without asking leave of anyone else, she is my equal, and the equal of all others."[29]

Lincoln had formed Genesis 3:19 and Psalm 128:2, with their powerful images of sweat, bread, labor of the hands, and toil of the ground into effective biblically based arguments against slavery. Enslaved people—who in the *Dred Scott* case the Supreme Court had recently declared had *no* rights—*did* have rights according to Lincoln, per the Bible and the Declaration of Independence. The Bible said every man had the right to the fruit of his labor, and the

Declaration said that everyone had the right to "life, liberty, and the pursuit of happiness." These two simple arguments were, for working class people—whether they were Democrats or Republicans—easy to grasp and difficult to dismiss. They suggest Psalm 90:17, a person's desire that <u>God establish the work of their hands</u>. It was Lincoln's skill at using the Declaration, the Bible, and his Euclidian logic that caused one Democrat to say about him that "He is a dangerous man, sir! A damned dangerous man! He makes you believe what he says, in spite of yourself!"[30]

Although Genesis 3:19 and Psalm 128:2 both allude to the slaves eating the bread they earned from their own labor, Lincoln preferred the image of "the labor of hands" to "the sweat of the face." He would primarily use Psalm 128:2, rather than Genesis 3:19 in dozens of speeches, both published and unpublished, for the next year and a half.

← ❋ →

Because of the Kansas-Nebraska Act, a series of violent civil confrontations between proslavery and free state forces in Kansas raged from 1856 to 1858. In September of 1857 an illegitimate proslavery legislature met in Lecompton to rig passage of a new constitution that would inaugurate slavery in Kansas. Outraged at this action, free-state supporters, who comprised a large majority of settlers in the territory, boycotted the vote. In spite of its fraudulent passage, on February 2, 1858, Democratic president James Buchanan approved the Lecompton Constitution and submitted it to Congress. Stephen A. Douglas, who had assured everyone that popular sovereignty would decide the legality of slavery in Kansas, sided with the more numerous free-state residents and condemned both the proslavery constitution and the actions of President Buchanan.

This resulted in a huge split of the Democratic Party, and Douglas supported Republicans' efforts to defeat the Lecompton Constitution. Powerful eastern Republicans such as the New-York *Tribune*'s mercurial editor Horace Greeley began praising the Little Giant for his anti-Lecompton actions, and suggested that the Republicans of Illinois should endorse his candidacy for the Senate rather than run a Republican challenger in the upcoming 1858 Senate election.

Although Douglas was the most powerful Democrat in the United States Senate, and would have a significant advantage over Lincoln in the Democrat-dominated state of Illinois, Lincoln wanted to be that Republican challenger. For the remainder of 1857 and into early 1858, Lincoln prepared for the upcoming canvass by writing letters, making speeches, and calling in political favors to secure the Republican Party's nomination for the US Senate.[31]

Before returning to political polemics with Douglas, Lincoln had an opportunity to demonstrate his knowledge of the Bible in a less confrontational venue than the debate stage. On April 6, 1858, Lincoln delivered the first of a two-part lecture on "Discoveries and Inventions" before an audience of the Young Men's Association in Bloomington, Illinois. Lincoln's address included over thirty biblical references, mostly from Genesis, Exodus, and Deuteronomy. He used scripture to illustrate human accomplishments—discoveries such as the properties of metals, and inventions such as the wheel and axle, and the plow.[32]

Although Lincoln referenced over thirty scriptures as his source for discoveries and inventions, the presentation was secular rather than religious or moral. Nevertheless, preparation by Lincoln for this lecture required a considerable amount of work, and to find all the "inventions" required extensive reading on Lincoln's part. He either read the entire books of Genesis, Exodus, Numbers, Deuteronomy, Job, Proverbs, Isaiah, and Matthew, or used a biblical aid such as a concordance to help his search.[33]

Believing that he was on solid footing with the Bible, Lincoln's speeches were becoming bolder and more moralistic. As Herndon said, Lincoln now had "the fervor of a new convert" and acted as if he "stood before the throne of eternal right." As evidenced by the popular reaction to his 1856 "lost speech" in Bloomington, his speeches had become increasingly captivating and motivational, and by 1857 he was the acknowledged leader of the Republican Party of Illinois. Although the Bible was not his only weapon in his battle against slavery, it was becoming a very reliable one. Consequently, his use of scripture was growing, and in his next campaign for Stephen A. Douglas's Senate seat his biblically based moral arguments against slavery would reach full force.

5. A HOUSE DIVIDED

DEBATING SLAVERY
AS A MORAL EVIL

Beat your plowshares into swords and your pruninghooks
into spears.

—Joel 3:10

In the spring of 1858, the Republican Party of Illinois rejected Horace Greeley's suggestion that they support Democratic senator Stephen A. Douglas in
his coming re-election bid and called for a convention on June 16, 1858. The
keynote speaker for the convention was to be Abraham Lincoln, whom they
would declare that day as "the first and only choice of the Republicans of Illinois
for the United States Senate."[1]

When Lincoln completed the draft of his speech, he decided to solicit William H. Herndon's opinion about using Christ's statement that "a house divided
against itself cannot stand." Herndon described their conversation:

> I remember what I said after hearing the first paragraph wherein
> occurs the celebrated figure of the house divided against itself. [Hern-
> don asked:] "It is true, but is it wise or politic to say so?" [Lincoln]
> responded: "That expression is a truth of all human experience, a
> house divided against itself cannot stand [Mark 3:25] and he that
> runs may read [Habakkuk 2:2]. The proposition also is true and has
> been for six thousand years. I want to use some universally known
> figure expressed in simple language as universally well-known, that
> may strike home to the minds of men in order to raise them up to
> the peril of the times. I do not believe I would be right in changing
> or omitting it. I would rather be defeated with this expression in the
> speech, and uphold and discuss it before the people, than be victo-
> rious without it."[2]

Herndon recalled that Lincoln had wanted to use this scripture in a political statement two years ago, but friends had talked him out of it because they considered it impolitic. But this time Mark 3:25 was a vision, and Lincoln could not be dissuaded from its use. Herndon explained: "Now, however, the situation had changed somewhat. There had been a shifting of scenes, so to speak. The Republican Party had gained some in strength and more in moral effectiveness and force. Nothing could keep back in Lincoln any longer."[3]

Again friends tried to talk Lincoln out of using this scripture, one of them calling it a "damned fool utterance." But despite their objections, Lincoln was adamant: "Friends, this thing has been retarded long enough. The time has come when these sentiments should be uttered; and if it is decreed that I should go down because of this speech, then let me go down linked to the truth; let me die in the advocacy of what is just and right."[4]

Lincoln had often used metaphors in the past, usually about something related to farming or farm animals. But now he had found a biblical metaphor and firm place to stand on the political, economic, and moral issue of his age. He had previously seen himself as powerless to do anything significant about slavery, but now saw clearly that with this scripture he could strike a meaningful blow at the evil institution.

At the Republican state convention in Springfield on June 16, 1858, after being nominated as his party's candidate for the US Senate, Lincoln proclaimed:

> "A house divided against itself cannot stand" [Mark 3:25].
> I believe this government cannot endure, permanently half slave and half free.
> I do not expect the Union to be dissolved—I do not expect the house to fall—but I do expect it will cease to be divided. It will become all one thing, or all the other. Either the opponents of slavery, will arrest the further spread of it, and place it where the public mind shall rest in the belief that it is in course of ultimate extinction; or its advocates will push it forward, till it shall become alike lawful in all the States, old as well as new—North as well as South. Have we no tendency to the latter condition?[5]

The House Divided Speech, as it became known, was indeed one of Lincoln's most influential addresses. Legal scholar Wilson Huhn said that with this speech Lincoln was pointing out that the country was at a crossroads, and it faced "a conflict of biblical proportions, and a moral choice of eternal significance." The House Divided Speech was Lincoln's clarion call to the nation to wake up and face the slavery question. Lincoln would use the house divided political allegory and associated biblical arguments in at least a dozen major speeches over the course of the next year—including several of the Lincoln-Douglas debates. Stephen A. Douglas denigrated the phrase claiming it was a call for war between the North and South, and demanded that Lincoln repudiate it. But Lincoln dismissed Douglas's accusations and continued to use "a house divided" in his biblically based moral arguments.[6]

Less than a month after he was nominated for the Senate, in a July 10, 1858, speech in Chicago, Lincoln employed yet another Bible passage to attack slavery. With this use of Matthew 5:48, Lincoln demonstrated a more integrated approach to tying the Declaration of Independence, scripture, and straightforward moral argument into his attack on slavery and support of the equality of men:

> My friend [Douglas] has said to me that I am a poor hand to quote Scripture. I will try it again, however. It is said in one of the admonitions of the Lord, "As your Father in Heaven is perfect, be ye also perfect" [Matthew 5:48]. The Savior, I suppose, did not expect that any human creature could be perfect as the Father in Heaven; but He said, "As your Father in Heaven is perfect, be ye also perfect." He set that up as a standard, and he who did most towards reaching that standard, attained the highest degree of moral perfection. So I say in relation to the principle that all men are created equal, let it be as nearly reached as we can. . . . Let us discard all this quibbling about this man and the other man—this race and that race and the other race being inferior, and therefore they must be placed in an inferior position—discarding our standard that we have left us. Let us discard all these things, and unite as one people throughout this land, until we shall once more stand up declaring that all men are created equal.[7]

The Kansan proslavery Lecompton Constitution was defeated in January 1858. On July 17, 1858, in a speech in Springfield, Lincoln denigrated Douglas's claim that he [Douglas], rather than the Republican Party, deserved most of the credit for the defeat of the proslavery Lecompton constitution:

> Does he [Douglas] place his superior claim to credit, on the ground that he performed a good act which was never expected of him? He says I have a proneness for quoting Scripture. If I should do so now, it occurs that perhaps he places himself somewhat upon the ground of the parable of the lost sheep which went astray upon the mountains,

and when the owner of the hundred sheep found the one that was lost, and threw it upon his shoulders, and came home rejoicing, it was said that there was more rejoicing over the one sheep that was lost and had been found, than over the ninety and nine in the fold. The application is made by the Saviour in this parable, thus, "<u>Verily, I say unto you, there is more rejoicing in heaven over one sinner that repenteth, than over ninety and nine just persons that need no repentance</u>" [Luke 15:7].

And now, if the Judge claims the benefit of this parable, *let him repent.* Let him not come up here and say: I am the only just person; and you are the ninety-nine sinners! *Repentance*, before *forgiveness* is a provision of the Christian system, and on that condition alone will the Republicans grant his forgiveness.[8]

In that same speech Lincoln continued his attack against Douglas and slavery, by again using the familiar verses that "<u>a House Divided against itself cannot stand</u>" [Mark 3:25], and also that, "in the right to put into his mouth <u>the bread that his own hands have earned</u>, he [the Black man] is the equal of every other man" [allusion to Psalm 128:2].[9]

On July 24 Lincoln proposed to his opponent that they enter formal debate. As in 1854, Lincoln had been following Douglas around to different events and after the Little Giant finished speaking would speak to the same audience. Douglas reluctantly agreed to the proposal of formal debate, and offered seven debates over the coming months at cities representing seven congressional districts. The debates were to be held in Ottawa, Freeport, Jonesboro, Charleston, Galesburg, Quincy, and Alton. The first debate at Ottawa was scheduled for August 21, 1858. The debate format agreed upon was for the first candidate's opening speech to last one hour, to be followed by an hour and a half rebuttal by the second candidate. The first candidate would then get another half an hour for his final rejoinder. The candidates would alternate turns as first speaker.

Douglas was wary of debating Lincoln, whom he described as "the strong man of his party—full of wit, facts, dates—and the best stump speaker, with his droll ways and dry jokes, in the West. He is as honest as he is shrewd, and, if I beat him, my victory will be hardly won."[10]

← ❊ →

Four days before the first debate at Ottawa, in a short speech at Lewistown, Illinois, on August 17, 1858, Lincoln employed a verse from the book of Genesis, along with the Declaration of Independence, in an inspiring moral argument:

"We hold these truths to be self-evident: that all men are created
equal; that they are endowed by their Creator with certain unalien-
able rights; that among these are life, liberty and the pursuit of happiness." This was their [the Founding Fathers's] majestic interpretation
of the economy of the Universe. This was their lofty, and wise, and
noble understanding of the justice of the Creator to His creatures.
Yes, gentlemen, to *all* His creatures, to the whole great family of man.
In their enlightened belief, nothing stamped <u>with the Divine image
and likeness</u> [allusion to Genesis 1:26–27] was sent into the world to
be trodden on, and degraded, and imbruted by its fellows.[11]

The Lewistown speech has special significance in that Lincoln identifies the
Declaration of Independence with the Bible's doctrine of the creation of man in
the divine image. Using Genesis 1:26–27, Lincoln tied the Declaration's proposition of the equality of man to scripture.[12]

Anticipation for the debates ran high, and at least one Lincoln correspondent believed the upcoming contest had spiritual significance. Abraham Smith
of Ridge Farm, Illinois, wrote to Lincoln saying he regarded the upcoming
debates as "a contest for the advancement of the kingdom of Heaven or the
kingdom of Satan—a contest for an advance or a retrograde in civilization."[13]

On August 21 the first debate took place before an audience of twelve thousand people in Ottawa, a town in north central Illinois. As with all future
Lincoln-Douglas debates there was a carnival-like atmosphere, replete with
decorative bunting, brass bands playing, and cannons booming.

In mid-afternoon, Douglas began his hour-long assault on Lincoln and what
he called the "Black Republican Party," using the usual polemics. He declared
Republicans to be radical abolitionists, he said that he himself did not care if
slavery went up or down in Kansas, he derided the Black man as not the equal
to the White man, and described the House Divided Speech as revolutionary
and destructive. He again sang the praises of popular sovereignty.

Lincoln hit back hard, claiming Douglas's acknowledged indifference toward slavery to be an assault on the principles of equality expressed in the Declaration of Independence. He argued that it was morally wrong for Douglas
to declare that the Black man was inferior and without human rights. Lincoln
admitted that while both he and most Whites at that time were unwilling to
make Black people politically and socially their equals, he nevertheless proclaimed they still had rights. He said that "in the right <u>to eat the bread</u>, without
leave of anybody else, <u>which his own hand earns</u> [allusion to Psalm 128:2], he
[the Black man] is my equal and the equal of Judge Douglas, and the equal of

every living man." He also argued that "there is no reason in the world why the negro is not entitled to all the natural rights enumerated in the Declaration of Independence, the right to life, liberty and the pursuit of happiness."[14]

Lincoln defended his claim that a house divided against itself cannot stand [Mark 3:25] and joked that if Judge Douglas did not believe that to be true, then he needed to take up his argument with "an authority of somewhat higher character." But this rebuttal by Lincoln was not overwhelming, and Douglas would continue to attack the House Divided Speech in future debates—claiming that Lincoln's declaration was a call for war. Lincoln denounced the Supreme Court's *Dred Scott* decision and admonished Douglas's willingness to blindly accept the *Dred Scott* decision as a "Thus saith the Lord" [Exodus 4:22] type of proclamation. Lincoln expressed his fear that if things were allowed to continue the present course, there may be another Supreme Court decision coming—one that made slavery legal everywhere.

Lincoln, in remembering words of warning once spoken by Henry Clay, observed that: "When [Douglas] invites any people, willing to have slavery, to establish it, he is blowing out the moral lights around us. When he says he 'cares not whether slavery is voted down or voted up'—that it is a sacred right of self-government—he is, in my judgment, penetrating the human soul and eradicating the light of reason and the love of liberty in this American people."[15]

The second debate with Douglas was held six days later in the tiny town of Freeport, barely twenty miles from the Wisconsin state line. This was Republican country, and most of the audience looked forward to watching Lincoln skewer Douglas. Nearly fifteen thousand people assembled in a grove outside of town.

Unlike the first debate at Ottawa, Lincoln made no reference to the house divided scripture in his speech. He spent his first hour answering seven questions Douglas had proposed to him in the first debate, and then went on the offensive asking Douglas four questions of his own. One of these questions would eventually prove fatal to the Little Giant's chances of winning the office of president of the United States.

With the *Dred Scott* decision in mind, Lincoln asked Douglas a critical question, "Can the people of a United States Territory, in any lawful way, against the wish of any citizen of the United States, exclude slavery from its limits prior to the formation of a State Constitution?" A number of Lincoln's contemporaries argued that this question was a trap. If Douglas answered in the negative, he was violating his own popular sovereignty principle. However, if he answered in the affirmative, he would be going against the *Dred Scott* decision and risked alienating the South.[16]

Douglas delivered his "emphatic" answer to Lincoln's question, saying that "in my opinion the people of a territory can, by lawful means, exclude slavery from their limits prior to the formation of a State Constitution." This affirmative answer, hereafter known as the Freeport Doctrine, would eventually cause a split between the northern and southern wings of the Democratic Party. Southerners wanted a presidential candidate who would *guarantee* their right to take slaves into the territories. Finally, Douglas attacked Lincoln's House Divided Speech again, but Lincoln did not respond to Douglas's attack in his final rejoinder.[17]

It would be a month before the debates continued in Jonesboro. But during that interim the candidates continued to stump the state separately, making dozens of independent appearances to crowds of supporters that wanted to hear more about the political issue that was setting the Prairie State on fire.

Although Lincoln had avoided the use of the house divided argument in the second debate at Freeport, he continued to refer to it in speeches made between debate appearances at Freeport and Jonesboro, including an August 31 speech at Carlinville, a September 2 speech at Clinton, and a September 4 speech in Bloomington. It is likely that he used the house divided metaphor and/or the reference to Psalm 128:2 in various other speeches in towns such as Macomb on August 21, Tremont on August 30, and Greenville on September 13, but the editors of small-town newspapers did not have the necessary resources to record and publish Lincoln's entire speeches.

In Bloomington on September 4, and then again in a speech in Edwardsville on September 11, Lincoln utilized a new Bible reference when he warned the South of the dangers of disparaging and enslaving Black people. He likened these actions to Christ's teachings at the Sermon on the Mount and the warning in Acts 19 regarding the dangers of casting out demons: "And when you have stricken down the principles of the Declaration of Independence, and thereby consigned the negro to hopeless and eternal bondage, are you quite sure that the demon will not <u>turn and rend you</u>?" [allusion to Matthew 7:6 and Acts 19:15–16].[18]

On September 14 Lincoln traveled from Greenville to Jonesboro, a small town only thirty-four miles north of the southernmost city of Illinois—Cairo. Whereas most of the people in Freeport and Ottawa had been sympathetic to the Republican cause, Jonesboro was in the heart of Douglas country, where the majority had Southern roots and were adamant supporters of slavery. Although the audience was small—fewer than two thousand people—on the morning of September 15 Douglas arrived with the customary hubbub, cannons booming and bands playing. Douglas crammed his speech with his usual arguments about the inferiority of Black people, an attack on Lincoln's House Divided Speech as being an incendiary for war, and his customary exaggerations about Lincoln and the "Black Republican Party." This crowd was pro-Douglas, and Lincoln, although he defended the rights of Black people and his position that "a house divided against itself cannot stand" [Mark 3:25], made little headway against this highly prejudiced audience.[19]

Likewise, at the fourth debate in Charleston on September 18 Lincoln was still on the defensive and made very little progress with his moral arguments. A little gun-shy over how Douglas had been attacking his House Divided Speech, he did not quote that verse. Douglas again attacked the House Divided Speech, vehemently arguing that the nation had been prosperous under the divided system established by the founding fathers, and there was no reason this could not continue. For unknown reasons, Lincoln did not quote the Bible at all in his speech, even in his final rejoinder. Douglas's verbal attacks forced Lincoln to focus on refuting Douglas's claims that he [Lincoln] and the "Black Republican Party" were focused on giving Black people political and social equality with White people.

After these two disappointing debate performances, Lincoln resolved to go on the offensive again. The *CW* includes a number of memoranda (fragments) that Lincoln jotted down, probably in late September or early October. They reveal Lincoln's thought process as he developed his plan for the use of biblical language and scripture in future attacks on Douglas's proslavery arguments:

> Suppose it is true, that the negro is inferior to the white, in the gifts of nature; is it not the exact reverse justice that the White should, for that reason, take from the negro, any part of the little which has been given him? "Give to him that is needy" [allusion to Matthew 5:42] is christian rule of charity; but "Take from him that is needy" is the rule of slavery.
>
> The sum of pro-slavery theology seems to be this: "Slavery is not universally *right*, nor yet universally *wrong*; it is better for *some* people to be slaves; and, in such cases, it is the Will of God that they be such."
>
> Certainly there is no contending against the Will of God [allusion to Job 23:13]; but still there is some difficulty in ascertaining, and applying it, to particular cases. For instance we will suppose the Rev. Dr. Ross [a prominent clergyman that used the Bible to defend slavery] has a slave named Sambo [a common slave name in the nineteenth century], and the question is "Is it the Will of God that Sambo shall remain a slave, or be set free?" The Almighty gives no audable answer

to the question, and his revelation—the Bible—gives none—or, at most, none but such as admits of a squabble, as to it's meaning. No one thinks of asking Sambo's opinion on it. So, at last, it comes to this, that *Dr. Ross* is to decide the question. And while he consider[s] it, he sits in the shade, with gloves on his hands, and subsists on the bread that Sambo is earning in the burning sun. If he decides that God Wills Sambo to continue a slave, he thereby retains his own comfortable position; but if he decides that God will's Sambo to be free, he thereby has to walk out of the shade, throw off his gloves, and delve for his own bread. Will Dr. Ross be actuated by that perfect impartiality, which has ever been considered most favorable to correct decisions?

But, slavery is good for some people!!! As a *good* thing, slavery is strikingly perculiar, in this, that it is the only good thing which no man ever seeks the good of, *for himself.*

Nonsense! Wolves devouring lambs, [allusion to Isaiah 11:6] not because it is good for their own greedy maws, but because it is good for the lambs![20]

One additional fragment, written perhaps a little earlier than the others, was his definition of democracy: "As I would not be a *slave*, so I would not be a *master.* This expresses my idea of democracy. Whatever differs from this, to the extent of the difference, is no democracy." Lincoln scholar Lucas Morel correctly points out that this statement of equality by Lincoln was another way of expressing the Golden Rule.[21]

The fifth debate was on October 7 in Galesburg and was held at Knox College in front of another large crowd of about fifteen thousand people. In his opening argument Douglas upstaged Lincoln again when he quoted Lincoln's House Divided Speech and used it to question whether that scripture applied when, after all, "we have prospered" since the days of the founding "thus divided." He also attacked the speech in his final rejoinder, and chided Illinois Republicans for being themselves divided over the issue. Again, Lincoln did not respond to Douglas's criticism, probably because he had not yet developed an effective counterargument.[22]

At the sixth debate in Quincy on October 13, rather than using his controversial house divided argument, Lincoln used his less inflammatory biblical argument that although the enslaved person may not be equal to the White man in all respects, in his "right to eat the bread without leave of anybody else which his own hand earns [allusion to Psalm 128:2], he is my equal and the equal of Judge Douglas, and the equal of every other man." He decried the *Dred Scott* decision as not only a potential means of spreading slavery into the new territories, but also of making slavery legal everywhere.[23]

October 15 found Lincoln and Douglas in the Mississippi River town of Alton, ready to begin the last of the seven debates. This town of six thousand residents was the former home of abolitionist Elijah P. Lovejoy, who in 1837 was murdered by a proslavery mob as he tried to protect his printing press from destruction. Whereas Douglas was nursing a cold and was unable to display his normal, booming voice and stage presence, Lincoln looked strong, confident, and the picture of health.

The usual polemics about slavery ensued, and Douglas again attacked the House Divided Speech, calling it "a slander" on the framers of the constitution and arguing that their provision for slavery was the right thing to do at the nation's founding. But Lincoln was ready for him this time, and began by poking fun at Douglas when he said: "Judge Douglas has again referred to a Springfield speech in which I said 'a house divided against itself cannot stand' [Mark 3:25]. The Judge has so often made the entire quotation from that speech that I can make it from memory." Lincoln quoted the appropriate excerpt from his original Springfield House Divided Speech, and began his response by quipping that the speech has "been extremely offensive to Judge Douglas. He has warred upon [it] as Satan does upon the Bible."[24]

Lincoln then launched into his response to Douglas's attack on the House Divided Speech, saying that although the founders first allowed slavery, they intended it to eventually die out rather than continue indefinitely. He proclaimed that they "placed that institution where the public mind *did* rest in the belief that it was in the course of ultimate extinction." He pointed out that the founders made provision that the African slave trade "should be cut off at the end of twenty years." He observed that the founders did not openly talk about slavery in the Constitution, but instead used "covert language" to merely allude to slavery so that "after the institution of slavery had passed from among us— there should be nothing on the face of the great charter of liberty suggesting that such a thing as negro slavery had ever existed among us."

He continued with his defense of the house divided argument that was, according to audience member Walter Hitt, "melting pathos." His words spewed forth quickly and with the authority of one who had mastered his argument:[25]

> And when I say that I desire to see the further spread of [slavery] arrested I only say I desire to see that done which the fathers have first done. When I say I desire to see it placed where the public mind will

rest in the belief that it is in the course of ultimate extinction, I only say I desire to see it placed where they placed it. It is not true that our fathers, as Judge Douglas assumes, made this government part slave and part free. Understand the sense in which he puts it. He assumes that slavery is a rightful thing within itself—was introduced by the framers of the Constitution. The exact truth is, that they found the institution existing among us, and they left it as they found it. But in making the government they left this institution with many clear marks of disapprobation upon it. They found slavery among them and they left it among them because of the difficulty—the absolute impossibility of its immediate removal. And when Judge Douglas asks me why we cannot let it remain part slave and part free as the fathers of the government made, he asks a question based upon an assumption which is itself a falsehood.[26]

Lincoln's performance was indeed riveting, as is evidenced by his declaration of what "the real issue" was between Republicans and Democrats of the day. In it he exclaimed that, unlike the Democrats, he and the Republican Party believed slavery was a "moral, social, and political wrong," and then placed the argument in the context of human history: "It is the eternal struggle between these two principles—right and wrong—throughout the world. They are the two principles that have stood face to face from the beginning of time; and will ever continue to struggle. The one is the common right of humanity and the other the divine right of kings. It is the same principle in whatever shape it develops itself. It is the same spirit that says, 'You work and toil and earn bread, and I'll eat it'" [allusion to Psalm 128:2].[27]

With the conclusion of the Alton event, undoubtedly Lincoln's finest performance, the debates were over. They had captured the attention of not only thousands of people in Illinois, but millions more in the rest of the country. Many newspapers had published the debates in their entirety and Lincoln had attained, by his successful stance against the Democrat who could be credibly called the most skilled debater in the United States Senate, the respect and admiration of the North's reading public.

Citizens went to the polls on November 2, 1858. Lincoln won the popular vote in Illinois by four thousand votes; however, he lost the Senate contest in the Democrat-controlled legislature by a vote of 46 to 54. Even though Lincoln's nation-wide venue with Stephen A. Douglas was over, he continued to rage against the injustice of slavery in both public and private correspondence. In a letter on April 6, 1859, to Henry L. Pierce of Boston, Lincoln closed with a statement reminiscent of the Golden Rule: "This is a world of compensations; and he who would <u>be no slave, must consent to have no slave</u> [allusion to Matthew 7:12]. Those who deny freedom to others, deserve it not for themselves; and, under a just God, can not long retain it."[28]

In proclaiming that a just God will not allow those who deny freedom to others to retain their own freedom for very long, Lincoln was demonstrating not only that he was using the Bible in an increasingly effective way for moral argument, but that he was also being transformed by what he read. Many ministers had used the Bible to support their claim that God was not against slavery, but Lincoln took a bold stand against their interpretation. Lincoln believed that robbing Black people of the fruits of their labor was morally wrong, and scripture like the Golden Rule—from the words of Jesus himself—reinforced this position by indicating each person should treat his or her neighbor equally. This was another declaration for a natural birthright of man: equality. Lincoln's use of the Bible was changing from simply quoting it for the purpose of authority in moral argument to quoting it from his own convictions of what the Bible said about right and wrong. To Lincoln the Bible was becoming less of a book of great quotations and more of a personal driving force.

Lincoln returned to his law practice, but he was now a national figure and continued to receive invitations to speak at various cities across the Northern states. The next time Lincoln quoted the Bible was a September 16, 1859, speech in Columbus, Ohio. The following excerpt from this speech contrasts Thomas Jefferson's fear of God's wrath for the sin of American slavery with Judge Douglas's frequent statements that he didn't care whether the people of new territories chose to "vote slavery up or down":

> He [Douglas] ought to remember that there was once in this country a man by the name of Thomas Jefferson, supposed to be a Democrat—a man whose principles and policy are not very prevalent amongst Democrats to-day, it is true; but that man did not take exactly this view of the insignificance of the element of slavery which our friend Judge Douglas does. In contemplation of this thing [slavery], we all know he [Jefferson] was led to exclaim, "I tremble for my country when I remember that God is just!" We know how he looked upon it when he thus expressed himself. There was danger to this country—danger of the avenging justice of God in that little unimportant popular sovereignty question of Judge Douglas. He supposed there was a question of God's eternal justice wrapped up in the enslaving of any race of men, or any man, and that those who did so braved <u>the arm of Jehovah</u>

[allusion to Isaiah 53:1]—that when a nation thus dared the Almighty every friend of that nation had cause to dread His wrath [allusion to 2 Kings 22:13 and 2 Chronicles 20:29]. Choose ye between Jefferson and Douglas as to what is the true view of this element among us.[29]

In a speech given on September 17, 1859, in Cincinnati, Ohio, Lincoln introduced one of his most meticulously prepared, biblically based arguments for the defense of the fundamental rights of enslaved people. He proclaimed what he believed God intended for all men, and quoted or alluded to five Bible verses:

If there is any one thing that can be proved to be the will of God by external nature around us, without reference to revelation, it is the proposition that what any one man earns with his hands and by the sweat of his brow, he shall enjoy in peace [allusion to Genesis 3:19]. I say that whereas God almighty has given every man one mouth to be fed, and one pair of hands adapted to furnish food for that mouth, if anything can be proved to be the will of Heaven, it is proved by this fact, that that mouth is to be fed by those hands, without being interfered with by any other man who has also his mouth to feed [and] his hands to labor with [allusion to Psalm 128:2]. I hold that if the Almighty had ever made a set of men that should do all the eating and none of the work, he would have made them with mouths only and no hands, and if he had ever made another class that he intended should do all the work and none of the eating, he would have made them without mouths and with all hands. But inasmuch as he has not chosen to make man in that way, if anything is proved, it is that those hands and mouths are to be co-operative through life and not to be interfered with. That they are to go forth and improve their position as I have been trying to illustrate, is the inherent right given to mankind directly by the Maker.[30]

In this same speech, he again referred to the house divided metaphor [Mark 3:25], and then, for the first time, alluded to Jesus's miracle of feeding the five thousand:

I think that we ought to keep in view our real purpose, and in none do anything that stands adverse to our purpose. If we shall adopt a platform that fails to recognize or express our purpose, or elect a man that declares himself inimical to our purpose, we not only take nothing by our success, but we tacitly admit that we act upon no [other] principle than a desire to have "the loaves and fishes" [allusion to John 6:26], by which, in the end our apparent success is really an injury to us.[31]

In closing he added a new biblical allegory, stating, "The good old maxims of the Bible are applicable, and truly applicable to human affairs, and in this as in other things, we may say here that he who is not for us is against us; he who gathereth not with us scattereth" [Luke 11:23].[32]

In a subsequent speech at the Wisconsin State Agricultural Society, Lincoln (the jester) again presented his argument in a humorous manner: "As each man has one mouth to be fed, and one pair of hands to furnish food, it was probably intended that that particular pair of hands should feed that particular mouth"[33] [allusion to Psalm 128:2].

← ❈ →

Beginning in 1854, Lincoln had started using the Bible as a sword to attack slavery. He became increasingly adept at this, and with his house divided scripture in 1858 he drew the nation's attention to the proposition that the time to end slavery had come. This may seem obvious today, but in the late 1850s there existed a significant danger that slavery would not only survive, but flourish. With his repeated use of the Biblical "house divided," Lincoln said "enough is enough," America cannot go on as a nation that proclaims liberty while keeping millions of people in chains. Stephen A. Douglas's attacks on the speech, claiming Lincoln was threatening war, put his Republican opponent on the defensive for a time, but Lincoln finally figured out his counterargument. In Alton and other small towns in central Illinois he transferred from defense to offense and never looked back.

Lincoln had crossed the Rubicon with the House Divided Speech, however it was not his most powerful scriptural argument for the humanity of all persons. This distinction belonged to the arguments that drew upon Genesis 3:19, Psalm 128:2, and Ecclesiastes 3:13. With these, God's curse that man must work the ground in Genesis 3:19 (In the sweat of thy face shalt thou eat bread, till thou return unto the ground; for out of it wast thou taken: for dust thou art, and unto dust shalt thou return) became a privilege in Psalm 128 (For thou shalt eat the labour of thine hands: happy shalt thou be, and it shall be well with thee). This privilege then became a gift in Ecclesiastes 3 (And also that every man should eat and drink, and enjoy the good of all his labour, it is the gift of God). In a nation where its Supreme Court had ruled that Black people had "no rights the White man was bound to respect," and a sizable minority of the people questioned the humanity of African Americans, Lincoln, as a transformational leader, used these scriptures to great effect.

Lincoln's transformational leadership is evidenced by citizens such as Henry G. McPike, who witnessed Lincoln's skilled use of the Bible in the debate in Alton:

> When [Lincoln] touched on the slavery feature of his address, it seemed to me there came an eloquence born of the earnestness of a heart convinced of the sinfulness—the injustice and the brutality of the institution of slavery, which made him a changed man . . . "A house divided against itself cannot stand," said he, "and this nation must be all free or all slave," suiting his words to those of the Christ when he denounced sin and said that sin and unrighteousness could not exist with righteousness in the heart of the same individual. He argued that the principles of slavery and freedom could not exist in the nation side by side . . . I forgot the ungainly form and homely face and seemed to see the great heart of Lincoln beating in its horror at the infamy of the institution against which he inveighed. Wild and long continued cheering from Republican throats punctuated the points of Lincoln . . . The Alton debate was a great one—some asserting it was the greatest of the seven . . . It made such an impression on my mind that today the tones of Lincoln are still vibrating in my ears, and it stirred my heart as nothing else did and made me a greater foe of the institution of slavery.[34]

The Bible informed Lincoln's transformational leadership again in an address at Petersburg, Illinois, in the fall of 1858. It was probably typical of the dozens of speeches Lincoln made in the summer and fall of that year that were never printed in newspapers or recorded in the *Collected Works of Abraham Lincoln*. James Miles, who was in the audience that day, was among many forever changed: "[Lincoln's] speech was a fine one and claimed the attention of Every one Democrat as well as the Republicans, but what thrilled the audience was his apostroph[e] to Liberty, Concluding with the Expression 'God gave me these hands (holding them up to the vast audience) to feed this mouth' (putting his hands to his mouth). This expression contained in the apostroph[e] was more than Convincing: it literally Electrified them and Carried the Crowd with him as if the people were Caught up in a Cyclone."[35]

President-elect Abraham Lincoln, 1861. *Library of Congress, Prints and Photographs Division, reprod. no. LC-USZ62–7334.*

Mary Lincoln, 1861. Mary described her husband as "a religious man always." *Library of Congress, Prints and Photographs Division, reprod. no LC-DIG-ppmsca-37856.*

Lincoln's lifelong friend Joshua Speed and his wife, Fanny. Speed, although a skeptic himself, attested to Lincoln's increasing faith in the Bible during his presidential years. *Courtesy of the Abraham Lincoln Presidential Library and Museum, Springfield, IL.*

Evangelist Peter Cartwright, whom Lincoln suspected of starting a "whispering campaign" against his religious beliefs in their 1846 campaign for Congress. *Courtesy of the Abraham Lincoln Presidential Library and Museum, Springfield, IL.*

Political rival Senator Stephen A. Douglas, who in 1858 told Lincoln that he was "a poor hand to quote scripture." *Library of Congress, Prints and Photographs Division, reprod. no LC-DIG-cwpbh-00880.*

Lincoln's law partner William H. Herndon, who could never quite make up his mind about Lincoln's religious beliefs. *Courtesy of the Abraham Lincoln Presidential Library, Springfield, IL.*

Rev. James Smith of First Presbyterian Church, Springfield. Smith, through preaching and his book *The Christian's Defense,* was probably the first to offer Lincoln erudite explanation of the Bible. *Courtesy of the Abraham Lincoln Presidential Library and Museum, Springfield, IL.*

White House babysitter
Julia Taft Bayne, who
wrote firsthand accounts
of Lincoln's Bible reading
in the White House.
*Courtesy of the Abraham
Lincoln Presidential
Library and Museum,
Springfield, IL.*

Rev. Phineas Gurley, Lincoln's
pastor at the New York Avenue
Presbyterian Church. Lincoln
said of him, "I like Gurley. He
don't preach politics. . . . When
I go to church, I like to hear
the gospel." *Courtesy of the New
York Avenue Presbyterian Church,
Washington, DC.*

Elizabeth Keckley, the formerly enslaved seamstress who became Mary Lincoln's friend, as well as a careful observer of Lincoln's Bible reading habits while in the White House. *Courtesy of the Abraham Lincoln Presidential Library and Museum, Springfield, IL.*

Rebecca Pomroy, nurse who shared her Christian faith with Lincoln after Willie died. *Library of Congress, Prints and Photographs Division, reprod. no LC-DIG-ppmsca-32248.*

Abolitionist and former slave Frederick Douglass, who recognized Lincoln's increasing interest in equality for Black Americans. *Library of Congress, Prints and Photographs Division, reprod. no LC-DIG-ppmsca-56175.*

Life-long friend and Supreme Court Justice David Davis, who said he didn't think "anyone knew what Lincoln thought about religion." *Library of Congress, Prints and Photographs Division, reprod. no LC-DIG-cwpbh-02279.*

Newspaper Correspondent Noah Brooks, who attested to Lincoln's frequent Bible reading and prayer in the White House. *Courtesy of the Abraham Lincoln Presidential Library and Museum, Springfield, IL.*

Lincoln taking the oath at the second inaugural ceremony. *Library of Congress, Prints and Photographs Division, reprod. no. LC-USZ62–2578.*

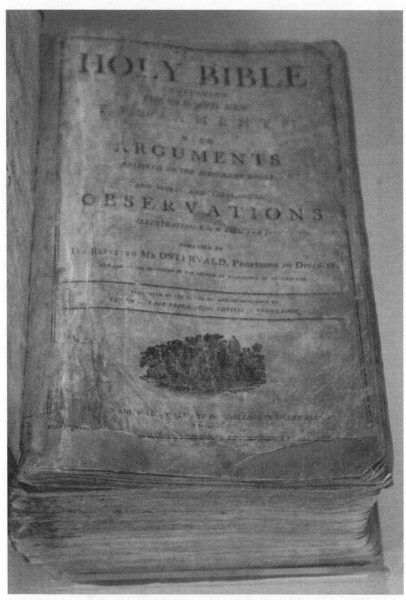

The Thomas Lincoln family Bible that Lincoln read as a youth. *Courtesy of the Abraham Lincoln Birthplace NHP, National Park Service.*

6. A HUMBLED INSTRUMENT

RISE TO THE PRESIDENCY

> I have called thee by thy name; thou art mine.
>
> —Isaiah 43:1

In early 1860, an increasing number of newspapers were suggesting Lincoln as a possible Republican candidate for the presidency. The entire country had been impressed by his oratory skills in the debates with Douglas, and the eastern Republican power brokers decided they wanted to see this Westerner for themselves. They invited him to speak at Rev. Henry Ward Beecher's Congregationalist church in Brooklyn on "any subject [Lincoln] pleased" (the venue was later switched to the Cooper Union in New York City). Lincoln accepted. Knowing that some of the most influential Republicans and journalists in the country would be in the audience, he prepared carefully for this presentation by poring over documents in the state library, including the official record of the proceedings of Congress, the *Congressional Globe*, and the six-volume *Debates on the Federal Constitution* by Jonathan Elliot.[1]

In Lincoln's February 27, 1860, lecture at Cooper Union, he examined the views of the thirty-nine signers of the Constitution regarding their position on the control of slavery in the territories. Lincoln's research revealed that most of them had believed that Congress should prevent slavery's expansion into the territories, which was a position that the Republican Party supported in 1860. Although he filled his speech with moral arguments against slavery, in the Cooper Union address Lincoln alluded to only one Bible verse, which he judiciously used in the speech's inspiring conclusion:

> Let us be diverted by none of those sophistical contrivances wherewith we are so industriously plied and belabored—contrivances such as groping for some middle ground between the right and the wrong, vain as the search for a man who should be neither a living man nor

a dead man—such as a policy of "don't care" on a question about which all true men do care—such as Union appeals beseeching true Union men to yield to Disunionists, reversing the divine rule, and calling, <u>not the sinners, but the righteous to repentance</u> [allusions to Luke 5:32]—such as invocations to Washington, imploring men to unsay what Washington said, and undo what Washington did. LET US HAVE FAITH THAT RIGHT MAKES MIGHT, AND IN THAT FAITH, LET US, TO THE END, DARE TO DO OUR DUTY AS WE UNDERSTAND IT.[2]

This electrifying closing brought the audience to their feet, and many of these sophisticated Easterners were so impressed that they stood on their chairs and cheered. Horace Greeley, editor of the *New-York Tribune*, hailed it as "one of the happiest and most convincing political arguments ever made in this City. . . . No man ever made such an impression on his first appeal to a New-York audience." Garry Wills points out that Lincoln included in his last sentence a "characteristic limitation" that he typically invoked—his dependence on God's revelation for his own wisdom.[3]

Lincoln was asked to speak in several eastern cities after his Cooper Union speech. In a speech in Hartford, Connecticut, Lincoln alluded to Luke 5:32 and continued with the biblical arguments he had used in his previous speeches delivered in the western states, such as Psalm 128:2. Lincoln's use of these scriptural anecdotes proved to be every bit as popular with the Bible-conscious eastern audiences as they had been with people in the West.

Upon his return to Illinois, Lincoln's political team began developing a plan to secure his nomination for president at the Republican National Convention in early May. They convinced the Republican National Committee to hold the convention in Chicago, which gave them the advantage of "home turf."

Knowing that William H. Seward would secure a large majority on the first ballot, Lincoln and his floor managers devised a strategy of allowing everyone to vote for their favorite candidates on the first ballot, and then arranging additional support from other state delegations on subsequent ballots. When explaining their intentions in a letter written before the event, Lincoln used a biblical illustration: "Our policy, then, is to give no offence to others—leave them in a mood to come to us, if they shall be compelled to <u>give up their first love</u>" [allusion to Revelation 2:4]. The strategy worked. On the third ballot Lincoln overtook Seward to receive the Republican Party's nomination for president, and the cannons boomed from the roof of the convention hall.[4]

But the real fireworks exploded after the Republican Convention ended. On June 23, thanks to Douglas's Freeport Doctrine, the Democratic Party split along North/South lines at their second presidential convention in Baltimore (the first convention in Charleston, South Carolina, had been inconclusive). This resulted in two Democratic presidential candidates, Stephen A. Douglas of Illinois and John C. Breckenridge of Kentucky. When a fourth party appealing to Southern Whigs emerged, Lincoln's opposition was split three ways, and he was virtually guaranteed victory in the November presidential election. In only six weeks, Lincoln had gone from a dark-horse Republican candidate to the nearly certain president-elect.[5]

Immediately after being nominated, Lincoln received tremendous pressure from politicians and newspaper editors to reveal his plans on important topics, especially what he was going to say to ease tensions with the South, and whom he planned to appoint to his cabinet. Assuring his friend Senator Lyman Trumbull that he would be keeping his own counsel on most of these issues, Lincoln wrote: "Remembering that Peter denied his Lord with an oath, after most solemnly protesting that he never would [allusion to Matthew 26:72], I will not swear that I will make no committals; but I do think I will not."[6]

Realizing he would probably be the next president, Lincoln tried to avoid provoking the South's increasingly belligerent leaders. Lincoln issued four communications during the summer and fall of 1860 that quoted scripture, none of which employed the strong antislavery sentiments found in scripture verses such as Mark 3:25, Psalm 128:2, or Genesis 3:19. Typical of these more subdued communications is the following letter written on October 30 to a concerned Southerner named William S. Speer:

> I appreciate your motive when you suggest the propriety of my writing for the public something disclaiming all intention to interfere with slaves or slavery in the States; but in my judgment, it would do no good. I have already done this many—many, times; and it is in print, and open to all who will read. Those who will not read, or heed, what I have already publicly said, would not read, or heed, a repetition of it.
>
> "If they hear not Moses and the prophets, neither will they be persuaded though one rose from the dead" [Luke 16:31].[7]

In late October, Lincoln wrote a similar note to George D. Prentice, who was editor of the Louisville, Kentucky, *Journal*. Prentice had asked Lincoln to prepare a letter "setting forth your conservative views . . . to take from the disunionists every excuse or pretext for treason." Lincoln responded that he would not mind communicating as requested "to the good men of the south" up to "seventy and seven times" [allusion to Matthew 18:22], but the "bad men" of both the North and the South would use his words as weapons for ill purpose. So, after considering whether it would do any good to write something for publication, he decided against it.[8]

The nation went to the polls on November 6, 1860, to decide one of the most critical elections in American history. The Republican ticket of Abraham Lincoln for president and Hannibal Hamlin for vice president won easily with 180 out of 303 votes in the electoral college and a plurality of 40 percent of the vote.

After the election, both the unionists and disunionists were still at each other's throats. Both sides misquoted, for their own political purposes, a November 20 public statement that had originated with Lincoln. In a letter to H. J. Raymond of the *New York Times* on November 28, Lincoln reacted to their vindictive, conflicting statements: "This is just as I expected, and just what would happen with any declaration I could make. These political fiends are not half sick enough yet. 'Party malice' and not 'public good' possesses them entirely." He finished with Christ's admonition to an "evil generation." "They seek a sign, and no sign shall be given them" [Luke 11:29].[9]

From November 1860 to February 1861 Lincoln spent the bulk of his time meeting with the public and choosing his cabinet. He wanted his cabinet to include strong leaders, and several of the men he selected were the political rivals that he had defeated at the Republican National Convention in Chicago. By the time he took office in March, he had established William H. Seward of New York as secretary of state, Salmon P. Chase of Ohio as secretary of the treasury, Simon Cameron of Pennsylvania as secretary of war, Edward Bates of Missouri as attorney general, Gideon Welles of Connecticut as secretary of the navy, and Montgomery Blair of Maryland as postmaster general.[10]

Sometime in early January 1861, Lincoln jotted down a few fragments regarding the Declaration of Independence, the Constitution, and the Union for use in a future speech. In these notes he compared the Declaration to an apple of gold, and the Union and Constitution to the picture of silver. Together these formed a reference to the Bible's "A word fitly spoken is like apples of gold in pictures of silver" [allusion to Proverbs 25:11]. This analogy was probably inspired by a recent letter from his old friend Alexander Stephens, the future vice president of the Confederacy, who had suggested to Lincoln that "a word fitly spoken by you now" about opposition to interference with the South's institution of slavery would be like 'apples of gold in pictures of silver.'"[11]

While Lincoln waited for his move from Springfield to Washington, he laid the groundwork for his new administration, and tried to assure everyone that the South's threatened secession was merely an "artificial crisis." However, the firestorm in Dixie was spreading rapidly from state to state. By the time

Lincoln was ready to leave Springfield, the states of South Carolina, Mississippi, Florida, Alabama, Georgia, Louisiana, and Texas each held referendums of secession.

A week before he left for Washington, Lincoln made a special trip to visit his 72-year-old stepmother and extended family in eastern Illinois. While saying goodbye to her stepson, Sarah's voice trembled as she expressed her fear that he would be killed by his enemies in Washington and that she would never be "permitted to see him again." He tried to comfort her, saying "No, no, Mama. Trust in the Lord and all will be well [allusion to Proverbs 3:5–6]. We will see each other again."[12]

Unfortunately, Sarah was right.

The president-elect was scheduled to depart Springfield for Washington on the morning of February 11. He had not planned to speak, but at the sight of the crowd of friends and well-wishers that were standing patiently in the rain at the train depot, he changed his mind. With his eyes full, Lincoln presented this short, impromptu farewell:

> My friends—No one, not in my situation, can appreciate my feeling of sadness at this parting. To this place, and the kindness of these people, I owe everything. Here I have lived a quarter of a century, and have passed from a young to an old man. Here my children have been born, and one is buried. I now leave, not knowing when, or whether ever, I may return, with a task before me greater than that which rested upon Washington. Without the assistance of that Divine Being, who ever attended him, I cannot succeed. With that assistance I cannot fail. Trusting in Him, who can go with me, and remain with you and be everywhere for good [allusions to Isaiah 41:10 and Proverbs 15:3], let us confidently hope that all will yet be well. To His care commending you [allusion to Acts 20:32], as I hope in your prayers you will commend me, I bid you an affectionate farewell.[13]

The journey to Washington took twelve days and followed a zigzag route eastward that allowed him to make short "whistle stops" at dozens of small towns, as well as overnight stays in major cities. It proved to be an invaluable trip for Lincoln, giving him an opportunity to connect with thousands of people who had read about him, but had never seen him. At each stop, people came out to see their president-elect and cheer him. Often the police force or soldiers who were guarding him in the train stations or hotels, particularly in the large cities, were inadequate, and Lincoln was nearly crushed by the exuberant crowds.

Future Lincoln biographer William Dean Howells observed that "the people who pushed upward to seize the great hand held out to everyone looked mostly like the country folk such as he had been of, and the best of him always was, and I could hear their hoarse or cracked voices as they hailed him, oftenest in affectionate joking, sometimes in fervent blessing."[14]

This ability to earn the trust and loyalty of followers was a hallmark of Abraham Lincoln's transformational leadership. John Nicolay observed that Lincoln's "whole bearing, manner, and utterance carried conviction to all beholders that the man was of them as well as for them." Nicolay said there existed a sort of "electrical communion" between Lincoln and the crowds. A teenage schoolboy named Smith Stimmel recalled that "to see Lincoln was to feel closely drawn to him," and his "freedom and good humor" persuaded all of the crowds "instinctively" that he was "a man of the people."[15]

In at least a dozen of his addresses on the way to Washington, Lincoln alluded to the Bible, petitioned the help of the Almighty, or both. He spoke of the North being "bound together" by Christianity, referred to himself as being an "instrument" of the Almighty, and several times expressed his trust in "that God who has never forsaken" the American people. Speaking to the state legislature in Indianapolis, he proclaimed that "When the people rise in masses in behalf of the Union and the liberties of their country, truly may it be said, "The gates of hell shall not prevail against them" [Matthew 16:18].[16]

In his address to the New Jersey Senate on February 21, Lincoln declared "I am exceedingly anxious that this Union, the Constitution, and the liberties of the people shall be perpetuated in accordance with the original idea for which that struggle was made, and I shall be most happy indeed if I shall be an humble instrument in the hands of the Almighty, and of this, his almost chosen people [allusion to Deuteronomy 7:6 and others], for perpetuating the object of that great struggle."[17]

Scholars have analyzed Lincoln's declaration of Americans being the "*almost* chosen" people as opposed to the "chosen people" and have offered different theories about his reasoning for this curious term. But I believe the reason is a fairly simple one. Lincoln had previously demonstrated his belief that the Bible did not support the institution of slavery, as practiced in America. So if human bondage continued, he could not countenance the idea that Americans were "God's chosen."[18]

During his stop at Independence Hall in Philadelphia, where both the Declaration of Independence and the Constitution had been adopted—he pledged his dedication to both of those documents, using a passage from the Psalms: "All my political warfare has been in favor of the teachings coming forth from that sacred hall. <u>May my right hand forget its cunning and my tongue cleave to the roof of my mouth</u> [Psalm 137:5–6], if ever I prove false to those teachings." He also added that he would rather be assassinated "on this spot" than see the country surrender the principles embodied in the Declaration of Independence. By the time Lincoln arrived in Washington on February 23, seven Southern states had seceded from the Union, elected Jefferson Davis their provisional president, and declared Richmond, Virginia, the capital of the Confederacy.[19]

At Abraham Lincoln's inauguration on March 4, 1861, he intended to use his inaugural address to reassure the Southern people that there was no need for secession. Hoping to avoid war, he quoted from his earlier speeches, stating once again that he had neither the intention nor, he believed, the constitutional authority to interfere with slavery where it legally existed. Yet he also insisted that under the Constitution no state had the right to secede from the Union without the consent of the others and warned Southerners that he was going "to hold, occupy, and possess" federal property in the South. He announced that "in your hands, my dissatisfied fellow countrymen, and not in mine, is the momentous issue of civil war," and promised that "The government will not assail you. You can have no conflict, without being yourselves the aggressors."[20]

Although he did not directly quote scripture, Lincoln reminded the South that they had a common biblical faith with the North: "Intelligence, patriotism, Christianity, and a firm reliance on Him, who has never yet forsaken this favored land, are still competent to adjust, in the best way, all our present difficulty."[21]

In closing, Lincoln offered a final, searching appeal to the Southern people: "We are not enemies, but friends. We must not be enemies. Though passion may have strained, it must not break our bonds of affection. The mystic chords of memory, stretching from every battle-field, and patriot grave, to every living heart and hearthstone, all over this broad land, will yet swell the chorus of the Union, when again touched, as surely they will be, by the better angels of our nature."[22]

Yet the better angels did not reach out. In spite of Lincoln's efforts to avoid inflaming Southern sensibilities, Southern leaders quickly rejected Lincoln's outstretched olive branch and moved forward with secession.

Soon after his inauguration, President Lincoln received a letter from Major Robert Anderson, the Union commander at Fort Sumter who was surrounded by hostile Confederate forces in Charleston harbor. Anderson gave the new president the news that he would soon be forced to surrender if the garrison was not resupplied. Lincoln wanted to reinforce the fort, but he had to consider the political loyalty of the states from the upper South. The slave states of Virginia, North Carolina, Tennessee, Arkansas, Missouri, Kentucky, Delaware, and Maryland had not seceded from the Union. Lincoln knew that if the North provoked them by a hostile act, they might join their Southern sisters in the Confederacy.

Finally, in early April Lincoln made his decision on Fort Sumter. He would not surrender it, but instead would advise the governor of South Carolina that he was sending a provisioning ship to Fort Sumter but would not attempt to reinforce the garrison with troops unless the ship was fired upon. That way, Lincoln reckoned, if the Southern forces attacked the ship, they would not only be firing the first shots of the war, but they would knowingly be attacking "a mission of humanity" that was "bringing food for hungry men."[23]

Secretary of state Seward disagreed with Lincoln's support of Fort Sumter, and (intentionally or not) he nearly ruined the president's plans. Circumnavigating secretary of the navy Gideon Welles, Seward took it upon himself to write orders for some of the ships that were to be sent to Fort Sumter, sending them instead to a different destination. Lincoln blindly signed the orders that Seward brought to him regarding these ships. If he had read them, he would have realized they conflicted with orders he had recently signed from navy secretary Welles for the same ships, which Welles intended to send to Fort Sumter in Charleston Harbor.[24]

Although Lincoln's plan worked out, he learned some valuable lessons from this experience. I agree with what William Lee Miller concludes about this incident, which is that Lincoln learned to never again sign important presidential orders or public documents that had his name on them without carefully reading and, if necessary, editing them.[25]

Jefferson Davis decided that he did not want to allow the Fort Sumter garrison to be resupplied and ordered the Confederate commander to begin bombardment on April 12, 1861. Fort Sumter returned fire, but the small contingent of men was soon defeated. The dreaded war had begun. The Southern people rejoiced over their "victory," and the Northern people were outraged at the firing on the American flag.

← ❋ →

During the war, Lincoln developed a close relationship with his pastor Phineas D. Gurley, who was a minister of "Old School" Presbyterianism at the New York

Avenue Presbyterian Church. The Presbyterian Church had split over issues like revivalism in 1837, with the Old School Presbyterians taking a more traditionally Calvinistic stance and the New School proponents accepting the revivalism of the Methodists and Congregationalist theologians such as Jonathan Edwards. In addition to Lincoln's affinity for Old School Presbyterian Church beliefs, he also admitted "I like Gurley. He don't preach politics. I get enough of that through the week. When I go to church, I like to hear the gospel."[26]

Lincoln frequently heard Gurley preach sermons that focused on one of the president's favorite subjects, the mystery of providence. Lincoln was present for worship on Sunday, April 14, the day that Fort Sumter was surrendered, and on that fateful morning he heard a sermon by Gurley that "God, in His merciful providence" had afforded another opportunity for counsel, for pause, for appeal to Him for assistance before letting loose upon the land "the direst scourge which He permits to visit a people—civil war."[27]

But Lincoln did not pause for long, despite Gurley's sermon. The next day, April 15, he issued a proclamation calling for the states to provide an aggregate of seventy-five thousand troops for the purpose of putting down the rebellion, and called for a special session of Congress to assemble on July 4, 1861. The response to Lincoln's call for troops was overwhelming, and thousands of Northern men had to be turned away from the recruiting offices.[28]

Lincoln's call to arms had counterproductive results in the South, whose people were enraged that an army was being formed to coerce their Southern sister states. By May 20, the states of Virginia, Arkansas, Tennessee, and North Carolina seceded and joined the Confederacy. Only the slave states of Missouri, Kentucky, Maryland, and Delaware remained in the union.

President Lincoln, facing a crisis that was unprecedented in the republic's history, was forced to make a number of imperative decisions. He declared a blockade of Southern ports, increased the size of the army and navy, authorized the purchase of ships and war material, and—since Congress was not in session—spent money without congressional authorization. Although many of these were decisions that Secretary of State Seward would later say could have "brought them all to the scaffold," Congress acknowledged the urgency of the situation Lincoln had faced and approved these actions later when they convened.[29]

Lincoln also took strong action to combat guerrilla activities in Maryland, where Southern sympathizers were destroying bridges and cutting telegraph lines to isolate the nation's capital. The United States Constitution provides for the suspension of habeas corpus "in cases of rebellion," and Lincoln took the position that he, as president, had the authority to do this. When Chief Justice

Taney disagreed, saying that only Congress could suspend the writ, Lincoln ignored him. In defense of these actions, Lincoln would later ask, "Are all the laws, but one, to go unexecuted, and the government itself go to pieces, lest that one be violated?" Through strong executive action, by the end of 1861 Lincoln would eliminate any possibility of Maryland's secession and the capture of the nation's capital.[30]

In addition to Maryland, Lincoln had to keep the border states of Kentucky and Missouri from joining the Confederacy. The governments and citizens of these slave states were divided in their loyalties, so Lincoln knew that he had to be careful to avoid provoking them into joining the rebellion. Kentucky officially declared itself neutral, so Lincoln kept Union forces out of this strategic border state in order to maintain friendly relations.

Congress assembled in special session on July 4 to hear Lincoln address the joint body. Lincoln realized that this was one of the most important state papers he would ever present. He had to defend the extraordinary war measures he had already taken, unite Republicans and Democrats in a common cause, and motivate the North into extraordinary war effort. In one of the most inspiring moments of the address, he proclaimed the significance of the American conflict in the course of human history: "This issue embraces more than the fate of these United States. It presents to the whole family of man, the question, whether a constitutional republic, or a democracy—a government of the people, by the same people—can, or cannot, maintain its territorial integrity, against its own domestic foes."[31]

Finally, after stating his case to Congress about the importance of the impending war for the Union, Lincoln concluded with a statement of faith: "And having thus chosen our course, without guile, and with pure purpose, let us renew our trust in God, and go forward without fear, and with manly hearts."[32]

The speech truly proved to be one of Lincoln's most transformational. Republicans and Democrats in Congress united to not only approve most of Lincoln's war measures taken thus far, but also voted a more significant increase in funding and manpower than their new president requested.

← ✻ →

The first major battle of the war took place on July 21, 1861, at Manassas, Virginia. At the battle of Manassas—also known as the Battle of Bull Run—Union forces under Brigadier General Irwin McDowell's command were defeated at the end of a daylong struggle. The North's green troops were forced back, and what began as an orderly retreat degenerated into a rout. Union forces continued retreating until they got all the way to the confines of Washington.

Lincoln quickly replaced McDowell with a man he had known in Illinois, George B. McClellan. McClellan, a graduate of the United States Military Academy and a major general of volunteers in Ohio, had recently won battles against Confederate forces in western Virginia, and had deftly courted the support of the press and Congress. McClellan was put in command of all Union troops around Washington, and immediately began organizing, drilling, and molding them into an effective army. His parades and pageantry paid off, and the morale and confidence of his men soared.

Lincoln loved to befriend the soldiers and frequently visited the army camps to give uplifting, motivational talks to the troops. Brigade commander Colonel William Tecumseh Sherman, who would later attain the rank of major general and command several Union armies, heard one of these talks. Sherman said Lincoln gave to his men "one of the neatest, best, and most feeling addresses I have ever listened to, referring to our late disaster at Bull Run, the high duties that still devolved upon us, and the brighter days yet to come."[33]

So far, Lincoln had made no use of scripture in his letters or speeches in 1861, but this was not because he wasn't reading the Bible. Lincoln's friend Senator Orville H. Browning recalled that the "closest thing [he and Lincoln] ever had "to any religious talk" was when the two of them spent a Sunday afternoon in the White House library in the late summer of 1861. According to Browning, Lincoln was reading the Bible "a good deal" and he [Browning] was reading "some other book." Browning said to Lincoln: "Mr. Lincoln we can't hope for the blessing of God on the efforts of our armies, until we strike a decisive blow at the institution of slavery. This is the great curse of our land, and we must make an effort to remove it before we can hope to receive the help of the Almighty."

Lincoln responded, saying, "Browning, suppose God is against us in our view on the subject of slavery in this country, and our method of dealing with it?"

Browning later recalled that he was "very much struck by this answer of his, which indicated to me for the first time that he [Lincoln] was thinking deeply of what a higher power than man sought to bring about by the great events then transpiring."[34]

As mentioned previously, another witness of Lincoln's Bible reading in 1861 was the White House babysitter Julia Taft. When an adult, she wrote a book that included many interesting observations of the president's day-to-day behaviors in the White House. Regarding his Bible reading she recalled: "It is well known, of course, that Mr. Lincoln was a great reader of the Bible . . . The big, worn leather-covered book stood on a small table ready to his hand and quite often, after the midday meal, he would sit there reading, sometimes in his stocking feet with one long leg crossed over the other, the unshod foot slowly waving back and forth, as if in time to some inaudible music."[35]

Julia recounted that once, when asked by his son Tad why he had to go to Sunday school, Lincoln replied, "Every educated person should know something about the Bible and Bible stories, Tad." Julia thought it an odd answer, because "it was not the conventional reason for attending Sunday-school, but I have thought since that it summed up the most useful result from attending Sunday-school in that day. We got a deal of creed and moral reflections, most of which have been forgotten. But the Bible stories still stick." Although this reason given to Tad for reading the Bible was not the most important one, Lincoln might have known that for his son, it was the most convincing.[36]

Lincoln issued his first proclamation of a National Fast Day on August 12, an excerpt of which follows. It includes references to five Bible verses:

> [W]hereas it is fit and becoming in all people, at all times, to acknowledge and revere the Supreme Government of God; to bow in humble submission to his chastisements; to confess and deplore their sins and transgressions in the full conviction that <u>the fear of the Lord is the beginning of wisdom</u> [Psalm 111:10, Proverbs 9:10, and Job 28:28]; and to pray, with all fervency and contrition, for the pardon of their past offences, and for a blessing upon their present and prospective action:
>
> And whereas, when our own beloved Country, once, by the blessing of God, united, prosperous and happy, is now afflicted with faction and civil war, it is peculiarly fit for us to recognize the hand of God in this terrible visitation, and in <u>sorrowful remembrance of our own faults</u> and crimes as a nation and as individuals, to <u>humble ourselves before Him</u>, [allusion to 2 Chronicles 7:14 and Ezekiel 20:43] and to pray for His mercy . . .
>
> Therefore, I, Abraham Lincoln, President of the United States, do appoint the last Thursday in September next, as a day of humiliation, prayer and fasting for all the people of the nation. And I do earnestly recommend to all the People, and especially to all ministers and teachers of religion of all denominations, and to all heads of families, to observe and keep that day according to their several creeds and modes of worship, in all humility and with all religious solemnity, to the end that the united prayer of the nation may <u>ascend to the Throne of Grace</u> [allusion to Hebrews 4:16] and <u>bring down plentiful blessings</u> [allusion to Ezekiel 34:26] upon our Country.[37]

Scholars have long debated whether it was Lincoln or Secretary of State Seward who authored the national proclamations of thanksgiving, fasting, and prayer, because both of their signatures appeared on many of these documents. Lincoln scholar Michael Burkhimer points out that even if Secretary Seward was the author of some of these proclamations, Lincoln still allowed them to carry his name. It is also important to remember the confusing orders given over the relief of Fort Sumter in early 1861. As a result of this experience, Lincoln had learned to never sign any important documents from the secretary of state, or from anyone else for that matter, without editing and approving them first.[38]

Other scholars argue that Lincoln may not have written all the proclamations for prayer and thanksgiving because of their inconsistencies in composition and tone. But historian Nicholas R. Parrillo, who has analyzed the proclamations, says that the differences could also have been due to the president's increasing apprehension of God's sovereignty.[39]

The remaining pages of the *CW* in 1861 reveal no additional use by Lincoln of scripture or significant Biblical language, but are instead crammed with the hundreds of diverse communications from a hard-pressed leader who was totally consumed with management of the war. This might have been the time an interviewer asked Lincoln what his policy was, and the exhausted president responded saying "I have none. I pass my life in preventing the storm from blowing down the tent, and I drive in the pegs as fast as they are pulled up."[40]

7. THE FIERY TRIAL

TRANSFORMING THE PURPOSE OF THE WAR

For the Lord thy God is a consuming fire.

—Deuteronomy 4:24

By December 31, 1861, General McClellan had done nothing with the army except train and drill them on the parade ground. In January of 1862 Lincoln's patience was exhausted and he decided to take more forceful action with the War Department to get things done. He started at the top by removing the unethical secretary of war Simon Cameron from office and replacing him with the scrupulously honest Edwin Stanton. After receiving invaluable council from quartermaster general Montgomery Miegs, Lincoln pressured McClellan to reveal when he was going to attack the Confederate army in Virginia, warning his commander that if he did not plan on using the army, he would "borrow it."[1]

Succumbing to presidential pressure, McClellan finally revealed his plans for military operations. Rather than marching his army south via a land route, he would use navy ships to transport his army down the Chesapeake Bay and attack Richmond by advancing westward up Virginia's James River Peninsula. This operation was to commence in early March.

In the meantime, a Confederate army under the command of General Gideon J. Pillow had violated Kentucky's neutrality by marching into that state and occupying the city of Columbus on the Mississippi River. This incurred the ire of many Kentuckians, including the Kentucky state legislature, which allowed Union Brigadier General Ulysses S. Grant to move his army into Kentucky as a countermove. Grant's army passed rapidly up the Tennessee River through Kentucky, and from February 6 through February 16 took Forts Henry and Donelson in northern Tennessee, capturing over twelve thousand prisoners. This forced the remaining Confederate armies in northwestern Kentucky and west-central Tennessee to retreat all the way to northern Mississippi.[2]

Although he finally had military operations in motion, Lincoln's troubles in 1862 were just beginning. Tragedy struck the Lincoln family in early February when both Tad and Willie came down with typhoid fever. Although Tad survived, Willie died on February 20. Lincoln and Mary were, of course, devastated. Recalling the terrible ordeal, Mary Lincoln's seamstress Elizabeth Keckley wrote:

> I assisted in washing him [Willie] and dressing him, and then laid him on the bed, when Mr. Lincoln came in. I never saw a man so bowed down with grief. He came to the bed, lifted the cover from the face of his child, gazed at it long and earnestly, murmuring, "My poor boy, he was too good for this earth. God has called him home. I know that he is much better off in heaven, but then we loved him so. It is hard, hard to have him die!"[3]

After Willie's death, Mary was inconsolable for weeks and emotionally unable to care for Tad. Dorothea Dix, the head of army nurses in Washington, sent one of her most skilled nurses, Rebecca Pomroy, to take care of the Lincoln family. Lincoln would later say that Pomroy was "one of the best women I ever knew."[4]

The distraught president found out about Pomroy's religious beliefs and at their first meeting he asked her many questions about her faith. She told him of her own sufferings, and how she had lost two children and a husband to sickness. Her biographer recounted their conversation:

> [The president asked her] "Did you always feel that you could say, 'thy will be done?'"
> And here the father's heart seemed agonized for a reply.
> She said, "No; not at the first blow, nor at the second. It was months after my affliction that God met me when at a camp-meeting."
> Here he showed great interest, and, she says, "While I was telling him my history, and, above all, of God's love and care for me through it all, he covered his face with his hands while the tears streamed through his fingers. Then he told me of his dear Willie's sickness and death. In walking the room, he would say: 'This is the hardest trial of my life. Why is it? Oh, why is it?' He sometimes hid his face in his hands and sobbed uncontrollably, asking "Will I see my boy soon?"

Lincoln met with her the next two nights, asking her how she had obtained her faith in God and about "the secret of placing herself in the Divine hands."[5]

Over the course of her time in the White House, Lincoln and Pomroy talked freely about the Bible. He told her that he thought the Psalms "were the best," for he found in them "something for every day in the week." He asked that she pray for Tad "that he may be spared, if it is God's will," admitted his need for "the prayers of many," acknowledged that the country needed "more praying and less swearing," and confessed that if he were near death he "should like to hear prayer."[6]

Pomroy's support was invaluable to Lincoln, because he could not afford to spend all his time grieving and comforting his family. As anyone who has lost a child understands, it results in an overwhelming sense of emptiness, along with a grief that comes in waves and robs you of strength. It is another sign of Lincoln's amazing fortitude that he was able to carry on. On March 9 he had to turn his attention to Hampton Roads, Virginia, where the most important naval battle of the American Civil War was being fought between the ironclad ships USS *Monitor* and CSS *Virginia*. The *Monitor* managed to defeat the *Virginia's* attempt to break the Union blockade of the James River, and afterward Lincoln was able to again spare time to care for Tad and Mary.

Recalling this family crisis, Mary Lincoln would later say that although her husband "was a religious man always," his ideas about "hope" and "faith" began to change after Willie died. According to one historian, Lincoln underwent "a process of crystallization" regarding his religious beliefs about this time. The *CW* reveals that although Lincoln's quoting of scripture did not significantly increase in 1862, he did in fact talk about God, his dependence on prayer, and God's will with greater frequency that year.[7]

At this time Lincoln was being well cared for by Reverend Gurley, whose sermons frequently addressed the ambiguity and mystery of Providence, themes that Lincoln had been wrestling with for most of his life. Gurley's funeral sermon for Willie illustrates this:

> Not a sparrow falls to the ground without His care much less one of the human family, for we are of more value than many sparrows. . . . What we need in the hour of trial, and what we should seek by earnest prayer is confidence in Him who sees the end from the beginning and doeth all things well. Let us bow in His presence with an humble and teachable spirit; let us be still and know that He is God; . . . In His light shall we see light; by His grace our sorrows will be sanctified and made a blessing to our souls, and by and by we shall have occasion to say with blended gratitude and rejoicing, "It is good for us that we have been afflicted."[8]

This message from Gurley was not one of "you shall see your boy again," but it was similar to the sort of comfort Lincoln himself gave people who had lost loved ones. Lincoln was encouraged, and asked Gurley to give him a copy of the eulogy. Lincoln and Gurley would grow quite close during his remaining presidential years. Lincoln would occasionally attend the midweek evening prayer service held in the main lecture room at New York Avenue Presbyterian Church, and sit in Gurley's study with the door partially ajar so he could listen without being disturbed.[9]

Lincoln issued another thanksgiving proclamation on April 10, 1862. Although he expressed gratitude for the Union's progress in the war, the proclamation was spiritless, reflecting the heart of a man still suffering from his terrible personal loss. Entitled "Proclamation of Thanksgiving for Victories," Lincoln did not quote any specific scripture in it.

In the spring of 1862, Lincoln began to seriously consider an action that would transform the purpose of the war. After the South fired on Fort Sumter in 1861, Lincoln had called the North to arms for the purpose of putting down the rebellion and saving the Union. He knew at that time that the majority of the Northern people were willing to fight to preserve the government, but were reluctant to fight for the abolition of slavery. This fact, plus knowing that it was essential to keep the upper slave states (Kentucky, Maryland, and Missouri) from seceding, had made him extremely cautious about any interference with slavery in 1861.

Lincoln closely monitored the attitudes of the people in Northern and border states, and he sensed that by the spring of 1862 there was a softening in their opposition to the abolition of slavery. He recognized that if he could weaken the South's enslaved work force, the Confederate war effort would be significantly undermined. He realized these factors might enable him to add the abolition of slavery as a war goal, and it might be possible to strike a blow at slavery without a constitutional amendment.[10]

Congress, with its Republican majority, was trying to help in the battle against slavery. In 1861 it had passed the First Confiscation Act, which was intended to retain enslaved people who had escaped to Union lines and keep them from being returned to their masters. But because of the reluctance of some Union army commanders to enforce it, and Lincoln's need for caution regarding the border states, the First Confiscation Act was not as effective as it might have been in the war against slavery. But Lincoln was persistent, trying various means of convincing the border states to give up their slaves, including a federal program to buy their freedom, colonization plans, and gradual emancipation schemes.

McClellan had transported the Army of the Potomac to the James River Peninsula in early March and began his advance toward Richmond, giving him plenty of opportunities to rescue enslaved people. But McClellan was a Democrat who did not believe in interfering with the institution of slavery. His progress toward Richmond was terribly slow, and even when enslaved people sought asylum within Union lines, he refused it.

While McClellan's army took ten weeks to crawl fifty miles westward up the peninsula, Grant's army rushed southward through the entire width of the state of Tennessee, about a hundred miles, in half the time. Grant used navy transports for most of his campaign, which culminated in a defeat of the South's principal western army at the Battle of Shiloh on April 6–7. With twenty-four thousand casualties, it was the bloodiest battle fought on American soil up until that time. The Confederates retreated from Shiloh to Corinth, Mississippi, and western Tennessee was suddenly under Union control.

Lincoln had convinced himself years ago that the Bible did not support American slavery and that God was going to put an end to the evil institution someday. He had always assumed this would be done through legislative action, without a war. But in the spring of 1862 the case for freeing enslaved people as a war measure grew stronger: an increasing number of them were running away from their masters and seeking asylum; Congress was continuing to support the confiscation of slaves; the border states were becoming less supportive of the South, and Lincoln realized that if enslaved people were freed, it would simultaneously weaken the South and strengthen the North. Events were progressing in such a manner that Lincoln began to suspect God's method and timing for the abolishment of slavery might be much sooner than he had expected—as a war measure.[11]

Through prayer, reading the Bible, and careful consideration of evolving events, Lincoln began to diligently seek God's will on what he should do about slavery. Lincoln talked with friends about this quest and discussed the will of God in multiple speeches and letters. His friend Noah Brooks said reading scripture was Lincoln's "constant habit," and while in the White House he kept up the practice of daily prayer. Lincoln's secretary John Nicolay said that the president often asked people to pray for him, and many others testified that Lincoln endeavored to read the Bible every day. White House secretary William O. Stoddard stated that "he [Lincoln] had an abiding faith in the overruling providence of God, [and] in His active interference in the affairs of men and nations."[12]

In addition to Lincoln's personal prayers and meditations, there are several public demonstrations of his pursuit of God's will in these difficult months. One example is from a visit with a group of Evangelical Lutherans on May 13, 1862. Lincoln said: "I now humbly and reverently, in your presence, reiterate the acknowledgment of that dependence, not doubting that, if it shall please the Divine Being who <u>determines the destinies of nations</u> [allusion to Job 12:23] that this shall remain a united people, they will, humbly seeking the Divine guidance, make their prolonged national existence a source of new benefits to themselves and their successors, and to all classes and conditions of mankind."[13]

In a May 15 letter to a Methodist conference in Baltimore, Lincoln wrote, "By the help of an all-wise Providence, I shall endeavor to do my duty; and I shall expect the continuance of your prayers for a right solution of our national difficulties."[14]

On June 20 he remarked to a delegation of Quakers that he "was deeply sensible of his need for Divine assistance," that he "might be an instrument in God's hands of accomplishing a great work," and that he had a "firm reliance upon the Divine arm" and was seeking "<u>light from above</u>" [allusion to Job 29:3] so that he could "do his duty in the place to which he had been called."[15]

On July 17 Lincoln said to a committee from the synod of the Reformed Presbyterian Church, "Feeling deeply my responsibility to my country and to that God to whom we all owe allegiance, I assure you I will try to do my best, and so may God help me."[16]

From March through the end of May 1862, General McClellan's army continued its glacial advance toward Richmond, finally getting within sight of the city's church steeples. But his overcautiousness allowed the Confederate commanders General Joseph Johnson and General Robert E. Lee to finally seize the initiative and counterattack, and by June 1, McClellan and the Army of the Potomac were in full retreat.

Fed up with McClellan's timidity and willingness to return to Southern planters the enslaved people who escaped to his lines, Congress began establishing harsher laws to impact Southern slave owners. On July 17, 1862, Congress passed the Second Confiscation Act. This act allowed the seizure of land and property from Southern landowners, as well as the emancipation of the enslaved people who came under Union control. Lincoln, who had known the Second Confiscation Act was in the works, attempted to minimize the financial shock to the slave owners in the border states. Hoping to assure their cooperation, he offered to compensate them for their slaves if they emancipated them voluntarily, but they refused.

After months of prayer, reading his Bible, and awaiting war developments Lincoln finally reached a place of personal peace on the slavery issue and on July 22 he presented a draft of the Emancipation Proclamation to his Cabinet. Surprisingly, not all of them were willing to support it. The Cabinet raised several objections, and Secretary of State Seward suggested that Lincoln wait until the North won a military victory before he announced it to the nation. Union victories, at least in the east, had been as scarce as the proverbial hen's teeth lately, but Lincoln saw value in Seward's argument that to announce it immediately would look like "our last shriek on the retreat." Lincoln put the proclamation back in his desk and waited for that elusive victory.[17]

After delaying the announcement of the Emancipation Proclamation, Lincoln seemed to go through a period of self-reflection. For instance, on July 26 he wrote to Reverdy Johnson, "I am a patient man—always willing to forgive on the Christian terms of repentance; and also, to give ample time for repentance" [allusion to Luke 17:3–4 and Colossians 3:13]. On July 28 he stated in a letter to Mr. Cuthbert Bullitt of New Orleans, "I shall do nothing in malice. What I deal with is too vast for malicious dealing." A few days later, he said something similar in a letter to Count Gasparin of Switzerland: "I can only say that I have acted upon my best convictions without selfishness or malice, and that by the help of God, I shall continue to do so."[18]

Lincoln was still concerned that civilians and soldiers alike would reject his emancipation efforts, and was wondering how he might assure the public's support. Providentially, Horace Greeley published in mid-August a newspaper editorial entitled "The Prayer of Twenty Millions." In this letter he criticized the president for not immediately enforcing the Second Confiscation Act and freeing enslaved people, and, perhaps unwittingly, gave Lincoln an excellent platform for introducing his support of this very cause.

Lincoln seized the opportunity to bolster public support for emancipation and responded on August 22 by publishing an article in a competing newspaper. In his brilliant rejoinder to Greeley, Lincoln started by stating that his primary goal was to save the Union. Everything he did concerning slavery would be for the purpose of supporting that primary goal. He sought to convince his readers that his next step—which only his Cabinet knew was his pending Emancipation Proclamation—would be done for that purpose. This conversation, Lincoln hoped, would help assure acceptance of his plan to add the abolition of slavery as a war goal, as well as ensure the army's support. He closed his article with "I have here stated my purpose according to my view of *official* duty; and I intend no modification of my oft-expressed *personal* wish that all men everywhere could be free."[19]

About a week after Lincoln's response to Greeley, the Army of the Potomac suffered another defeat by Confederate forces. Lee had concluded that McClellan was no longer a threat to Richmond, and in mid-August he turned his back on the Army of the Potomac and marched most of his men to northern Virginia. On August 28–30 at the old Manassas Battlefield he defeated a recently formed Union army under the command of General John Pope. In spite of twenty-one thousand casualties between the two armies, Lee decided to invade western Maryland on September 4. After the loss at Manassas, Lincoln ordered McClellan to return to Washington and take command of the army there.[20]

Lincoln described McClellan as having "the slows" and was understandably concerned about his general's ability to successfully repulse the Confederate army that was marching rapidly toward Pennsylvania. It was at this moment that the hand of Providence seemed to intervene. Two Union soldiers stumbled across a copy of Lee's invasion plans, which had been lost by a Confederate officer in a field near Frederick, Maryland. These plans revealed that Lee's army was widely dispersed, and McClellan gleefully declared that with the Confederate leader's plans, he would now be able to "whip Bobbie Lee." Unfortunately, rather than marching immediately, the slothful McClellan waited eighteen critical hours before ordering his army to force its way through the mountain passes toward Lee.[21]

On September 13, the day that the Union soldiers found Lee's lost orders, Lincoln had received a delegation of men who represented "Chicago Christians of all denominations." They had recently adopted a memorial in favor of emancipation, and announced to a rather impatient president that they believed God had told them he should free the enslaved people. Lincoln, who was frequently pestered by visiting ministers who claimed to know what God wanted him to do, offered a response that revealed more about his thoughts on the will of Providence than his plans on emancipation:

> I am approached with the most opposite opinions and advice, and that by religious men, who are equally certain that they represent the Divine will. I am sure that either the one or the other class is mistaken in that belief, and perhaps in some respects both. I hope it will not be irreverent for me to say that if it is probable that God would reveal his will to others, on a point so connected with my duty, it might be supposed he would reveal it directly to me; for, unless I am more deceived in myself than I often am, it is my earnest desire to know the will of Providence in this matter. And if I can learn what it is I will do it! These are not, however, the days of miracles, and I suppose

it will be granted that I am not to expect a direct revelation. I must study the plain physical facts of the case, ascertain what is possible and learn what appears to be wise and right. The subject is difficult, and good men do not agree. . . .

I have not decided against a proclamation of liberty to the slaves, but hold the matter under advisement. And I can assure you that the subject is on my mind, <u>by day and night </u>[Exodus 13:21], more than any other. Whatever shall appear to be God's will I will do.[22]

The editors of the *CW* believe that it was at about this time Lincoln wrote an undated meditation about the will of God. Known as the "Meditation on the Divine Will," it was a short note to himself, another of the kind the *CW* editors frequently refer to as fragments, that revealed the depth of his evolving theological deliberations on the role of Providence in the war.

Many years after he died, Lincoln's secretaries John G. Nicolay and John Hay found the meditation memorandum, written in Lincoln's script, among the president's private papers. They theorized that Lincoln penned this document "in September 1862, while his mind was burdened with the weightiest question of his life [the Emancipation Proclamation]."[23]

However, Douglas Wilson has made a compelling argument that the meditation was written by Lincoln after 1862—perhaps as late as 1864. Consequently, the text of the document and a more detailed discussion of the meditation will be presented in chapter 9.[24]

McClellan and the Army of the Potomac finally attacked Lee and the Army of Northern Virginia at Sharpsburg, Maryland, on September 17. This furious, daylong slaughter of men in blue and gray is known today as the Battle of Antietam. McClellan sent his men forward in a series of disjointed attacks, and Lee was able to stand his ground by shifting troops from one point of the battlefield to another. The result was the bloodiest single day battle in American history, with a ghastly twenty-five thousand casualties between the two armies. Lee's invasion was halted, and the Confederate army retreated to Virginia. At last Lincoln had the "victory" he had been seeking, and once again brought his draft Emancipation Proclamation to his Cabinet.[25]

This time, however, rather than asking his Cabinet's opinion as to whether the Emancipation Proclamation should be issued, he told them that he had made up his mind to go forward with it. All he wanted from them were suggestions for improvements. Two of Lincoln's Cabinet members, secretary of the treasury

Salmon Chase and secretary of the navy Gideon Welles, recorded in their respective diaries the events of that September 22 Cabinet meeting. The following is an excerpt from Chase's diary of what Lincoln said. It reveals the mind of a man who was faithfully acting on a promise made to God. After bringing up some of his previous reservations, he announced his decision to the Cabinet:

> When the rebel army was at Frederick, I determined, as soon as it should be driven out of Maryland, to issue a proclamation of emancipation, such as I thought most likely to be useful. I said nothing to any one, but I made the promise to myself and (hesitating a little) to my Maker [Job 36:3]. The rebel army is now driven out, and I am going to fulfill that promise. I have got you together to hear what I have written down. I do not wish your advice about the main matter, for that I have determined for myself.[26]

Secretary of the navy Gideon Welles also recorded in his diary what Lincoln said that day. The following is an excerpt from Welles's diary regarding the Cabinet meeting. It differs from Chase's account slightly in that he says Lincoln made a vow or covenant with God in lieu of a "promise":[27]

> In the course of the discussion on this [Emancipation Proclamation] paper, which was long, earnest, and, on the general principle involved, harmonious, he remarked that he had made a vow—a covenant— that if God gave us the victory in the approaching battle, he would consider it *an indication of Divine will*, and that it was his duty to move forward in the cause of emancipation. It might be thought strange, he said, but there were times when he felt uncertain how to act, that he had in this way submitted the disposal of matters—when the way was not clear to his mind what he should do. *God had decided this question* in favor of the slaves. He was satisfied it was right—was confirmed and strengthened in his action by the vow and the results. His mind was fixed, his decision made.[28]

On September 22, Lincoln issued his preliminary Emancipation Proclamation, announcing that all enslaved people held by states still in rebellion as of January 1, 1863, would be "thenceforward and forever free." At last Abraham Lincoln, the man who had "always hated slavery," had amassed sufficient moral, political, and popular support to be able to strike the first of two powerful, fatal blows at the institution of slavery. Just as importantly, he had—through prayer and reading the Bible—reached the conclusion that he was to be God's instrument in this momentous task.[29]

Lincoln's promise, or vow, to his "Maker" that he would emancipate the enslaved people if God gave the North a military victory demonstrated a significant increase in his biblical faith. Yet this decision was still unsettling to Lincoln. Would the Northern people sustain him? Two days after he had issued the preliminary Emancipation Proclamation, he responded to a serenade given to him by a crowd on the White House lawn. On this occasion he divulged that "what I did [the Emancipation Proclamation], I did after very full deliberation, and under a very heavy and solemn sense of responsibility. I can only trust in God I have made no mistake."[30]

In late September, Lincoln was visited in the White House by four Quakers, led by Mrs. Eliza P. Gurney, an ordained Quaker minister. They had felt led to seek an interview with the president for the purpose of comforting and encouraging him. As evidenced by his earlier conference with the deputation of Chicago Christians, Lincoln was often wary of meeting with ministers because of their tendency to lecture him about God's will. But Lincoln strongly suspected that some of his ancestors might have been Quakers, and had a soft spot for this pacifist Christian sect.

They sat down together, and Mrs. Gurney presented a short sermon of encouragement to the president, and then knelt with him and her companions in prayer. Lincoln was profoundly touched by their sincerity and in a letter to Gurney on October 26, he quoted or alluded to three Bible verses in his thoughts about Providence:[31]

> I am glad of this interview, and glad to know that I have your sympathy and prayers. We are indeed going through a great trial—a fiery trial [1 Peter 4:12]. In the very responsible position in which I happen to be placed, being a humble instrument in the hands of our Heavenly Father, as I am, and as we all are, to work out his great purposes, I have desired that all my works and acts may be according to his will, and that it might be so, I have sought his aid—but if after endeavoring to do my best in the light which he affords me [allusion to Job 29:3], I find my efforts fail, I must believe that for some purpose unknown to me, He wills it otherwise. If I had had my way, this war would never have been commenced; If I had been allowed my way this war would have been ended before this, but we find it still continues;

and we must believe that He permits it for some wise purpose of his own, mysterious and unknown to us; and though with our limited understandings we may not be able to comprehend it, yet we cannot but believe, that <u>he who made the world still governs it</u> [allusion to Colossians 1:16–17].[32]

↞ ❋ ↠

Immediately after General Lee began his September 18 retreat from Antietam to Virginia, Lincoln urged McClellan to vigorously pursue and attack if a favorable opportunity presented itself. But McClellan, always the snail, offered Lincoln a plethora of excuses for inaction. After Lee successfully retreated into Virginia and McClellan abandoned all pursuit of him, Lincoln's patience was finally exhausted. On November 7, the day after the November elections, Lincoln replaced McClellan with a new commander for the Army of the Potomac, Major General Ambrose E. Burnside.

On December 1 Lincoln began his second annual message to Congress with an acknowledgment of his continued trust in God and an allusion to scripture, saying: "Since our last annual assembling another year of health and bountiful harvests has passed. And while it has not pleased the Almighty to bless us with a return of peace, we can but press on, guided by <u>the best light He gives us</u> [allusion to Job 29:3], trusting that in His own good time, and wise way, all will yet be well."[33] Although the main body of the speech constituted the typical facts and figures that comprise present day State of the Union addresses, it is atypical of modern-day speeches in that Lincoln included the aforementioned allusion and two subsequent quotations from the Bible. For the first quotation (in the main body of the speech not presented here), Lincoln made use of a simple illustration, saying: "<u>One generation passeth away, and another generation cometh, but the earth abideth forever</u>" [Ecclesiastes 1:4].[34] Then, in his iconic conclusion to this speech, Lincoln quoted scripture to proclaim an inspiring challenge to his generation:

> We can succeed only by concert. It is not "can *any* of us *imagine* better?" but "can we *all* do better?" Object whatsoever is possible, still the question recurs "can we do better?" The dogmas of the quiet past, are inadequate to the stormy present. The occasion is piled high with difficulty, and we must rise with the occasion. As our case is new, so we must think anew, and act anew. We must disenthrall our selves, and then we shall save our country.

... Fellow-citizens, we cannot escape history. We of this Congress and this administration, will be remembered in spite of ourselves. No personal significance, or insignificance, can spare one or another of us. The fiery trial [1 Peter 4:12] through which we pass, will light us down, in honor or dishonor, to the latest generation. We say we are for the Union. The world will not forget that we say this. We know how to save the Union. The world knows we do know how to save it. We—even we here—hold the power, and bear the responsibility. In giving freedom to the slave, we assure freedom to the free— honorable alike in what we give, and what we preserve. We shall nobly save, or meanly lose, the last best, hope of earth. Other means may succeed; this could not fail. The way is plain, peaceful, generous, just—a way which, if followed, the world will forever applaud, and God must forever bless.[35]

While Lincoln looked forward to a day of peace, the war bludgeoned on. Burnside—Lincoln's new commander of the Army of the Potomac—proved to be a well-meaning, yet inept battlefield commander. From December 11 to 13, this tunnel-visioned leader threw his men against an impenetrable position held by Lee's army at Fredericksburg, Virginia. Union losses were thirteen thousand men—twice that of the Confederate losses, and Lincoln was despondent over the massive casualties. When Pennsylvania governor Andrew Curtin brought him the battle news, Lincoln groaned and wrung his hands in agony, asking, "What has God put me in this place for?" According to Curtin, Lincoln lamented, "If there is a worse place than hell, I am in it."[36]

It was not only the war with the Confederate armies that gave Lincoln such anguish. He also was called upon, as president, to approve the mass execution of 303 Dakota warriors who had been convicted by a military tribunal for their part in killings and massacres of hundreds of white settlers in the Minnesota territory. Lincoln, who believed mercy was one of the greatest attributes, demanded that a "full and complete record" of the convictions be sent to him for his review. After incurring a thorough review of each case, Lincoln determined that 264 of them (nearly 90 percent) were not guilty of the killings, rapes, and massacres that they had been convicted of, and commuted their sentences.[37]

As distressing as these events were, there was still one more bloody battle in 1862 that Lincoln would have to endure. The Battle of Stones River in central Tennessee, which began on December 31 and ended two days later, had even more casualties than the Battle of Fredericksburg. The only bright spot in that desperate conflict was that the Union commander, General William

Rosecrans, stood his ground. The Confederate army under the command of General Braxton Bragg retreated toward Chattanooga, leaving virtually all of Tennessee in Union hands.

← ❋ →

The year 1862 had been transformational, not only for Lincoln's decision about the war's purpose, but for Lincoln himself. The year's events solidified his Old School Presbyterian conception of Providence, as well as his commitment to study both the war events and his Bible in order to be an effective instrument of God. Although he despised the terrible cost of war, he was beginning to wonder whether it was God's way of imposing retribution for the sin of slavery. As evidenced by his annual message to Congress on December 1, he had become convinced that it was his generation's duty to endure war for the sake of future generations.[38]

Lincoln did not quote the Bible as often in his presidential years as he had before, but his biblical language became more pervasive in his speeches, proclamations, and state papers. He was pondering and living the Bible every day. At a New Year's Eve meeting with a group of abolitionists, Lincoln admitted his impatience with the continuation of slavery and confessed that he was "not so certain that God's views and feeling" in respect to slavery "are the same as mine." Job-like, Lincoln wondered "if his feelings were like mine, how could he have permitted it to remain so long?"[39]

8. TO HIGHLY RESOLVE

THE TIDE OF WAR CHANGES

Thus says the Lord, the God of Israel, "Let my people go."
—Exodus 5:1

New Year's Day, 1863—the long-awaited moment for Lincoln to sign the final Emancipation Proclamation—finally arrived. Some had feared that the president would change his mind at the last minute and not go through with it. But when he sat down to sign the document, he said resolutely, "I never in my life felt more certain that I was doing right than I do in signing this paper. If my name goes into history, it will be for this act, and my whole soul is in it." He paused a moment, composed himself, and boldly signed his full name. "That will do," he remarked with satisfaction.[1]

The Emancipation Proclamation announced that as of January 1, 1863, all enslaved people in the states still in rebellion would be "thenceforward, and forever free." Although most of these enslaved people were currently out of the reach of Lincoln's long arms, at least twenty thousand of them in the Union-occupied regions of the Confederacy were immediately emancipated. Before the war was over, four hundred thousand more were freed by advancing Union armies.[2]

Hundreds of messages of thanks and congratulations from around the world flooded into the White House. On January 5, Lincoln responded to a note of gratitude from two representatives of a Quaker organization in Iowa who had expressed their appreciation and pledged their ongoing prayers and support. Lincoln gratefully responded:

> It is most cheering and encouraging for me to know that in the efforts which I have made and am making for the restoration of a righteous peace to our country, I am upheld and sustained by the good wishes and prayers of God's people. No one is more deeply than myself aware

that <u>without His favor our highest wisdom is but as foolishness</u> [allusion to 1 Corinthians 1:20–21] and that our most strenuous efforts would avail nothing in the shadow of His displeasure. I am conscious of no desire for my country's welfare, that is not in consonance with His will, and of no plan upon which we may not ask His blessing.[3]

The Emancipation Proclamation not only broadened the purpose of the war and elevated those who supported it to a higher moral plane, it also brought military reinforcements. Before the war was over, nearly 180,000 Black men would enlist in the Union army, adding significant strength to "Father Abraham's" mighty host.[4]

← ❀ →

Lincoln removed the inept General Burnside from command of the Army of the Potomac on January 26, and replaced him with "Fighting Joe" Hooker. General Hooker made effective changes to improve the health and morale of the troops after the slaughter at Fredericksburg and was soon brimming with confidence. "I hope God has mercy on Bobby Lee, for I will have none," he proclaimed. Unimpressed, Lincoln reminded him that in the next battle he should "put in all of your men."[5]

Responding to a Senate resolution, Lincoln issued his next "Proclamation of Appointing a National Fast Day" on March 30, setting Thursday, April 30, as the day of prayer. In this remarkable announcement, he proclaimed that America had forgotten God, and urged the people to confess their sin, repent, and pray for God's mercy:

> Whereas it is the duty of nations as well as of men, to own their dependence upon the overruling power of God, to confess their sins and transgressions, in humble sorrow, yet with assured hope that genuine repentance will lead to mercy and pardon; and to recognize the sublime truth, announced in the Holy Scriptures and proven by all history, <u>that those nations only are blessed whose God is the Lord</u> [Psalm 33:12].
>
> And, insomuch as we know that, by His divine law, <u>nations like individuals are subjected to punishments and chastisements</u> in this world, [allusion to Isaiah 34: 2] may we not justly fear that the awful calamity of civil war, which now desolates the land, may be but a punishment, inflicted upon us, for our presumptuous sins, to the needful end of our national reformation as a whole People? We have

been the recipients of the choicest bounties of Heaven. We have been preserved, these many years, in peace and prosperity. We have grown in numbers, wealth and power, as no other nation has ever grown. But we have forgotten God [allusion to Jeremiah 3:21]. We have forgotten the gracious hand which preserved us in peace, and multiplied and enriched and strengthened us; and we have vainly imagined, in the deceitfulness of our hearts, that all these blessings were produced by some superior wisdom and virtue of our own. Intoxicated with unbroken success, we have become too self-sufficient to feel the necessity of redeeming and preserving grace, too proud to pray to the God that made us! It behooves us then, to humble ourselves before the offended Power, to confess our national sins, and to pray for clemency and forgiveness [allusion to 2 Chronicles 7:14].[6]

Nicholas Parrillo cogently observes that this proclamation was far more focused on sin than the proclamation of 1861. It reminded Northerners that they were presumptuous, deceitful, "intoxicated" with success, had forgotten God, and were too proud to pray. Absent in this list of sins, however, was any suggestion that slavery was a sin. Apparently at the end of March 1863, Lincoln was still not absolutely convinced that slavery was the *national* sin that had caused the war.[7]

The War Department placed Union general Burnside in command of the Department of the Ohio, where it was hoped he would see less fighting and stay out of trouble. But in early May, Burnside managed to give Lincoln yet another headache when he arrested Democratic politician Clement L. Vallandigham for making speeches that the general thought were encouraging desertions, and thereby subversive to the war effort. Lincoln did not countenance Vallandigham's imprisonment, but rather than simply release him from prison he decided to banish him to the Confederacy. Justifying this punitive action against Vallandigham, Lincoln asked, "Must I shoot a simple-minded soldier boy who deserts, but must not touch a hair of the wiley agitator who induces him to desert?" Lincoln refused to allow Vallandigham to return through Union lines, so on June 11 the Democrats chose to run him in the 1863 election for governor of Ohio, in absentia.[8]

Lincoln's statement about shooting "a simple-minded soldier boy" was in reference to the law that required soldiers who committed serious crimes such as desertion, cowardice in battle, or sleeping on guard duty to be sentenced to death by firing squad. Lincoln understood that most of his volunteer army was composed of young men who had not received the months of training and military discipline normally drilled into professional soldiers. Although the army willingly sentenced men to death—even boys under eighteen years of age—the president, who once said that he thought "mercy bears richer fruits than any other attribute," strongly objected.[9] Consequently, he attempted to personally review every instance of court-martial that had resulted in a soldier being sentenced to death, and he spent hours reading cases one by one, searching for reasons to pardon the men. Once, when reproached for his refusal to allow a soldier to be shot for cowardice, Lincoln stood by his decision and stated, "I am just as God made me, and cannot change." In another instance, when told that a condemned prisoner had been previously wounded in battle, Lincoln shrewdly asked, "Did you say this boy was once badly wounded? Since the scriptures say that in <u>the shedding of blood is remission of sins</u> [allusion to Hebrews 9:22], I guess we'll have to let him off."[10]

Unfortunately, the Union forces were about to suffer another tragic defeat. On May 6, a few miles west of Fredericksburg Virginia, the Army of the Potomac was again beaten by Lee at the Battle of Chancellorsville. With over seventeen thousand Union casualties, the loss was even more devastating than Fredericksburg. Lincoln was beside himself with grief. He paced his office, asking mournfully, "What will the country say? Oh, what will the country say?" General Hooker, so confident in himself beforehand, lost his nerve in the heat of battle. Lincoln soon replaced him as commander of the Army of the Potomac with General George Gordon Meade.[11]

It was during this time that Mary's friend Elizabeth Keckley saw Lincoln rejuvenated by reading from the book of Job in the family quarters of the White House. Having lost two sons and nearly his country, Lincoln might indeed have identified with Job, who lost nearly everything. Job is a book in the Bible that delves into tragedy and suffering of the innocent, and Lincoln had learned that with its questions directed to God, it was a book of deep water.

Seeking divine reason behind catastrophes, a preacher named Charles Spurgeon, who was the most popular Calvinist minister in Britain while Lincoln was president, preached dozens of sermons on Job over the years—including one a few days before Willie and Tad came down with typhoid fever. Spurgeon often said that Job 1:21 ("Naked I came from my mother's womb, and naked shall I return. The Lord gave, and the Lord has taken away; blessed be the name of the Lord") "means that the Lord is to be blessed both for giving and taking." He comforted listeners who had lost loved ones, saying that they must "let God be Master in his own house; where we are only the children, he shall take whatever he pleases of all he has lent us for a while." To Spurgeon and other Calvinist preachers like Phineas D. Gurley, as well as diligent Bible readers like Lincoln, the message of Job was one of encouragement in time of tragedy.[12]

← ✳ →

General Lee did not wait long after his victory at Chancellorsville to make his next move. In June he began his second invasion of the North, and by the first of July he was facing General Meade and the Army of the Potomac at the little village of Gettysburg, Pennsylvania. From July 1 through July 3, the greatest land battle on the North American continent was fought, resulting in a horrendous fifty thousand casualties between the two armies. But victory on Northern soil again eluded Lee, and he was forced to retreat to Virginia.

Gettysburg was not the only military defeat the South suffered on July 3, 1863. While Lee's army was fighting in Pennsylvania, another large Confederate army commanded by General John Pemberton was fighting a desperate battle for survival in Vicksburg, Mississippi. The Union army they faced was commanded by the North's most capable generals, U.S. Grant and William Tecumseh Sherman. After five separate battles and a seven-week siege, Pemberton surrendered his entire army of thirty thousand men to Grant on July 3.[13]

The victories at Gettysburg and Vicksburg had significant strategic impact on the course of the war. Lee's army was greatly reduced in strength, and would never again return to the strategic offensive. Vicksburg was the last Southern stronghold on the Mississippi River. The Confederacy was cut in two, and the North now had uninterrupted river commerce from Ohio to the Gulf of Mexico.

On July 15 Lincoln issued the following Proclamation of Thanksgiving:

> I do set apart Thursday the 6th. day of August next, to be observed as a day for National Thanksgiving, Praise and Prayer, and I invite the People of the United States to . . . render the homage due to the Divine Majesty, for the wonderful things he has done in the Nation's behalf, and invoke the influence of His Holy Spirit to subdue the anger, which has produced, and so long sustained a needless and cruel rebellion, . . . and to visit with tender care and consolation throughout the length and breadth of our land all those who, through the vicissitudes of marches, voyages, battles and sieges, have been brought to suffer in mind, body or estate, and finally to lead the whole nation, through the paths of repentance and submission to the Divine Will, back to the perfect enjoyment of Union and fraternal peace.[14]

This proclamation manifests Lincoln's lack of malice and inveterate sense of equanimity. Parrillo believes the nature of this Thanksgiving Proclamation indicates that Lincoln still thought the war was "needless," a result of man's selfish actions, rather than an event ordained by God.[15] It was proclamations like this that inspired Lincoln's secretary John Hay to write: "I am growing more and more firmly convinced that [Lincoln] should be kept where he is until this thing is over. There is no man in the country so wise, so gentle, so firm. I believe the hand of God placed him where he is."[16]

In August Lincoln's old friend James C. Conkling invited him to speak to an assembly of "unconditional Union men" in Springfield, Illinois. Lincoln had to decline, but he sent a superb letter defending his administration's actions and demonstrating faith in the providence of God:

> Peace does not appear so distant as it did. I hope it will come soon, and come to stay; and so come as to be worth the keeping in all future time. It will then have been proved that, among free men, there can be no successful appeal from the ballot to the bullet. And then, there will be some black men who can remember that, with silent tongue, and clenched teeth, and steady eye, and well-poised bayonet, they have helped mankind on to this great consummation; while, I fear, there will be some white ones, unable to forget that, with malignant heart, and deceitful speech, they have strove to hinder it.
>
> Still let us not be over-sanguine of a speedy final triumph. Let us be quite sober. Let us diligently apply the means, never doubting that a just God, in his own good time, will give us the rightful result.[17]

On August 10, the famous abolitionist and former enslaved man Frederick Douglass made his first trip to the White House to meet with President Lincoln. Douglass was concerned that Black soldiers were not getting equal treatment when compared to White soldiers. He recalled that "Mr. Lincoln asked me to state particulars.... [he] listened with patience and silence to all I had to say. He was serious and even troubled by what I had said, and by what he had evidently thought himself before upon the same points. He impressed me with the solid gravity of his character, by his silent listening not less than by his earnest reply to my words."[18]

Although Lincoln could not take immediate action to accommodate Douglass's request on issues like equal pay for Black soldiers, Douglass concluded that "though I was not entirely satisfied with his views, I was so well satisfied with the man and with the educating tendency of the conflict, I determined to go on with the recruiting." Douglass may have been the first person to recognize that Lincoln was progressing from being simply a kind White man who hated slavery to one who was becoming a proponent of equal rights and social status for Black people. Lincoln had indeed come a long way from his debates with Stephen A. Douglas in 1858, when he feared that there would never be equality of the races because of the extreme prejudice of the White people in Illinois.[19]

About a month after Douglass met with Lincoln, the Union cause suffered a serious reversal of fortune. Union armies had enjoyed a series of military victories in the West, but on September 19 Confederate general Braxton Bragg launched a surprise attack on General William Rosecrans's army along Chickamauga Creek in northern Georgia. This resulted in a calamitous two-day battle with thirty-five thousand casualties and the Union army's rapid retreat to Chattanooga, Tennessee. Lincoln decided it was time to promote General Grant to command of all Union armies between the Appalachian Mountains and the Mississippi River. Grant fired Rosecrans and headed for Chattanooga to take command of the besieged army there.

Thanks to the efforts of magazine editor Sara Josepha Hale, 1863 would be the year that Thanksgiving was transformed into a "National and fixed Union Festival." Occasional proclamations of thanksgiving had been issued previously by many presidents, including Lincoln, but Hale, editor of *Godey's Lady's Book*, wrote to Lincoln on September 28 asking for the establishment of a permanent Thanksgiving holiday. The idea was well received by the president, who asked the secretary of state to draft the proclamation. In the proclamation, dated October 3, Lincoln observed how the nation was prospering despite the war and enumerated the many blessings the Northern people were experiencing. He concluded:[20]

> No human counsel hath devised nor hath any mortal hand worked out these great things. They are the gracious gifts of the <u>Most High God, who, while dealing with us in anger for our sins, hath nevertheless remembered mercy</u> [allusion to Psalm 78:38, 56]. It has seemed to me fit and proper that they should be solemnly, reverently and gratefully acknowledged as with one heart and one voice by the whole American People.

> I do therefore invite my fellow citizens . . . [to] commend to His
> tender care all those who have become widows, orphans, mourners
> or sufferers in the lamentable civil strife in which we are unavoidably
> engaged, and fervently implore the interposition of the Almighty
> Hand to heal the wounds of the nation and to restore it as soon as
> may be consistent with the Divine purposes to the full enjoyment
> of peace, harmony, tranquility and Union.[21]

His request that the nation "implore the interposition of the Almighty Hand"
to heal the nation's wounds and restore it "as soon as may be consistent with
the Divine purposes" hints that Lincoln was still not convinced that the war
was from the Almighty.

Lincoln continued to confess his dependence on God's guidance in late
1863, as evidenced by his October 24 response to the Baltimore Presbyterian
Synod, which had been introduced to the president by Lincoln's pastor Phineas
D. Gurley. Lincoln closed that meeting admitting that "I have often wished that
I was a more devout man than I am," and acknowledged that "amid the greatest
difficulties of my Administration, when I could not see any other resort, I would
place my whole reliance in God, knowing that all would go well, and that He
would decide for the right [allusion to Proverbs 3:5-6]."[22]

Lincoln was able to escape from the pressures of Washington beginning
November 18, when he traveled to Gettysburg in response to an invitation to
"make a few appropriate remarks" at the battlefield dedication ceremony. It was
about this time in his life that Mary Lincoln said her husband started feeling
"religious more than ever."[23]

At the ceremony the next day, the main speaker for the event, Edward Everett, delivered a two-hour long oration describing in detail the course of the
battle that had taken place the first week of July. After Everett finished, Lincoln
rose to present the short speech he had written over the course of the previous
two weeks. This, his Gettysburg Address, became what is arguably the most
famous presidential speech in American history. Inspired by biblical precepts
as well as the Declaration of Independence, Lincoln used it to reinforce his
transformation of the Civil War from one that had been exclusively for the
purpose of maintaining the Union to one that was also to eliminate slavery.
What had previously been merely a "proposition" of equality in the Declaration
of Independence had now, through the North's dedication to emancipation,
become a fact. Lincoln utilizes language of the King James Bible to present the
biblical theme of birth—death—rebirth throughout.[24]

The Gettysburg Address:

Four score and seven years ago [allusion to Genesis 16:16 and Psalm 90:10] our fathers brought forth on this continent, a new nation [allusion to Leviticus 25:38 and Luke 1:57], conceived in Liberty, and dedicated to the proposition that all men are created equal. Now we are engaged in a great civil war, testing whether that nation, or any nation so conceived and so dedicated, can long endure. We are met on a great battle-field of that war. We have come to dedicate a portion of that field, as a final resting place for those who here gave their lives that that nation might live [allusion to John 15:13]. It is altogether fitting and proper that we should do this.

But, in a larger sense, we can not dedicate—we can not consecrate—we can not hallow—this ground. The brave men, living and dead, who struggled here, have consecrated it, far above our poor power to add or detract. The world will little note, nor long remember what we say here, but it can never forget what they did here. It is for us the living, rather, to be dedicated here to the unfinished work which they who fought here have thus far so nobly advanced. It is rather for us to be here dedicated to the great task remaining before us—that from these honored dead we take increased devotion to that cause for which they gave the last full measure of devotion—that we here highly resolved that these dead shall not have died in vain—that this nation, under God, shall have a new birth of freedom [allusion to John 3:3]—and that government of the people, by the people, for the people, shall not perish from the earth [allusion to Job 18:17, Jeremiah 10:11].[25]

Numerous scholars have noted how the language of the Gettysburg Address emulates the style and cadence of the King James Bible, and how its underlying theme of "life—death—rebirth" is reminiscent of Christ's teachings from the Gospel of John. Lincoln's choice of words such as "dedicate," "consecrate," and "hallow," and expressions such as "brought forth" were also reminiscent of the King James Bible as well as, according to scholar E. A. Elmore, the *Book of Common Prayer*. Through the sacrifice of the men that died, the nation—as well as the cause of freedom for the enslaved people in America—was given new life and purpose.[26]

Less than a week after Lincoln's address at Gettysburg, General Grant, who had been reinforcing and resupplying his army in Chattanooga, was finally ready to break out of the siege. On November 25, Grant launched an overwhelming assault on the Confederate lines surrounding him, and this time it was the Confederates' turn for a hasty retreat. Not long afterward, Jefferson Davis replaced General Bragg with Confederate general Joseph E. Johnston, who took charge of opposing the Union army's advance on Atlanta.

By the close of 1863, Lincoln had significantly changed the character of the war. Support for his acts of emancipating enslaved people and enlisting them in the army continued to grow, and by December the use of Black troops was supported by most Northerners. Lincoln had not only successfully secured the border states for the Union, but had also been instrumental in the admission of the new free state of West Virginia. The navy's blockade of Confederate ports was strangling the Confederacy, and everywhere Union armies advanced, thousands of enslaved people left their masters, never to return to bondage. The leaders of Great Britain, who had for two years been contemplating intervention in the war on behalf of the South, changed their minds. Lincoln's ambassador Charles Francis Adams, who had previously been critical of his chief's leadership skills, reported happily from London that the recent military victories had put "all idea of intervention" on the part of Great Britain "at an end."[27]

Military leaders realized that if the war continued the way it was going, Union victory was inevitable. But a great deal of the North's population did not fully grasp the significance of the army and navy's accomplishments. Thanks to the myopic press, who focused their attentions primarily on the war in Virginia, many people thought only of the fact that Jefferson Davis still ruled defiantly from the Confederate capital of Richmond. As long as Richmond remained unconquered, Lincoln's political situation would remain tenuous.

9. THE WILL OF GOD

SEEKING GOD'S PURPOSE FOR AMERICA

Thy will be done, as in heaven, so in earth.

—Luke 11:2

In early 1864 the president of the United States, concerned about gigantic issues but nevertheless attentive to small details he deemed important, endorsed a basic principle of the Christian faith in an order to Secretary of War Edwin Stanton. On February 5, the president stated his disapproval of a government decree requiring Tennessee residents who were seeking state office to swear that they had never supported the Confederacy. In his message to Stanton, he said: "I dislike an oath which requires a man to swear he has not done wrong. It rejects the Christian principle of <u>forgiveness on terms of repentance</u> [allusion to Luke 17:3–4, Colossians 3:13]. I think it is enough if the man does no wrong hereafter."[1]

On February 11, a coalition of Christians, including well-known theologian Horace Bushnell, met with Lincoln to seek his support for a Christian amendment to acknowledge God in the preamble of the Constitution. They proposed that the preamble be changed to the following (additions italicized):

> We, the people of the United States, *humbly acknowledging Almighty God as the source of all authority and power in civil government, the Lord Jesus Christ as the Ruler among the nations, His revealed will as the supreme law of the land, in order to constitute a Christian government, and* in order to form a more perfect union, establish justice, insure domestic tranquility, provide for the common defense, promote the general welfare, and secure *the inalienable rights and* the blessings of life, liberty, *and the pursuit of happiness* to ourselves [and] our posterity, *and all the people,* do ordain and establish this Constitution for the United States of America.[2]

After hearing their proposed amendment, Lincoln responded: "The general aspect of your movement I cordially approve. In regard to particulars I must ask time to deliberate, as the work of amending the Constitution should not be done hastily. I will carefully examine your paper in order more fully to comprehend its contents than is possible from merely hearing it read, and will take such action upon it as my responsibility to our Maker and our country demands." The amendment was formally introduced to Congress and supported by powerful Republican senators such as Charles Sumner and John Sherman, but it did not pass.[3]

On the war front, Grant's overwhelming victory in Chattanooga convinced Lincoln that it was time to bring his most successful general eastward to fight the Confederacy's most successful general, Robert E. Lee. In early March of 1864, Lincoln ordered U. S. Grant to Washington, promoted him to the rank of lieutenant general, and put him in command of all Union armies. Grant, in turn, appointed General William T. Sherman to command of the Division of the Mississippi and placed him at the head of his old army in northern Georgia. Lincoln and Grant decided together that Grant would accompany General Meade and the Army of the Potomac in its field campaigns rather than direct the war from a desk in Washington. Meanwhile, Sherman would press on toward Atlanta and focus on defeating the Confederate army commanded by General Joseph Johnston.

The president frequently spoke at events that raised money for the care of wounded soldiers. At one of these events held on March 18 in Baltimore, known as a Sanitary Fair, Lincoln quoted a new scripture. He praised the dedication and efforts of civilians in the war effort, and then concluded with a special tribute to the soldiers. Quoting the book of Job in his closing remarks, he observed, "For it has been said, all that a man hath will he give for his life [Job 2:4]; and while all contribute of their substance the soldier puts his life at stake, and often yields it up in his country's cause. The highest merit, then, is due to the soldier."[4]

In late March of 1864, Lincoln addressed representatives of a charitable organization known as the New York Workingmen's Democratic Republican Association. Hoping to offer some encouragement to this bipartisan group, he quoted the book of Revelation in his closing remarks: "The strongest bond of human sympathy, outside of the family relation, should be one uniting all working people, of all nations, and tongues, and kindreds" [Revelation 13:7].[5]

Lincoln's transformative speeches, letters, and words of encouragement were making a decisive difference in the war effort. According to Douglas

Wilson, in 1864 the Northern people's support for the abolition of slavery dramatically increased. This is partially evidenced by diarist George Templeton Strong, who had in 1860 sharply criticized Lincoln's qualifications for the office of president. But like many others, the nation's premier diarist had seen the light. Reflecting on Lincoln's patient policy of saving the Union first and eliminating slavery second, Strong wrote in his diary on February 24, 1864, that "the change of opinion on this slavery question since 1860 is a great historical fact . . . I think this great and blessed revolution is due, in no small degree, to A. Lincoln's sagacious policy."[6]

In an April 4 letter to Albert G. Hodges, editor of the Frankfort, Kentucky *Commonwealth*, Lincoln wrote one of his most influential letters as president. Beginning with his famous acknowledgment "I am naturally anti-slavery. If slavery is not wrong, nothing is wrong. I cannot remember when I did not so think, and feel," he explained his reasoning and the process for his presidential actions over the preceding months to eliminate slavery. He closed the letter with this acknowledgement of his dependence on God:

> In telling this tale I attempt no compliment to my own sagacity. I claim not to have controlled events, but confess plainly that events have controlled me. Now, at the end of three years struggle the nation's condition is not what either party, or any man devised, or expected. God alone can claim it. Whither it is tending seems plain. If God now wills the removal of a great wrong, and wills also that we of the North as well as you of the South, shall pay fairly for our complicity in that wrong, impartial history will find therein new cause to attest and revere the justice and goodness of God [allusion to Psalm 52:1 and Psalm 19:9].[7]

This letter reveals that Lincoln seems to have concluded that God saw slavery as a national sin, and that he wanted it ended now—with this war—rather than decades hence through legislation. Lincoln accepted that he was going to be the Almighty's instrument for its elimination. It is noteworthy that Lincoln's statement that God is removing the "great wrong" of slavery and requiring that both the North and South "pay fairly for our complicity in that wrong" is prescient of the second inaugural's conclusion that "he gives to both North and South, this terrible war, as the woe due to those by whom the offence came."[8]

Lincoln quickly followed up the Hodges letter with other communications about the will of God. On April 5 he replied to a letter from a Mrs. Mann, who had submitted a petition signed by 195 children from Concord, Massachusetts, asking that "all slave children" be freed. He said that although he did not have the power to "grant all they [the children] asked," he trusted that they would remember that "God has" the power, and "as it seems, He wills to do it."[9]

When speaking at another Sanitary Fair in Baltimore on April 18, Lincoln quoted scripture that would have been typically used by Calvinist preachers: "When the war began, three years ago, neither party, nor any man, expected it would last till now. Each looked for the end, in some way, long ere to-day. Neither did any anticipate that domestic slavery would be much affected by the war. But here we are; the war has not ended, and slavery has been much affected—how much needs not now to be recounted. So true is it that man proposes, and God disposes" [allusion to Proverbs 19:21]. In this same speech, he acknowledged his own responsibility to the Almighty regarding his decision to employ Black troops: "Upon a clear conviction of duty I resolved to turn that element of strength [Black troops] to account; and I am responsible for it to the American people, to the christian world, to history, and on my final account to God" [allusion to Romans 14:12].[10]

In the first week of May, Grant and Lee fought their first battle—a desperate, three-day engagement known today as the Battle of the Wilderness—immediately west of the old Chancellorsville battlefield. Despite twenty-nine thousand casualties between the two armies, Grant continued pressing southward to Richmond rather than retreating as preceding commanders of the Army of the Potomac had done after encounters with Lee. Grant's resolve to keep up the fight was certainly not lost on Lincoln. On May 9, the president proclaimed "to the friends of Union and Liberty" the following brief, heartfelt request for Thanksgiving and prayer: "Enough is known of Army operations within the last five days to claim our especial gratitude to God; while what remains undone demands our most sincere prayers to, and reliance upon, Him, without whom, all human effort is vain. I recommend that all patriots, at their homes, in their places of public worship, and wherever they may be, unite in common thanksgiving and prayer to Almighty God."[11]

Even this late in the war, Lincoln continued his moral crusade against slavery. In a remarkable May 30 response to Rev. George B. Ide and a visiting delegation of Baptists, Lincoln explained not only his biblical reasons for why he thought slavery morally wrong, but also what he thought of those "professing Christianity" who believed it was right. In this sermon-like letter he combined two of his favorite scriptures about slavery—Genesis 3:19 and Mathew 7:12—with four additional scriptures. Lincoln knew that, as with all his public letters, it would be passed on to a larger audience:

> Indeed, it is difficult to conceive how it could be otherwise with any one professing christianity, or even having ordinary perceptions of right and wrong. To read in the Bible, as the word of God himself, that "In the sweat of thy face shalt thou eat bread["] [Genesis 3:19], and to preach there-from that, "In the sweat of other mens faces shalt thou eat bread," to my mind can scarcely be reconciled with honest sincerity. When brought to my final reckoning [allusion to 2 Corinthians 5:10], may I have to answer for robbing no man of his goods [allusion to 1 Samuel 12:3]; yet more tolerable even this, than for robbing one of himself, and all that was his. When, a year or two ago, those professedly holy men of the South, met in the semblance of prayer and devotion, and, in the name of Him who said "As ye would all men should do unto you, do ye even so unto them" [Matthew 7:12] appealed to the christian world to aid them in doing to a whole race of men, as they would have no man do unto themselves, to my thinking, they contemned and insulted God and His church, far more than did Satan when he tempted the Saviour with the Kingdoms of the earth [allusion to Matthew 4:8–10]. The devils attempt was no more false, and far less hypocritical. But let me forbear, remembering it is also written "Judge not, lest ye be judged" [Matthew 7:1].[12]

Dissatisfied with Lincoln, the Radical Republicans on May 31 attempted to launch a new political party that would halt Lincoln's renomination as a presidential candidate and replace him with John C. Frémont. This event, which was attended by four hundred delegates in Cleveland, proved quite short-lived. Hearing of their failed effort, a bemused Lincoln was reminded of 1 Samuel 22:2 describing the supporters of David at the cave of Adullam: "And every one that was in distress, and every one that was in debt, and every one that was discontented, gathered themselves unto him, and he became a captain over them, and there were with him about four hundred men."[13]

← ❋ →

The terrible carnage on the battlefield never ceased. Grant repeatedly hammered Lee in a series of costly battles including Spotsylvania Court House and Cold Harbor during his advance southward, and he finally reached the vicinity of Richmond in early June. Repulsed by Lee at Petersburg, Richmond's major railroad and supply center, Grant and the Army of the Potomac entrenched and settled into a siege of the Confederate capital. In the meantime, Sherman inched closer and closer to Atlanta, continuously outflanking Johnston and forcing him to retreat.

Anxious about the slow progress of the war, Lincoln issued a Proclamation for a Day of Prayer to be observed on August 4. In addition to a confession of national sin, and a request for mercy and help, he also acknowledged the nation's need to seek and follow the will of God. In the following excerpt from the proclamation, he called on the Northern people to:

> confess and to repent of their manifold sins; to implore the com-
> passion and forgiveness of the Almighty, that, if consistent with His
> will, the existing rebellion may be speedily suppressed, and the su-
> premacy of the Constitution and laws of the United States may be
> established throughout all the States; to implore Him as the Supreme
> Ruler of the World, not to destroy us as a people, nor suffer us to be
> destroyed [allusion to Isaiah 34:2] by the hostility or connivance of
> other Nations, or by obstinate adhesion to our own counsels, which
> may be in conflict with His eternal purposes, and to implore Him to
> enlighten the mind of the Nation to know and do His will.[14]

One of Lincoln's favorite things to do during the war was to talk to the soldiers, thank them for their sacrifice, and encourage them to continue their support of the Northern cause. His faithfulness and sincerity earned him the respect and admiration of the men. One private in the Army of the Potomac spoke for many of his comrades when he said that "we have learned to love him as well as he appears to love his boys in blue, and we all would be willing to sacrifice anything for such a man."[15]

On August 22, 1864, he had an opportunity to talk to the men of the 166th Ohio Regiment, who had recently completed their tour of duty and were going home. It is yet another example of how Lincoln, as a transformational leader, always sought to elevate his listeners to a higher moral plane:

> I suppose you are going home to see your families and friends. For
> the service you have done in this great struggle in which we are
> engaged I present you sincere thanks for myself and the country. I
> almost always feel inclined, when I happen to say anything to sol-
> diers, to impress upon them in a few brief remarks the importance

of success in this contest. It is not merely for to-day, but for all time to come that we should perpetuate for our children's children this great and free government, which we have enjoyed all our lives. I beg you to remember this, not merely for my sake, but for yours. I happen temporarily to occupy this big White House. I am a living witness that any one of your children may look to come here as my father's child has. It is in order that each of you may have through this free government which we have enjoyed, an open field and a fair chance for your industry, enterprise and intelligence; that you may all have equal privileges in the race of life, with all its desirable human aspirations. It is for this the struggle should be maintained, that we may not lose our birthright—not only for one, but for two or three years. The nation is worth fighting for, to secure such an inestimable jewel.[16]

Though typical of his communications to soldiers, this speech does not directly quote scripture. However, like many of his other communications (including the Gettysburg Address) it is awash in familiar biblical phrases and terms. For instance, it includes "living witness" [Acts 1:8], "the race of life" [1 Corinthians 9:24], and "lose our birthright" [Genesis 27:36]. Communication using biblical language had become second nature with President Lincoln.

The fact that 1864 was a presidential election year brought increasing public scrutiny of the Lincoln administration's war effort. Despite seventy-five thousand casualties between their two armies since the spring campaign began, by late summer Grant had failed to take Richmond and Sherman had not yet captured Atlanta. The Democratic Party made much of this dilemma by claiming that there was no end to the war in sight. They nominated General George B. McClellan for president and drafted a peace platform for him to run on. Lincoln knew that a McClellan administration would be obligated by his party to sue for peace immediately, which would allow the South to become a separate nation and keep its enslaved people. Lincoln, an astute politician, was convinced that it was "exceedingly probable" that he would lose the election. Lincoln needed a miracle.[17]

Lincoln was willing to talk to the Southern leaders about peace, but as a precondition for these talks, he required the South's willingness to emancipate their enslaved people and rejoin the Union. In the summer of 1864 Lincoln came under increasing pressure from Republicans and Democrats alike to drop this requirement for peace talks. Responding in mid-August to two visitors about this subject, Lincoln said, "There have been men who have proposed to me to return to slavery the black warriors [soldiers] of Port Hudson & Olustee to their masters to conciliate the South. I should be damned in time & in eternity for so doing. The world shall know that I will keep my faith to friends & enemies, come what will."[18]

Lincoln was adamant on this point. As was evident in Welles's diary entry on September 22, 1862, about the Emancipation Proclamation, Lincoln had learned the concept of covenant from the Bible, and he refused to reverse his Emancipation Proclamation. In his annual message to Congress on December 6 he declared that if forced to re-enslave Black people, he would resign his office: "I repeat the declaration made a year ago, that 'while I remain in my present position I shall not attempt to retract or modify the emancipation proclamation, nor shall I return to slavery any person who is free by the terms of that proclamation, or by any of the Acts of Congress.' If the people should, by whatever mode or means, make it an Executive duty to re-enslave such persons, another, and not I, must be their instrument to perform it."[19]

Many Southerners realized that with Grant at the outskirts of Richmond, and Sherman nearing Atlanta, the South's best hope for victory was Lincoln's defeat in the November elections. If Southern armies could hold onto Atlanta and Richmond until Election Day, Lincoln would probably lose the election and a negotiated peace assuring the continuation of slavery would likely result. Surprisingly, at this moment Jefferson Davis made a huge political blunder and replaced the patient, defensive-minded General Joseph Johnson with the reckless, offensive-minded General John Bell Hood. Hood made four quick assaults on Sherman's army, all of which were repulsed, and the Confederate army defending Atlanta suffered nearly 50 percent casualties.

Hood fell back into the fortifications that surrounded Atlanta, and Sherman prepared to lay siege. But Hood, rather than waiting Sherman out, evacuated his army from Atlanta on the night of September 1, and the city fell to Sherman on September 2. With this news trumpeted throughout the North, the people's morale and optimism for ultimate victory immediately soared. Instead of a Democratic Party victory and the triumph of slavery, it was now Lincoln's re-election and the death of slavery that was virtually guaranteed.[20]

Not bothering to acquire secretary of state Seward's signature, Lincoln quickly followed Sherman's victory announcement with a Proclamation of Thanksgiving and Prayer on September 3. In it he acknowledged the work of God's hands and gave the credit for recent military successes to "Divine Providence":

The signal success that Divine Providence has recently vouchsafed... resulting in the capture of the City of Atlanta, call for devout acknowledgement to the Supreme Being in whose hands are the destinies of nations [allusion to Psalm 22:28 and Isaiah 2:4]. It is therefore requested that on next Sunday, in all places of public worship in the United-States, thanksgiving be offered to Him for His mercy in preserving our national existence against the insurgent rebels who so long have been waging a cruel war against the Government of the United-States, for its overthrow; and also that prayer be made for the Divine protection to our brave soldiers ... and for blessing and comfort from the Father of Mercies to the sick, wounded, and prisoners, and to the orphans and widows of those who have fallen in the service of their country, and that he will continue to uphold the Government of the United-States against all the efforts of public enemies and secret foes.[21]

It is noteworthy that although he spoke of the war as a cruel one, Lincoln no longer referred to it as "needless." He had evidently concluded that God had his own good purpose for the war.[22]

As mentioned in chapter 7, Lincoln's well-known, undated note called the "Meditation on the Divine Will" had been placed chronologically by Nicolay and Hay, and the editors of the *CW*, in the September 1862 timeframe. Nicolay and Hay said that they thought the meditation "was not written to be seen of men. It was penned in the awful sincerity of an honest soul trying to bring itself into closer communion with its maker" about the "the weightiest question of his life," the Emancipation Proclamation.[23]

But as I said before, I believe that Douglas Wilson is correct when he says the date of the meditation should be much later. For reasons I will soon offer, I believe the spring of 1864 is likely. Lincoln's Meditation on Divine Will reads as follows:

The will of God prevails [allusion to Job 23:13]. In great contests each party claims to act in accordance with the will of God. Both *may* be, and one *must* be wrong. God can not be *for*, and *against* the same thing at the same time. In the present civil war it is quite possible that God's purpose is something different from the purpose of either party—and yet the human instrumentalities, working just as they do, are of the best adaptation to effect His purpose. I am almost ready to say this is probably true—that <u>God wills this contest, and wills that it shall not end yet</u> [allusion to Isaiah 14:24]. By his mere quiet power, on the minds of the now contestants, He could have either saved or destroyed the Union without a human contest. Yet the contest began. And having begun He could give the final victory to either side any day. Yet the contest proceeds.[24]

Rather than focusing on the problem of emancipation in this meditation, Lincoln seems to be more focused on the war and its extended duration as a "contest" that only God can end. Lincoln sounds perplexed that it has not ended.

Lincoln would have had less reason for frustration on the subject of the war's duration in 1862 than in 1864. In the summer of 1863, the South had won the Battles of Chancellorsville and Second Manassas, and then invaded the North in September. The North, not the South, was the fighter "on the ropes" and complete military victory was not even a remote possibility for the North at that time. Contrast this situation with the fact that by the summer of 1864 Grant had already forced the surrender of two entire Southern armies, Northern forces were on the outskirts of Richmond and nearing Atlanta, and the blockade was strangling the Confederacy. And yet total victory still seemed out of reach.[25]

Another important indicator that the meditation might have been written in 1864 is its similarity to other things Lincoln wrote that year. To perceive this, it is instructive to expand on what Ronald C. White did in his juxtaposition of the Meditation of the Divine Will to the second inaugural address, and add in the comparison two additional 1864 communications. Below I have taken White's table comparing "the similarity of ideas" between the meditation and the second inaugural and added excerpts of the April 4, 1864, letter to Hodges and the October 4, 1864, letter to Gurney. I believe that all four of these documents show similar continuity and development. If one considers the meditation a fragment, it is quite possible it was written sometime shortly before or after the Hodges letter.[26]

Several scholars have recognized the significance of Lincoln's meditation. Lincoln scholar Allen C. Guelzo calls it "the most radically metaphysical question ever posed by an American President." Mark Noll believes the meditation is the "most remarkable theological commentary" on the Civil War. Noll points out that Lincoln's conclusions in the meditation were both conventional and nonconventional. They were conventional in the belief that God ruled over all events, but unconventional in that Lincoln was evidently questioning the

Table 9.1 Comparison of the Major Lincoln Communications of 1864/65.

Meditation (Undated)	Letter to A. Hodges (April 4, 1864)	Letter to E. Gurney (September 4, 1864)	Second Inaugural Address (March 4, 1865)
The will of God prevails.	[I] confess plainly that events have controlled me.... God alone can claim it.	The purposes of the Almighty are perfect, and must prevail,	The Almighty has His own purposes.
Both may be, and one must be wrong. God can not be for, and against, the same thing at the same time.	Now, at the end of three years struggle the nation's condition is not what either party, or any man devised, or expected.	though we erring mortals may fail to accurately perceive them in advance.	The prayers of both could not be answered; that of neither has been answered fully.
I am almost ready to say that this is probably true— that God wills this contest, and wills that it shall not end.	If God now wills the removal of a great wrong, and wills also that we of the North as well as you of the South, shall pay fairly for our complicity in that wrong,	We hoped for a happy termination of this terrible war long before this; but God knows best, and has ruled otherwise.	He now wills to remove ... Yet, if God wills that it continue,

commonly held belief that the United States was a uniquely "chosen" nation, and that God would always support the preservation of the Union. To Lincoln, God's purposes were far beyond man's comprehension. Lincoln's Calvinist concept of a sovereign God was stronger than ever.[27]

On September 4, 1864, Lincoln wrote a long-delayed reply to Quaker minister Eliza P. Gurney, who had written him on August 3, 1863. Lincoln wrote:

I have not forgotten—probably never shall forget—the very impressive occasion when yourself and friends visited me on a Sabbath forenoon two years ago. Nor has your kind letter, written nearly a year later, ever been forgotten. In all, it has been your purpose to strengthen my reliance on God. I am much indebted to the good christian people of the country for their constant prayers and consolations;

and to no one of them, more than to yourself. <u>The purposes of the Almighty are perfect, and must prevail</u> [allusion to Job 23:13], though we erring mortals may fail to accurately perceive them in advance. We hoped for a happy termination of this terrible war long before this; but God knows best, and has ruled otherwise. We shall yet acknowledge His wisdom and our own error therein. Meanwhile we must work earnestly <u>in the best light He gives us</u> [allusion to Job 29:3 and Psalm 119:105], trusting that so working still conduces to the great ends He ordains. Surely He intends some great good to follow this mighty convulsion, which no mortal could make, and no mortal could stay.[28]

In comparing this 1864 letter to his 1862 letter to Gurney, it is obvious that Lincoln is now much more certain about God's intentions, and confidently states that those intentions "are perfect."

On September 7, a group of Black men representing what they called the Loyal Colored People of Baltimore gave Lincoln a beautiful presentation Bible. Considering that the Bible had influenced his life more than any other single book, Lincoln's remarks on the occasion, although brief, were certainly sincere. Speaking to the visiting delegation in the White House, he said, "In regard to this Great Book, I have but to say, it is the best gift God has given to man. All the good the Saviour gave to the world was communicated through this book. But for it we could not know right from wrong. All things most desirable for man's welfare, here and hereafter, are to be found portrayed in it." In this acknowledgment of the preeminence of the Bible, Lincoln demonstrated how far he had come from the New Salem days, when he was reading Thomas Paine and questioning the Bible's veracity. For at least two decades now, he had looked to the Bible for answers.[29]

Thanks again to the encouragement of the editor of *Godey's Lady's Book*, Sarah Josepha Hale, Lincoln issued on October 20, 1864, what would prove to be his last proclamation of Thanksgiving, which was to be celebrated, like the previous year, on the last Thursday of November. Lincoln closed with a note of humble optimism:

> I . . . appoint and set apart the last Thursday in November next as a day, which I desire to be observed by all my fellow-citizens wherever they may then be as a day of Thanksgiving and Praise to Almighty God

the beneficent Creator and Ruler of the Universe. And I do farther recommend to my fellow-citizens aforesaid that on that occasion they do reverently humble themselves in the dust [allusion to Job 42:6] and from thence offer up penitent and fervent prayers and supplications to the Great Disposer of events for a return of the inestimable blessings of Peace, Union, and Harmony throughout the land, which it has pleased him to assign as a dwelling place for ourselves and for our posterity throughout all generations.[30]

Americans went to the polls on November 8 to choose their next president, and Lincoln won the 1864 election by a landslide. He defeated McClellan 212 to 21 in the electoral college, and nearly 80 percent of the soldier vote went for Lincoln. Lincoln accepted this result as a vindication of his emancipation policy. It looked as if his 1854 plea in Peoria, Illinois, for the people to "re-adopt the Declaration of Independence" was finally being embraced. Northern voters not only returned Lincoln to office, but maintained a Republican Party majority in both houses of Congress as well.[31]

About a week after the election, Sherman placed half his army under the command of General George H. Thomas and ordered them back to a defensive position in central Tennessee. Then he took the other half of his army, about sixty thousand men, and marched eastward from Atlanta toward Savannah. Virtually unopposed, he cut a swath of destruction sixty miles wide across the state of Georgia, destroying or consuming Southern produce and livestock along the way. Rather than attempting to follow Sherman through Georgia, Confederate general Hood decided to head westward and attack General Thomas's force in Tennessee.

Still intent on reinforcing his moral argument against slavery, on December 6 the president invited his friend Noah Brooks to the White House Library. Brooks was a newspaper correspondent and, some would say, Lincoln's surrogate son. Lincoln wrote out a little story, in which he quoted one of his favorite scripture verses, and suggested that Brooks publish it:

> On Thursday of last week two ladies from Tennessee came before the President asking the release of their husbands held as prisoners of war at Johnson's Island. They were put off till Friday, when they came again; and were again put off to Saturday. At each of the interviews one of the ladies urged that her husband was a religious man. On

Saturday the President ordered the release of the prisoners, and then said to this lady "You say your husband is a religious man; tell him when you meet him, that I say I am not much of a judge of religion, but that, in my opinion, the religion that sets men to rebel and fight against their government, because, as they think, that government does not sufficiently help some men to <u>eat their bread on the sweat of other men's faces</u> [allusion to Genesis 3:19] is not the sort of religion upon which people can get to heaven!"[32]

Lincoln probably asked that the story be published because he knew that a large element of society still supported slavery, and he wanted to reinforce his Biblical argument against that institution. Lincoln was preparing for what he hoped would be his final, death-dealing blow to slavery in January—the passing of the abolition amendment.

Although Lincoln was looking forward to inflicting slavery's death blow in January, he still had to await the progress of arms. Good news regarding this progress soon arrived from both General Thomas in Tennessee and General Sherman in Georgia. On December 15, 1864, General Thomas defeated General Hood's Confederate army in Nashville. After this battle, which was an annihilation of Hood's force, only two Confederate armies remained east of the Mississippi, General Robert E. Lee's at Richmond, and a much smaller one under General Joseph Johnson in the Carolinas. On December 20 Sherman and his army finished their trek through Georgia, arriving at the coastal city of Savannah. He sent a telegram to Lincoln, offering him the city as a "Christmas gift."[33]

Lincoln responded to Sherman with a note of thanks that includes another quote from the Bible, telling him that Sherman's and Thomas's military victories "[bring] <u>those who sat in darkness, to see a great light</u>" [allusion to Isaiah 9:2]. After refitting his army, Sherman would soon make his final push northward through the Carolinas toward Grant and Lee in Richmond.[34]

A war-weary Abraham Lincoln had good reason to anticipate victory in the coming year.

10. THE JUDGMENTS
OF THE LORD

LINCOLN'S SERMON FOR AMERICA,
THE SECOND
INAUGURAL ADDRESS

Recompense to no man evil for evil.

—Romans 12:17

With Sherman in the deep South virtually unopposed, and Grant laying siege to Richmond, the end of the war was drawing near. But Lincoln still had one additional major task to accomplish before his presidential war powers came to an end. He wanted to pass a constitutional amendment that would legally abolish slavery. The Emancipation Proclamation had effectively freed enslaved people during the war, but Lincoln feared that once the fighting was over, slave owners would be able to use the courts to return previously enslaved people to bondage. Consequently, in January 1865 Lincoln's top political priority was to convince Congress to quickly pass the Thirteenth Amendment, which he called "a King's cure for all evils" (an allusion to Shakespeare's King Edward the Confessor in *Macbeth*). Once Congress had accomplished this, it could be sent to the states for ratification. Anxious to push this through, Lincoln requested that Republican leadership in Congress introduce the amendment in the House of Representatives in early January and to bring it to a vote before February 1.[1]

Although the Senate had passed the Thirteenth Amendment several months prior, the House of Representatives of the 38th Congress had rejected the amendment in June 1864 because of nearly unanimous opposition by Democrats. In the November 1864 elections the Republican Party increased its majority in the House of Representatives, but the 39th Congress would not be seated until December 1865. Considering that the war could end before this, Lincoln did not want to wait on the 39th Congress for passage of the Thirteenth

Amendment. He instead decided to try to convince the lame duck Democrats of the 38th Congress to change their minds and support passage of the Thirteenth Amendment immediately. Thanks to Lincoln's extraordinary leadership skills, his plan succeeded.

Lincoln signed the Thirteenth Amendment abolishing slavery on February 1, 1865, and it was immediately sent to the states for ratification. Although the last state to ratify did not do so until December of 1865, the amendment had immediate momentum, and by late spring the danger that slavery would be reinstated after the war had been virtually eliminated.[2]

While these political maneuverings took place in Washington, General Sherman left Savannah and marched his army northward. His force of sixty thousand men advanced steadily through South and North Carolina. Although they had to force their way through swamps, burned bridges, and blockaded roads, they faced very little fighting from General Joseph Johnston and his small force of fifteen thousand troops. As Sherman advanced northward, Lee and Grant prepared for what they both knew would be their final spring campaign in Virginia.

Inauguration Day, March 4, 1865, arrived—overcast and drizzly. But when Lincoln approached the podium on the steps of the Capitol building to begin his inaugural address, the sun broke through the clouds and bathed the audience in light. The parting of the clouds seemed to be a gift from heaven, and Noah Brooks said, "Every heart beat quicker at the unexpected omen." For the occasion Lincoln prepared a seven-hundred-word masterpiece, which now is considered the most famous inaugural address in American history.[3]

In previous inaugural speeches the presidents-elect usually focused on their past accomplishments and future plans. But Lincoln would say very little about these things. His address would be, in effect, a sermon that dwelled almost exclusively on the sin of slavery, the need for national repentance, and charity toward enemies.

Preceding inaugural addresses rarely mentioned God, but in this address Lincoln would mention God fourteen times including God-related pronouns and synonyms. He would also include three direct quotes of scripture and six allusions to the Bible.[4]

Enveloped in sunlight, Lincoln put on his spectacles, pulled his manuscript out of his coat pocket, and began reading his address. In the first half of the address, which was as unremarkable in spirit as the second half would be extraordinary, Lincoln spoke briefly of the events of the last four years, and pointed out that slavery was "somehow, the cause of the war." After finishing this introduction, Lincoln launched into the second half of his address, beginning what one Biblical scholar calls a theological statement "of rare depth:"[5]

Neither party expected for the war, the magnitude, or the duration, which it has already attained. Neither anticipated that the *cause* of the conflict might cease with, or even before, the conflict itself should cease. Each looked for an easier triumph, and a result less fundamental and astounding. Both read the same Bible, and pray to the same God; and each invokes His aid against the other. It may seem strange that any men should dare to ask a just God's assistance in wringing their bread from the sweat of other men's faces [allusion to Genesis 3:19]; but let us judge not that we be not judged [Matthew 7:1]. The prayers of both could not be answered; that of neither has been answered fully. The Almighty has His own purposes [allusion to Job 23:13]. "Woe unto the world because of offences! for it must needs be that offences come; but woe to that man by whom the offence cometh!" [Matthew 18:7]. If we shall suppose that American Slavery is one of those offences which, in the providence of God, must needs come, but which, having continued through His appointed time, He now wills to remove, and that He gives to both North and South, this terrible war, as the woe due to those by whom the offence came, shall we discern therein any departure from those divine attributes which the believers in a Living God always ascribe to Him?

Fondly do we hope—fervently do we pray—that this mighty scourge of war may speedily pass away. Yet, if God wills that it continue, until all the wealth piled by the bond-man's two hundred and fifty years of unrequited toil shall be sunk, and until every drop of blood drawn with the lash, shall be paid by another drawn with the sword, as was said three thousand years ago, so still it must be said "the judgments of the Lord, are true and righteous altogether" [Psalm 19:9].[6]

Lincoln's sequitur was that it was an unquestionable judgment from God that the bloodshed of slavery must be paid for by the bloodshed of war. This Old Testament "eye for an eye" was a conclusion that most of the Bible-conscious nineteenth-century American audience could understand. But then Lincoln launched into his peroration, which was much more difficult for the war-weary audience to embrace:[7]

With malice toward none; with charity for all [allusion to Colossians 3:8 and 14]; with firmness in the right, as God gives us to see the right, let us strive on to finish the work we are in; to bind up the nation's wounds [allusion to Psalm 147:3]; to care for him who shall have borne the battle, and for his widow, and his orphan [allusion to James 1:27]—to do all which may achieve and cherish a just, and a lasting peace, among ourselves, and with all nations [allusion to Romans 12:18].[8]

These last seventy-five words were Lincoln's final plea for the nation to ascend to a higher moral plane. To appreciate their significance we must consider the words of Henry Ward Beecher, the most popular Northern preacher of that day. In 1864, Beecher had vehemently declaimed, "I charge the whole guilt of this war upon the ambitious, educated, plotting political leaders of the South . . . A day will come when God will reveal judgment, and arraign at his bar these mighty miscreants." Beecher looked forward to the day when "these most accursed and detested of all criminals" would be "caught up in black clouds full of voices of vengeance and lurid with punishment" and "plunged downward forever in an endless retribution."[9]

Unlike Beecher, Lincoln was not a popular preacher; he was America's consummate transformational leader. Had he known what Beecher said about punishment for the Southern leaders, he would have surely recoiled. Lincoln's understanding of the Bible was that it elicited a more gracious response to human offences. Christ told his followers that when they were struck they were to turn the other cheek [Matthew 5:39], they were to forgive up to seventy times seven times [Matthew 18:22], they should do unto others as they would have others do unto them [Matthew 7:12], and they should judge not lest they be judged [Matthew 7:1]. Lincoln had evoked the spirit of these scriptures many times in his life, and in his second inaugural address he did once again. Mark Noll correctly says that the theologians of Lincoln's day paled in comparison to Abraham Lincoln when it came to understanding the theological aspects of the war.[10]

In seven minutes, Lincoln's address was over. It was received with polite applause by the White attendees. By contrast, Black people in the audience granted hearty "amens" and "bless de Lord's" after nearly every sentence. Frederick Douglass was, at last, extremely satisfied with a speech from President Lincoln and recalled, "[I] clapped my hands in gladness and thanksgiving at their utterance." He resolved to go to the White House reception later that day and pay his respects.[11]

In front of the White House that evening Douglass stood in a long line of well-wishers, and like everyone else he wanted to shake the president's hand and congratulate him on his speech. But when he got to the front door, the Washington policemen on duty refused him entrance because of his race. Douglass understood this was from habit, and asked a friend to tell the president about it. Henceforth, he was immediately admitted.

As Douglass approached Lincoln in the crowd of White well-wishers, the president saw him and announced loudly enough for all those nearby to hear, "Here comes my friend Douglass." He shook Douglass's hand and said to him warmly, "I am glad to see you. I saw you in the crowd today," and asked Douglass how he liked the speech.

Douglass demurred, "Mr. Lincoln, I must not detain you with my poor opinion, when there are thousands waiting to shake hands with you."

Lincoln rejoined, "No, no. You must stop a little, Douglass; there is no man in the country whose opinion I value more than yours. I want to know what you think of it?"

Douglass related exactly what he felt: "Mr. Lincoln, that was a sacred effort."[12]

← ❄ →

Less than two weeks after the second inaugural, Lincoln responded to a note from New York political boss Thurlow Weed. In this short March 15 letter, Lincoln demonstrated the quiet confidence of a man who believes he is following the will of God. His message connoted a balance of self-assurance and humility:

> I expect the latter [the second inaugural address] to wear as well as—perhaps better than—anything I have produced; but I believe it is not immediately popular. Men are not flattered by being shown that there has been a difference of purpose between the Almighty and them. To deny it, however, in this case, is to deny that there is a God governing the world [allusion to Psalm 22:28]. It is a truth which I thought needed to be told; and as whatever of humiliation there is in it, falls most directly on myself, I thought others might afford for me to tell it.[13]

A number of scholars have compared and contrasted Lincoln's second inaugural with the Gettysburg Address, and at least two of them believe the second inaugural is Lincoln's completion of his quest to understand the Almighty's purpose for the United States of America. I believe that the Gettysburg

Address was Lincoln's conclusion that God had a distinct purpose for the Republic—the establishment and survival of a democratic government that assured the equality of men. But by war's end Lincoln realized that even this noble objective was one that fell short of God's purposes. In the second inaugural, Lincoln asserted that the Bible says God requires not only atonement for sin, but also forgiveness of enemies.[14]

← ✳ →

On April 1 Union forces won the decisive battle known as Five Forks on the right flank of Lee's army, rendering his continuing defense of Richmond impossible. During the night of April 2 Lee was forced to evacuate his entrenchments around Richmond, and to retreat toward the town of Danville, in western Virginia. He hoped he could eventually unite with the small army under the command of General Joseph Johnson in North Carolina, but Lee's retreat was cut off by the hard-marching Union troops under the command of General Phil Sheridan. On April 9, 1865, Lee surrendered his army to General Grant at Appomattox Court House, Virginia.

Grant complied with Lincoln's directions for an easy peace, and offered highly magnanimous surrender terms to the Army of Northern Virginia. Men and officers were promptly paroled. Any soldier who claimed to own a horse was allowed to keep it, and within a few days most men had left for home. Officers and men, even Lee, were free to leave, "not to be disturbed by U.S. authority so long as they observe their paroles and the laws in force where they may reside." Per Lincoln's direction, there were to be no trials or hangings of the Confederate army leaders.[15]

The evening of April 11, Lincoln was called upon by a crowd of well-wishers who were standing on the White House lawn. Lincoln addressed them from the balcony, and began his speech, saying: "The evacuation of Petersburg and Richmond, and the surrender of the principal insurgent army, give hope of a righteous and speedy peace whose joyous expression can not be restrained. In the midst of this, however, He, from Whom all blessings flow, must not be forgotten. A call for a national thanksgiving is being prepared, and will be duly promulgated."[16]

In the remainder of his speech, Lincoln discussed the question of how he hoped to re-admit the Southern states, beginning with Louisiana, and restore them to their "proper practical relation" with the federal government. To do this, Lincoln suggested that some Black men in Louisiana, including "the very intelligent" and "those who serve our cause as soldiers," be given the right to vote. This proposition for black suffrage was undoubtedly shocking to most of the audience, and the last straw for the Southern sympathizer and actor John Wilkes Booth, who was among those listening from the White House lawn. Angered that Lincoln was going to give African Americans the right to vote, he is purported to have sworn to his companion, "That is the last speech he will ever give."[17]

Booth was right. It was in fact his last speech. But this address was an indicator of what Lincoln had in mind for his next transformational task. He had saved the Union and won the terrible war against slavery, but he now had a new vision before him. As part of the reconstruction of the South, Lincoln began to lay the groundwork for enslaved people to receive not only their freedom, but also—one day—political and social equality with Whites. Lincoln had already been making modest efforts toward social equalization through his own personal actions, such as welcoming different organizations of Black people and well-known spokespersons like Frederick Douglass and Sojourner Truth to the White House. There were countless acts of kindness that Lincoln had been showering on Black people who worked in the nation's capital or came to the White House for help. Finally, there is also the example of his second inaugural reception, when he publicly welcomed Frederick Douglass and told him and everyone else within hearing distance that there "was not a man in the country" whose opinion he valued more. These acts of benevolence may sound small today, but in that day the president was, as Frederick Douglass would say, a "statesman" that was "swift, zealous, radical, and determined." Frederick Douglass had been right about the "educating tendency" of the war on the president. Lincoln had successfully transformed the war's purpose, and in the process, Lincoln himself had changed.[18]

Lincoln's last day as president was April 14, Good Friday. Lincoln invited General Grant to attend his 11:00 AM Cabinet meeting, and at the president's request, Grant shared details regarding the surrender of the Confederate forces at Appomattox. Lincoln told his Cabinet about a dream he had had the night before, in which he seemed to be on a ship that was "moving with great rapidity toward a dark and indefinite shore." He shared that he was not alarmed, because this was a dream that had recurred many times, usually before a Union military victory. Lincoln speculated that it might have to do with General Joseph Johnston's anticipated surrender in North Carolina and said, "I think it must be from Sherman." Lincoln expressed his desire that Jefferson Davis and other Confederate leaders be allowed to leave the country unmolested, and the Cabinet meeting broke up at 2:00 PM.[19]

Afterward, Lincoln had a relaxed, hour-long lunch with Mary. He then met with a few other political leaders, including Vice President Johnson at

3:00 PM. He assisted former enslaved person Mrs. Nancy Bushrod, who had pushed her way past White House guards to ask for help in reinstating her soldier-husband's pay. After a few more informal meetings, he and Mary went for a carriage ride. They talked about their future, which might one day include a trip to Europe and the Holy Land. She expressed her surprise at how relaxed and cheerful her "dear husband" seemed to be.[20]

Lincoln had good cause to be relaxed and cheerful. The war was all but over, the Union intact, slavery was on a short road to extinction, and—still a jester—he was taking his wife to Ford's Theatre that evening, to enjoy a comedy.

CONCLUSION

... for the tree is known by his fruit.

—Matthew 12:33

The preceding chapters have examined Lincoln's life through the lens of the Bible, reviewing how Lincoln used the Bible, what he said about it and God, and how it informed his leadership.

While the preponderance of oral testimony indicates that Lincoln went through a period of skepticism early in adulthood, his subsequent writings and speeches in the *CW* reveal that as Lincoln aged, he increasingly relied on the Bible for guidance and justification of many of his key proclamations. By the time he was president he was reading the Bible nearly every day for pleasure as well as guidance, and publicly acknowledged that he considered the Bible to be the most valuable "gift" that God had given to man.[1]

Lacking unequivocal evidence or personal testimony by Lincoln, it is prudent to avoid absolute conclusions about his personal faith, i.e., whether he was or was not a Christian. Yet it is natural to wonder why a man who relied on the Bible so much would not have articulated to others any definite conclusions about the state of his soul.

Since the 1970s, one expects to hear about the Christian's born again conversion experience—a point in time when he or she decided to accept Christ as his or her Savior and follow him. Although this type of testimony was not unheard of in nineteenth-century America, being born again was an expression not often used. Often when people talked about their faith, they defined it in terms of their church membership or being "converted" rather than whether they had been "born again."[2]

Lincoln knew about Methodist revivalism and sometimes seemed to identify with it, particularly during his Springfield years in speeches like the Temperance Address. There is always the possibility that Lincoln confessed Christ privately, but William E. Barton believed that Lincoln's religious faith was at "rock-bottom" the Calvinism of his youth and that he had never "ceased to be a

Predestinarian." To Lincoln, the Almighty had his own purposes. He believed God was omniscient, omnipotent, and beneficent. Yet he also believed God was sovereign, and like many Old School Presbyterians, Lincoln may have wondered if he had been "chosen."[3]

As attested by his close associates William H. Herndon and Judge David Davis, Lincoln was a very private man about many of his personal beliefs. Herndon said that Lincoln was "the most secretive, reticent, shut-mouthed man that ever existed," and Supreme Court Justice David Davis, who had known Lincoln since the days they rode the Illinois Eighth Judicial Circuit together, said that Lincoln was "the most reticent,—Secretive man that I ever Saw—or expect to see." Davis concluded he did "not know anything about Lincoln's religion" and didn't think "anybody else" knew either.[4]

This book generally avoided using any of the scores of personal testimonies by Lincoln's friends and associates regarding his religious faith. This was not simply because of their conflicting conclusions, but also because to do them justice would require a book that was nearly the size of the Bible itself. For example, a supporter of the view that Lincoln was not an orthodox Christian was Lincoln's law partner William H. Herndon, a Unitarian who described Lincoln's religious belief in so many ways that he becomes an unreliable witness. David Donald said Herndon "overstated his case." On the opposite side of the debate was Herndon's nemesis Newton Bateman, the Illinois superintendent of public instruction. Bateman was a devout Christian who probably exaggerated Lincoln's testimony, proclaiming that the president declared "Christ is God." In fact, Barton's book *The Soul of Abraham Lincoln* reveals that most of the witnesses about Lincoln's faith had their own agendas. Typically, the skeptics wanted Lincoln to be a skeptic, the atheists wanted him to be an atheist, and the Christians wanted him to be a Christian.[5]

However there is one witness who, even though he does not provide the irrefutable answer, offers a less biased insight into Lincoln's personal faith during his late presidential years. This testimony is from the man who is widely accepted as Abraham Lincoln's closest lifelong friend, Joshua F. Speed. Ronald C. White says that "Speed described himself as a skeptic. In his reminiscences, he may well have wanted to magnify his relationship with Lincoln, but he would seem to have little incentive [as a skeptic] to build up Lincoln's use of the Bible."[6]

Speed said:

> I have often been asked what were Mr. Lincoln's religious opinions. When I knew him, in early life, he was a skeptic. He had tried hard to be a believer, but his reason could not grasp and solve the great

problem of redemption as taught. He was very cautious never to give expression to any thought or sentiment that would grate harshly upon a Christian's ear. For a sincere Christian he had great respect. He often said that the most ambitious man might live to see every hope fail; but no Christian could live to see his fail, because fulfillment could only come when life ended. But this was a subject we never discussed. The only evidence I have of any change, was in the summer before he was killed.

I was invited out to the Soldier's Home to spend the night. As I entered the room, near night, he was sitting near a window intently reading his Bible. Approaching him I said, "I am glad to see you so profitably engaged."

"Yes," said he, "I *am* profitably engaged."

"Well," said I, "If you have recovered from your skepticism, I am sorry to say that I have not."

Looking me earnestly in the face, and placing his hand on my shoulder, he said, "You are wrong Speed, take all of this book upon reason that you can, and the balance on faith, and you will live and die a happier and better man."[7]

While it does not conclusively reveal to us whether President Lincoln was a Christian, this testimony is significant, nonetheless. First, it validates the movement of Lincoln's reliance on the scriptures and his own understanding of and belief in God over his lifetime. Second, although Speed admits that he and Lincoln "never discussed" the president's faith in detail, it offers important insight into Lincoln's religious beliefs less than a year before the president died.

Speed's statement that Lincoln had been a skeptic back when he first knew him is not surprising. As has already been stated, this theory is widely accepted by scholars regarding Lincoln's New Salem and early Springfield days. His testimony that Lincoln "tried hard to be a believer" is more intriguing, but again, not totally surprising. In his remarks to the Baltimore Presbyterian Synod in 1864 Lincoln admitted, "I have often wished that I were a more devout man than I am." Speed's explanation that Lincoln's reason for not being able to become a believer because he "could not grasp and solve the great problem of redemption as taught," and that "no Christian could live to see [his hope] fail," are revealing statements. The former statement reveals that as a young man Lincoln was pondering the mystery of the Cross, and the latter that Lincoln realized the Christian's ultimate reward is a life with Christ in heaven, not treasure or success on Earth.[8]

Speed's testimony that Lincoln was "cautious never to give expression to any thought or sentiment that would grate harshly upon a Christian's ear" could be understood in either of two ways. People who thought Lincoln simply "played a sharp game" and disingenuously used biblical language to make himself more popular with the religious public could take it uncharitably and claim that "Honest Abe" was a great deceiver of men. But there is a more likely interpretation. The sentence that follows it, "but for a true Christian he had great respect," strengthens the argument that Lincoln was an honest and honorable man who sincerely respected the religious faith of others.

Up until this moment in the narrative, Speed speaks about Lincoln before he was president. Speed then switches to Lincoln as president when he says that the "only evidence of change" he saw was during a brief visit with Lincoln at the Soldiers' Home in the summer of 1864.

Lincoln's advice for Speed to "take all of [the Bible] upon reason that you can, and the balance on faith," strongly suggests that Lincoln himself had overcome his skeptical attitude toward precepts of the Bible. However, even this statement to Speed may not be about redemption. To tell Speed that he will "live and die a happier and better man" is not a statement about eternity.

There is a second insight into Lincoln's faith from Joshua Speed. This occurred only two weeks before his assassination, when Speed made his last visit with Lincoln in the White House. Speed was in the room when two women asked Lincoln to pardon their men—the husband of one and the son of the other—who were currently in a Pennsylvania jail for evading the draft. Speed listened to the conversation and then, after Lincoln pardoned the men:

> The old woman walked to him, wiping with her apron the tears that were coursing down her cheeks. She gave him her hand, and looking into his face said, "Good-bye, Mr. Lincoln, we will never meet again till we meet in Heaven." A change came over his sad and weary face. He clasped her hand in both of his, and followed her to the door, saying as he went, "With all that I have to cross me here, I am afraid that I will never get there; but your wish that you will meet me there has fully paid for all I have done for you."[9]

It is curious that Lincoln was not able to gratefully say, even to an old woman he had just met in the White House, that he would one day see her in heaven. Historian Robert Bruce has correctly observed that when Lincoln attempted to comfort people who had lost someone in the war, he rarely encouraged them by saying anything to them about seeing their loved ones again in the hereafter.

Bruce's theory is that this is because Lincoln did not believe in heaven. But this goes too far. Lincoln believed in heaven—he had told Speed to take the Bible on faith, he had told his father that he could look forward to reuniting with "loved ones gone before" after he died, he had engraved "of such is the kingdom of heaven" on his son Eddy's tombstone, and had talked of his son Willie being "much better off" in heaven. Even his law partner, Herndon, acknowledged that "he [Lincoln] believed in heaven—a place." Rather than questioning the existence of heaven, Lincoln might have instead been questioning whether God was going to send him there after he died.[10]

Why would Lincoln be so uncertain about this? If Lincoln really believed in Calvinism's predestinarian message, he would probably have agreed with sermons he had heard over the years that were based on scripture such as "ye have not chosen me, but I have chosen you" (John 15:16) and "he chose us in him, before the foundation of the world . . . he predestined us to be adopted as sons" (Ephesians 1:4–5). It is quite possible that his Calvinist roots and unmitigated honesty would not allow him to say that he knew he was predestined for heaven.

Even though they are not conclusive, the stories recounted above by Speed are a strong indicator that Lincoln, although probably a skeptic as a young man, had undergone a significant change of heart before the last year of his life. Per his own admission to Speed, he was now able to accept in faith those parts of the Bible with which he might have been previously skeptical. Even more significant is the trust Lincoln had in the Bible, as revealed in the CW. Those nine volumes of his writings show no trace of atheism. What is more, as has already been established by various individuals such as his secretary John Nicolay, President Lincoln prayed and asked for prayer—indicating he was probably at least a biblical monotheist, who believes that God answers prayer, rather than a deist, who does not.[11]

William Herndon testified this about Lincoln's biblical faith: "If at any time in [Lincoln's] life he was sceptical of the divine origin of the Bible he ought not for that reason to be condemned; for he accepted the practical precepts of that great book as binding alike upon his head and his conscience." Regarding life in heaven Herndon said: "Whether orthodox or not, he believed in God and immortality; and even if he questioned the existence of future eternal punishment, he hoped to find a rest from trouble and a heaven beyond the grave."[12]

To answer our question from chapter 1 about what would become of Lincoln's biblical faith, I return to the introduction's methodology of examining how he used the Bible, what he said about it, and how it informed his leadership.

Abraham Lincoln fully accepted the moral authority of the Bible. *The Collected Works of Abraham Lincoln* reveal to us that he relied on the Bible to support many of his most profound declarations in state papers and speeches, that he spoke highly of the Bible and never criticized it, and that he used essential biblical principles and teachings to lead his followers to a higher moral plane. Finally, in his daily readings of scripture such as the book of Job, Lincoln was able to find peace in his fiery trial as an "instrument" of the Almighty. Clearly, with the Bible, Abraham Lincoln had found his firm place to stand.

APPENDIX

NOTES

BIBLIOGRAPHY

INDEX

APPENDIX:
LINCOLN'S USE OF THE BIBLE
IN THE *COLLECTED WORKS*

NOTE: The 34 scripture references for the "First Lecture on Discoveries and Inventions" were used by Lincoln for historical references in a secular lecture rather than for moral argument, expression of his personal faith, political allegory or metaphor, theological illustration, or exhibitive purpose—as the other 167 scriptures were.

Book	Verse	See Also[1] S: Supplemental A: Alternative	KJV quote	CW Ref	CW Quote	Who and Where	CW Date
Genesis	1.26		Let us make man in our image and after our likeness.	2.546	nothing stamped with the Divine image and likeness was sent into the world to be trodden on, and degraded, and imbruted by its fellows.	Speech at Lewistown, IL	8/17/58
Genesis	2.15		And the Lord God took the man, and put him into the garden of Eden to dress it and to keep it.	2.440	Man put in the Garden to "dress it, and to keep it" [Lincoln quoted the Bible but did not specify verse number]	First Lecture on Discoveries and Inventions	4/6/58
Genesis	3.1		Now the serpent was more subtil than any beast of the field which the Lord God had made. And he said unto the woman, Yea, hath God said, Ye shall not eat of every tree of the garden?	2.500	Turn in whatever way you will—whether it come from the mouth of a King, an excuse for enslaving the people of his country, or from the mouth of men of one race as a reason for enslaving the men of another race, it is all the same old serpent	Speech in Chicago	7/10/58
Genesis	3.1–3		And he said unto the woman, Yea, hath God said, Ye shall not eat of every tree of the garden? And the woman said unto the	2.278	God did not place good and evil before man, telling him to make his choice. On the contrary, he did tell him there was one tree, of the fruit	Speech at Peoria, IL	10/16/54

		serpent, We may eat of the fruit of the trees of the garden: But of the fruit of the tree which is in the midst of the garden, God hath said, Ye shall not eat of it, neither shall ye touch it, lest ye die.		of which, he should not eat, upon pain of certain death.		
Genesis	3.7	And the eyes of them both were opened, and they knew that they were naked; and they sewed fig leaves together, and made themselves aprons.	2.437	his first invention was the fig-leaf apron. [Lincoln did not specify verse but it is implied]	First Lecture on Discoveries and Inventions	4/6/58
Genesis	3.17–19	And unto Adam he said, Because thou hast hearkened unto the voice of thy wife, and hast eaten of the tree, of which I commanded thee, saying, Thou shalt not eat of it. cursed is the ground for thy sake; in sorrow shalt thou eat of it all the days of thy life	3.462	the effort of some to shift their share of the burthen on to the shoulders of others, is the great, durable, curse of the race.	Fragment on free labor	9/17/59

1. The scripture listed in this column is not intended to be an exhaustive list. I typically list only one or two supplemental/alternate scripture.

Book	See Also S: Supplemental A: Alternative — Verse	KJV quote	CW Ref	CW Quote	Who and Where	CW Date
Genesis	3.19	In the sweat of thy face shalt thou eat bread, till thou return unto the ground; for out of it wast thou taken: for dust thou art, and unto dust shalt thou return.	1.411	In the early days of the world, the Almighty said to the first of our race "In the sweat of thy face shalt thou eat bread"; and since then, if we except the light and the air of heaven, no good thing has been, or can be enjoyed by us, without having first cost labour	Fragment on Tariff Discussion	12/1/47
Genesis	3.19	In the sweat of thy face shalt thou eat bread, till thou return unto the ground; for out of it wast thou taken: for dust thou art, and unto dust shalt thou return.	7.368	To read in the Bible, as the word of God himself, that "In the sweat of thy face shalt thou eat bread[,"] and to preach there-from that, "In the sweat of other mans faces shalt thou eat bread," to my mind can scarcely be reconciled with honest sincerity.	Letter to Delegation of Baptists: Ide, Doolittle and Hubbell	5/30/64
Genesis	3.19	In the sweat of thy face shalt thou eat bread, till thou return unto the ground; for out of it wast thou taken: for dust thou art, and unto dust shalt thou return	8.155	"You say your husband is a religious man; tell him when you meet him, that I say I am not much of a judge of religion, but . . . men to eat their bread on the sweat of other men's faces, is not the sort of religion upon which people can get to heaven!"	Story for Noah Brooks entitled The President's Last, Shortest, and Best Speech	12/6/64

Genesis	3.19	In the sweat of thy face shalt thou eat bread, till thou return unto the ground; for out of it wast thou taken. for dust thou art, and unto dust shalt thou return.	8.333	It may seem strange that any men should dare to ask a just God's assistance in wringing their bread from the sweat of other men's faces; but let us judge not that we be not judged.	Second Inaugural Address	3/4/65
Genesis	3.19	In the sweat of thy face shalt thou eat bread, till thou return unto the ground; for out of it wast thou taken. for dust thou art, and unto dust shalt thou return;	9.044 Suppl 1	. . . one thing that can be proved to be the will of God . . . What any one man earns with his hands and by the sweat of his brow, he shall enjoy in peace.	Speech at Cincinnati, OH	9/17/59
Genesis	3.21	Unto Adam also and to his wife did the Lord God make coats of skins, and clothed them.	2.438	At the first interview of the Almighty with Adam and Eve, after the fall, He made coats of skins, and clothed them Gen 3.21.	First Lecture on Discoveries and Inventions	4/6/58
Genesis	4.10	And he said, What hast thou done? the voice of thy brother's blood crieth unto me from the ground.	1.439	I more than suspect already, that he [President Polk] is deeply conscious of being in the wrong—that he feels the blood of this war, like the blood of Abel, is crying to Heaven against him	Speech in the House of Representatives	1/12/48

Book	Verse	See Also S: Supplemental A: Alternative	KJV quote	CW Ref	CW Quote	Who and Where	CW Date
Genesis	4.22		And Zillah, she also bare Tubalcain, an instructer of every artificer in brass and iron: and the sister of Tubalcain was Naamah.	2.439	Tubal-cain was "an instructer of every artificer in brass and iron["]—Gen;4–22.	First Lecture on Discoveries and Inventions	4/5/58
Genesis	5.24		And Enoch walked with God: and he was not; for God took him.	2.141	and Enoch walked with God; and he was not, for God took him	Speech to the Springfield Scott Club	8/14/52
Genesis	6.14		Make thee an ark of gopher wood; rooms shalt thou make in the ark, and shalt pitch it within and without with pitch.	2.438	How could the "gopher wood" for the Ark, have been gotten out without an axe? It seems to me an axe, or a miracle, was indispensable. [Lincoln does not mention specific scripture, but gopher wood is in only one place].	First Lecture on Discoveries and Inventions	4/6/58
Genesis	9.23		And Shem and Japheth took a garment, and laid it upon both their shoulders, and went backward, and covered the nakedness of their father; and their faces were backward, and they saw not their father's nakedness.	2.438	The Bible makes no other alusion to clothing, before the flood. Soon after the deluge Noah's two sons covered him with a garment. Gen. 9–23.	First Lecture on Discoveries and Inventions	4/6/58

Book	Verse	Cross-ref	Bible text	No.	Lincoln text	Source	Date
Genesis	14.23		That I will not take from a thread even to a shoelatchet, and that I will not take any thing that is thine, lest thou shouldest say, I have made Abram rich.	2.438	Abraham mentions "thread" in such connection as to indicate that spinning and weaving were in use in his day—Gen. 14.23.	First Lecture on Discoveries and Inventions	4/6/58
Genesis	16.16	Psalm 90.10 (A) Exodus 77 (A)	And Abram was fourscore and six years old, when Hagar bare Ishmael to Abram.	7.023	Four score and seven years ago our fathers brought forth upon this continent a new Nation,	Gettysburg Address	11/19/63
Genesis	22.3		And Abraham rose up early in the morning, and saddled his ass, and took two of his young men with him,	2.441	"Abraham rose up early in the morning, and saddled his ass,["] Gen. 22–3.	First Lecture on Discoveries and Inventions	4/6/58
Genesis	24.61		And Rebekah arose, and her damsels, and they rode upon the camels, and followed the man: and the servant took Rebekah, and went his way.	2.441	Rebekah arose, and her damsels, and they rode upon the camels, and followed the man. Gen 24–61.	First Lecture on Discoveries and Inventions	4/6/58

Book	Verse	See Also S: Supplemental A: Alternative	KJV quote	CW Ref	CW Quote	Who and Where	CW Date
Genesis	27.28		Therefore God give thee of the dew of heaven, and the fatness of the earth, and plenty of corn and wine.	5.223	This proposal makes common cause for a common object, casting no reproaches upon any. It acts not the pharisee. The change it contemplates would come gently as the dews of heaven, not rending or wrecking anything.	Proclamation revoking General Hunter's military order of emancipation	5/19/62
Genesis	41.43		And he made him to ride in the second chariot which he had; and they cried before him, Bow the knee: and he made him ruler over all the land of Egypt.	2.439	The oldest recorded allusion to the wheel and axle is the mention of a "chariot" Gen: 41–43.	First Lecture on Discoveries and Inventions	4/6/58
Genesis	42.26		And they laded their asses with the corn, and departed thence.	2.441	It would soon occur that they could also bear other burthens. Accordingly we find that Joseph's brethren, on their first visit to Egypt, "laded their asses with the corn, and departed thence" Gen. 42–26	First Lecture on Discoveries and Inventions	4/6/58
Genesis	46.29		And Joseph made ready his chariot, and went up to meet Israel his father, to Goshen, and presented	2.441	Also it would occur that animals could be made to draw burthens after them, as well as to bear them	First Lecture on Discoveries and Inventions	4/6/58

Book	Ref	No.	Bible Text	Commentary	Occasion	Date
			himself unto him; and he fell on his neck, and wept on his neck a good while.	upon their backs; and hence plows and chariots came into use early enough to be often mentioned in the books of Moses—Deut. 22-10. Gen. 41–43. Gen. 46–29. Exo. 14–25.	First Lecture on Discoveries and Inventions	4/6/58
Genesis	49.13	2.440	Zebulun shall dwell at the haven of the sea; and he shall be for an haven of ships; and his border shall be unto Zidon.	the first notice we have of watercraft, is the mention of "ships" by Jacob—Gen. 49-13.		
Exodus	4.22 (A) / 2 Samuel 7.5 (A)	3.028	And thou shalt say unto Pharaoh, Thus saith the Lord, Israel is my son, even my firstborn.	not that he [Douglas] judges at all of its [the Supreme Court's] merits, but because a decision of the court is to him a "Thus saith the Lord."	Debate at Ottawa, IL	8/21/58
Exodus	12.29–30	1.278	And it came to pass, that at midnight the Lord smote all the firstborn in the land of Egypt, from the firstborn of Pharaoh that sat on his throne unto the firstborn of the captive that was in the dungeon; and all the firstborn of cattle.	He ever seems to have gone forth, like the Egyptian angel of death, commissioned to slay if not the first, the fairest born of every family.	Temperance Address	2/22/42

Book	Verse	See Also S: Supplemental A: Alternative	KJV quote	CW Ref	CW Quote	Who and Where	CW Date
Exodus	12.37	Numbers 1.45–46(A) Judges 20.2 (A)	And the children of Israel journeyed from Rameses to Succoth, about six hundred thousand on foot that were men, beside children.	2.409	not against our interest, to transfer the African to his native clime, and we shall find a way to do it, however great the task may be. The children of Israel, to such numbers as to include four hundred thousand fighting men, went out of Egyptian bondage in a body.	Speech at Springfield	6/26/57
Exodus	13.21	Numbers 9.21 (A) Isaiah 28.19 (A)	And the Lord went before them by day in a pillar of a cloud, to lead them the way; and by night in a pillar of fire, to give them light; to go by day and night.	5.425	And I can assure you that the subject is on my mind, by day and night, more than any other.	Reply to Chicago Christians	9/13/62
Exodus	14.9		But the Egyptians pursued after them, all the horses and chariots of Pharaoh, and his horsemen, and his army, and overtook them encamping by the sea, beside Pihahiroth, before Baalzephon.	2.439	mention of chariots in connection with horses, in the same chapter, verses 9 and 23.	First Lecture on Discoveries and Inventions	4/6/58
Exodus	14.13	2 Chronicles 20.17	And Moses said unto the people, Fear ye not, stand still, and see the salvation of the Lord, which he	1.289	I believe God made me one of the instruments of bringing your Fanny and you together, which union, I	Letter to Joshua Speed	7/4/42

		will shew to you to day: for the Egyptians whom ye have seen to day, ye shall see them again no more for ever.		have no doubt He had fore-ordained. Whatever he designs, he will do for me yet. "Stand still and see the salvation of the Lord" is my text just now.		
Exodus	14:23	And the Egyptians pursued, and went in after them to the midst of the sea, even all Pharaoh's horses, his chariots, and his horsemen.	2.439	mention of chariots in connection with horses, in the same chapter, verses 9 and 23.	First Lecture on Discoveries and Inventions	4/6/58
Exodus	14:25	And took off their chariot wheels, that they drave them heavily: so that the Egyptians said, Let us flee from the face of Israel; for the Lord fighteth for them against the Egyptians.	2.439	sufficiently evidenced by the mention of chariot-wheels, at Exod. 14–25.	First Lecture on Discoveries and Inventions	4/6/58
Exodus	14:25	And took off their chariot wheels, that they drave them heavily: so that the Egyptians said, Let us flee from the face of Israel; for the Lord fighteth for them against the Egyptians.	2.441	Also it would occur that animals could be made to draw burthens after them, as well as to bear them upon their backs; and hence plows and chariots came into use early enough to be often mentioned in the books of Moses—Deut. 22–10. Gen. 41–43. Gen. 46–29. Exo. 14–25	First Lecture on Discoveries and Inventions	4/6/58

Book	Verse	See Also S: Supplemental A: Alternative	KJV quote	CW Ref	CW Quote	Who and Where	CW Date
Exodus	14.28		And the waters returned, and covered the chariots, and the horsemen, and all the host of Pharaoh that came into the sea after them; there remained not so much as one of them.	2.132	Pharaoh's country was cursed with plagues, and his hosts were drowned in the Red Sea for striving to retain a captive people who had already served them more than four hundred years.	Eulogy on Henry Clay	7/6/52
Exodus	15.1		Then sang Moses and the children of Israel this song unto the Lord, and spake, saying, I will sing unto the Lord, for he hath triumphed gloriously: the horse and his rider hath he thrown into the sea.	2.441	The horse, and his rider hath he thrown into the sea. Exo. 15–1.	First Lecture on Discoveries and Inventions	4/6/58
Exodus	28.42		And thou shalt make them linen breeches to cover their nakedness; from the loins even unto the thighs they shall reach.	2.438	Linen breeches, are mentioned,— Exod. 28.42.	First Lecture on Discoveries and Inventions	4/6/58
Exodus	35.25		all the women that were wise hearted, did spin with their hands.	2.438	All the women that were wise hearted, did spin with their hands (35–25).	First Lecture on Discoveries and Inventions	4/6/58

Book	Verse	Scripture	Citation	Lincoln's Text	Source	Date
Exodus	35.26	And all the women whose heart stirred them up in wisdom spun goats' hair.	2.438	and, all the women whose hearts stirred them up in wisdom, spun goat's hair (35–26).	First Lecture on Discoveries and Inventions	4/6/58
Exodus	35.35	Them hath he filled with wisdom of heart, to work all manner of work, of the engraver, and of the cunning workman, and of the embroiderer, in blue, and in purple, in scarlet, and in fine linen, and of the weaver, even of them that do any work, and of those that devise cunning work.	2.438	The work of the "weaver" is mentioned— (35–35).	First Lecture on Discoveries and Inventions	4/6/58
Leviticus	25.38	I am the Lord your God, which brought you forth out of the land of Egypt, to give you the land of Canaan, and to be your God.	7.017 Luke 1.57 (A) Matthew 1.25 (A)	Our fathers brought forth, upon this continent, a new nation,	Gettysburg Address	11/19/63
Numbers	35.16	And if he smite him with an instrument of iron, so that he die, he is a murderer: the murderer shall surely be put to death.	2.439	Thus "instrument of iron" at Num: 35–16.	First Lecture on Discoveries and Inventions	4/6/58
Deuteronomy	3.11	For only Og king of Bashan remained of the remnant of giants; behold his bedstead was a bedstead of iron;	2.439	"bed-stead of iron" at Deut. 3–11.	First Lecture on Discoveries and Inventions	4/6/58

Book	Verse	See Also S: Supplemental A: Alternative	KJV quote	CW Ref	CW Quote	Who and Where	CW Date
Deuteronomy	4.20		But the Lord hath taken you, and brought you forth out of the iron furnace, even out of Egypt, to be unto him a people of inheritance, as ye are this day.	2.439	"the iron furnace["] at 4–20.	First Lecture on Discoveries and Inventions	4/6/58
Deuteronomy	7.6	1 Peter 2.9 (A) 1 Kings 3.8 (A)	For thou art an holy people unto the Lord thy God: the Lord thy God hath chosen thee to be a special people unto himself, above all people that are upon the face of the earth.	4.236	I shall be most happy indeed if I shall be an humble instrument in the hands of the Almighty, and of this, his almost chosen people	Address to the New Jersey Senate	2/21/61
Deuteronomy	8.9		A land wherein thou shalt eat bread without scarceness, thou shalt not lack any thing in it; a land whose stones are iron, and out of whose hills thou mayest dig brass.	2.439	at 8–9, the promised land is described as "a land whose stones are iron, and out of whose hills thou mayest dig brass."	First Lecture on Discoveries and Inventions	4/6/58
Deuteronomy	19.5		As when a man goeth into the wood with his neighbour to hew wood, and his hand fetcheth a stroke with the axe to cut down the tree,	2.439	At 19–5—very distinct mention of "the ax to cut down the tree" is made.	First Lecture on Discoveries and Inventions	4/6/58

Deuteronomy	22.10	Thou shalt not plow with an ox and an ass together.	2.441	Also it would occur that animals could be made to draw burthens after them, as well as to bear them upon their backs; and hence plows and chariots came into use early enough to be often mentioned in the books of Moses—Deut. 22–10. Gen. 41–43. Gen. 46–29. Exo. 14–25.	First Lecture on Discoveries and Inventions — 4/6/58
Deuteronomy	27.5	and there shalt thou build an altar unto the Lord thy God, an altar of stones: thou shalt not lift up any iron tool upon them.	2.439	"iron tool" at 27-5.	First Lecture on Discoveries and Inventions — 4/6/58
Deuteronomy	32.39	See now that I, even I, am he, and there is no god with me: I kill, and I make alive; I wound, and I heal: neither is there any that can deliver out of my hand.	5.118	I know that the Divine hand that has wounded, is the only one that can heal.	Letter to Queen Victoria regarding death of Prince Albert — 2/1/62
1 Samuel	12.3	Behold, here I am: witness against me before the Lord, and before his anointed: whose ox have I taken? or whose ass have I taken? or whom have I defrauded? whom have I oppressed? or of whose hand have I received any bribe to blind mine eyes therewith? and I will restore it you.	7.368	... May I have to answer for robbing no man of his goods.	Letter to Ide and Doolittle — 5/30/64

Book	Verse	See Also S: Supplemental A: Alternative	KJV quote	CW Ref	CW Quote	Who and Where	CW Date
2 Kings	22.13	2 Chron 20.29 (S)	Go ye, enquire of the Lord for me, and for the people, and for all Judah, concerning the words of this book that is found: for great is the wrath of the Lord that is kindled against us, because our fathers have not hearkened unto the words of this book, to do according unto all that which is written concerning us.	3.410	when a nation thus dared the Almighty every friend of that nation had cause to dread His wrath. Choose ye between Jefferson and Douglas as to what is the true view of this element among us.	Speech at Columbus, OH	9/16/59
2 Chronicles	7.14	1 Peter 5.6 (A) James 4.10 (A) Ezekiel 20.43 (S)	If my people, which are called by my name, shall humble themselves, and pray, and seek my face, and turn from their wicked ways; then will I hear from heaven, and will forgive their sin, and will heal their land.	4.482	in sorrowful remembrance of our own faults [. . .] to humble ourselves before Him, and to pray for his mercy.	Proclamation of a National Fast Day	8/12/61
2 Chronicles	7.14	1 Peter 5.6 (A) James 4.10 (A)	If my people, which are called by my name, shall humble themselves, and pray, and seek my face, and turn from their wicked ways; then will I hear from heaven, and will forgive their sin, and will heal their land.	6.155–156	It behooves us then, to humble ourselves before the offended Power, to confess our national sins, and to pray for clemency and forgiveness.	Proclamation of National Fast Day	3/30/63

Book	Reference	Scripture	No.	Lincoln's Use	Document	Date
2 Chronicles	30.9	The Lord your God is gracious and merciful, and will not turn away his face from you, if ye return unto him.	2.097	Tell him to remember to call upon, and confide in, our great, and good, and merciful Maker; who will not turn away from him in any extremity.	Letter to John D. Johnston	1/12/51
Esther	7.10	So they hanged Haman on the gallows that he had prepared for Mordecai. Then was the king's wrath pacified.	1.477	Taylor's nomination takes the locos on the blind side. It turns the war thunder against them. The war is now to them, the gallows of Haman, which they built for us, and on which they are doomed to be hanged themselves.	Letter to Herndon	6/12/48
Esther	7.10	So they hanged Haman on the gallows that he had prepared for Mordecai. Then was the king's wrath pacified.	2.321	If, like Haman, they should hang upon the gallows of their own building, I shall not be among the mourners for their fate.	Letter to Joshua Speed	8/24/55
Job	2.4	And Satan answered the Lord, and said, Skin for skin, yea, all that a man hath will he give for his life.	7.254	For it has been said, all that a man hath will he give for his life; and while all contribute of their substance the soldier puts his life at stake, and often yields it up in his country's cause. The highest merit, then, is due to the soldier.	Remarks at closing of the Sanity Fair in Washington	3/18/64

Jeremiah 32.40 (A)

Book	Verse	See Also S: Supplemental A: Alternative	KJV quote	CW Ref	CW Quote	Who and Where	CW Date
Job	7.6		My days are swifter than a weaver's shuttle, and are spent without hope.	2.438	In the book of Job, a very old book, date not exactly known, the "weavers shuttle" is mentioned. [Scripture verse not given by Lincoln].	First Lecture on Discoveries and Inventions	4/6/58
Job	12.23	Matthew 25.32 (A)	He increaseth the nations, and destroyeth them: he enlargeth the nations, and straiteneth them again.	5.213	if it shall please the Divine Being who determines the destinies of nations that this shall remain a united people	Response to Evangelical Lutherans	5/13/62
Job	18:17	Jeremiah 10:11 (A)	His remembrance shall perish from the earth, and he shall have no name in the street.	7.023	shall not perish from the earth	The Gettysburg Address	11/19/63
Job	23.13	2 Chronicles 20.6 (A) Isaiah 14.27 (A)	But He is in one mind, and who can turn Him? and what His soul desireth, even that He doeth.	3.204–205	Certainly there is no contending against the Will of God; but still there is some difficulty in ascertaining, and applying it, to particular cases.	Fragment on Proslavery Theology	10/1/58
Job	23.13	2 Chronicles 20.6 (A) Isaiah 14.27 (A)	But He is in one mind, and who can turn Him? and what His soul desireth, even that He doeth.	5.403–404	The will of God prevails.	Meditation on the Divine Will	9/2/62 or 1864?

Book	Reference	Cross-references	Bible text	No.	Lincoln quote	Source	Date
Job	23:13	2 Chronicles 20.6 (A) Isaiah 14.27 (A)	But He is in one mind, and who can turn Him? and what His soul desireth, even that He doeth.	8.333	The Almighty has his own purposes.	Second Inaugural Address	3/4/65
Job	29:3	Psalm 119.105 (A) 2 Samuel 22.29 (A)	When his candle shined upon my head, and when by his light I walked through darkness;	5.279	It would be his earnest endeavor, with a firm reliance upon the Divine arm, and seeking light from above, to do his duty in the place to which he had been called.	Remarks to a Delegation of Progressive Friends	6/20/62
Job	29:3	Psalm 119.105 (A) 2 Samuel 22.29 (A)	When his candle shined upon my head, and when by his light I walked through darkness;	5.518	We can but press on, guided by the best light He gives us	Annual Message to Congress	12/1/61
Job	29:3	Psalm 119.105 (A) 2 Samuel 22.29 (A)	When his candle shined upon my head, and when by his light I walked through darkness;	7.535	Meanwhile we must work earnestly in the best light He gives us	Letter to Eliza P. Gurney	9/4/64
Job	40:15		Behold now behemoth, which I made with thee; he eateth grass as an ox.	2.270	But being, as it is, the great Behemoth of danger,	Speech at Peoria, IL	10/16/54

Book	Verse	See Also S: Supplemental A: Alternative	KJV quote	CW Ref	CW Quote	Who and Where	CW Date
Job	42.6	2 Chronicles 7.14 (S)	Wherefore I abhor myself, and repent in dust and ashes.	8.55–56	And I do farther recommend to my fellow-citizens aforesaid that on that occasion they do reverently humble themselves in the dust and from thence offer up penitent and fervent prayers and supplications	Proclamation of Thanksgiving	10/20/64
Psalms	19.9	Revelation 16.7 (A)	The fear of the Lord is clean, enduring for ever: the judgments of the Lord are true and righteous altogether.	8.333	as was said three thousand years ago, so still it must be said "the judgments of the Lord, are true and righteous altogether."	The Second Inaugural Address	3/4/65
Psalms	19.9	Revelation 16.7 (A)	The fear of the Lord is clean, enduring for ever: the judgments of the Lord are true and righteous altogether.	8.367	"the judgments of the Lord, are true and righteous altogether."	Letter to Amanda H. Hall	3/20/65
Psalms	22.28	Psalm 103.19 (A)	For the kingdom is the Lord's: and he is the governor among the nations.	8.356	To deny it, however, in this case, is to deny that there is a God governing the world	Letter to Thurlow Weed	3/15/65
Psalms	22.28	Psalm 103.19 (A)	For the kingdom is the Lord's: and he is the governor among the nations.	7.533	For devout acknowledgement to the Supreme Being in whose hands are the destinies of nations.	Proclamation of Thanksgiving and Prayer	9/3/64

Psalms	33.12	Blessed is the nation whose God is the Lord; and the people whom he hath chosen for his own inheritance.		6.155	to recognize the sublime truth, announced in the Holy Scriptures and proven by all history, that those nations only are blessed whose God is the Lord	Proclamation of National Fast Day	3/30/63
Psalm	52.1	52: Why boastest thou thyself in mischief, O mighty man? the goodness of God endureth continually. 33: He loveth righteousness and judgment: the earth is full of the goodness of the Lord.	Psalm 33.5 (A)	7.282	…wills also that we of the North as well as you of the South, shall pay fairly for our complicity in that wrong, impartial history will find therein new cause to attest and revere the justice and goodness of God.	Letter to Albert G. Hodges, et. al.	4/4/64
Psalm	78.38, 56	38: But he, being full of compassion, forgave their iniquity, and destroyed them not: yea, many a time turned he his anger away, and did not stir up all his wrath. 56: Yet they tempted and provoked the most high God, and kept not his testimonies		6.496–97	They are the gracious gifts of the Most High God, who, while dealing with us in anger for our sins, hath nevertheless remembered mercy.	Proclamation of Thanksgiving	10/3/63
Psalms	111.10	The fear of the Lord is the beginning of wisdom: a good understanding have all they that do his commandments: his praise endureth for ever.	Prov 9.10(A) Job 28.28(A)	4.482	to confess and deplore their sins and transgressions in the full conviction that the fear of the Lord is the beginning of wisdom	Proclamation of National Fast Day	8/18/61

Book	Verse	See Also S: Supplemental A: Alternative	KJV quote	CW Ref	CW Quote	Who and Where	CW Date
Psalms	128.2	Ecclesiastes 3:13 (A)	For thou shalt eat the labour of thine hands: happy shalt thou be, and it shall be well with thee.	2.405	but in her natural right to eat the bread she earns with her own hands without asking leave of any one else, she is my equal, and the equal of all others.	Speech at Springfield	6/26/57
Psalms	128.2	Ecclesiastes 3:13 (S) Genesis 3:13–14 (A)	For thou shalt eat the labour of thine hands: happy shalt thou be, and it shall be well with thee.	2.500	That is their argument, and this argument of the Judge is the same old serpent that says you work and I eat, you toil and I will enjoy the fruits of it.	Speech in Chicago	7/10/58
Psalms	128.2	Ecclesiastes 3:13 (A)	For thou shalt eat the labour of thine hands: happy shalt thou be, and it shall be well with thee.	2.520	still, in the right to put into his mouth the bread that his own hands have earned, he is the equal of every other man.	Speech at Springfield	7/17/58
Psalms	128.2	Ecclesiastes 3:13 (A)	For thou shalt eat the labour of thine hands. happy shalt thou be, and it shall be well with thee.	3.016	But in the right to eat the bread, without leave of anybody else, which his own hand earns, he is my equal and the equal of Judge Douglas, and the equal of every living man.	Debate at Ottawa, IL	8/21/58

Psalms	128.2	Ecclesiastes 3.13 (A)	For thou shalt eat the labour of thine hands. happy shalt thou be, and it shall be well with thee.	3.249	but in the right to eat the bread without leave of anybody else which his own hand earns, he is my equal and the equal of Judge Douglas, and the equal of every other man.	Debate at Quincy, IL	10/13/58
Psalms	128.2	Ecclesiastes 3.13 (A)	For thou shalt eat the labour of thine hands: happy shalt thou be, and it shall be well with thee.	3.315	"You work and toil and earn bread, and I'll eat it."	Debate at Alton, IL	10/15/58
Psalms	128.2	Ecclesiastes 3.13 (A)	For thou shalt eat the labour of thine hands: happy shalt thou be, and it shall be well with thee.	3.402	But in the right to eat the bread, without leave of anybody else, which his own hand earns, he is my equal and the equal of Judge Douglas and the equal of every living man	Speech at Columbus, OH	9/16/59
Psalms	128.2	Ecclesiastes 3.13 (A)	For thou shalt eat the labour of thine hands: happy shalt thou be, and it shall be well with thee.	1st Suppl 44–45	that that mouth is to be fed by those hands, without being interfered with by any other man who has also his mouth to feed [and] his hands to labor with.	Speech at Cincinnati, OH	9/17/59

Book	Verse	See Also S: Supplemental A: Alternative	KJV quote	CW Ref	CW Quote	Who and Where	CW Date
Psalms	128.2	Ecclesiastes 3.13 (A)	For thou shalt eat the labour of thine hands: happy shalt thou be, and it shall be well with thee.	3.479	The old general rule was that educated people did not perform manual labor. They managed to eat their bread, leaving the toil of producing it to the uneducated	Speech at Wisconsin State Agricultural Society	9/30/59
Psalms	128.2	Ecclesiastes 3.13 (A)	For thou shalt eat the labour of thine hands: happy shalt thou be, and it shall be well with thee.	3.204	And while he consider[s] it, he sits in the shade, with gloves on his hands, and subsists on the bread that Sambo is earning in the burning sun.	Fragment on proslavery theology	10/1/58
Psalms	137.5–6		If I forget thee, O Jerusalem, let my right hand forget her cunning. 6: If I do not remember thee, let my tongue cleave to the roof of my mouth; if I prefer not Jerusalem above my chief joy.	4.239	I have never asked anything that does not breathe from those walls. All my political warfare has been in favor of the teachings coming forth from that sacred hall. May my right hand forget its cunning and my tongue cleave to the roof of my mouth, if ever I prove false to those teachings.	Speech on hotel balcony in Philadelphia	2/21/61
Psalms	147.3		He healeth the broken in heart, and bindeth up their wounds.	8.333	...to bind up the nation's wounds;	The Second Inaugural Address	3/4/65

Book	Reference		Verse	No.	Usage	Context	Date
Proverbs	3:5–6		Trust in the Lord with all thine heart; and lean not unto thine own understanding. In all thy ways acknowledge him, and he shall direct thy paths.	6.536	when I could not see any other resort, I would place my whole reliance in God, knowing that all would go well, and that He would decide for the right.	Remarks to Baltimore Presbyterian Synod	0/24/63
Proverbs	6.6		Go to the ant, thou sluggard; consider her ways, and be wise.	2.437	Ants, and honey-bees, provide food for winter; but just in the same way they did, when Solomon refered the sluggard to them as patterns of prudence.	First Lecture on Discoveries and Inventions	4/6/58
Proverbs	16.9	Prov 16.33(A)	A man's heart deviseth his way. but the Lord directeth his steps.	7.301	slavery has been much affected— how much needs not now to be recounted. So true is it that man proposes, and God disposes.	Address at a Sanity Fair, Baltimore, MD	4/18/64
Proverbs	25.11		A word fitly spoken is like apples of gold in pictures of silver.	4.169	The assertion of that principle, at that time, was the word, "fitly spoken" which has proved an "apple of gold" to us. The Union, and the Constitution, are the picture of silver . . .	Fragment on the Constitution	1/1/61
Proverbs	30.5		Every word of God is pure: he is a shield unto them that put their trust in him.	2.097	and He will not forget the dying man, who puts his trust in Him.	Letter to John D. Johnston	1/12/51

Book	Verse	See Also S: Supplemental A: Alternative	KJV quote	CW Ref	CW Quote	Who and Where	CW Date
Proverbs	31.28	Luke 1.48(A) Revelation 22.13 (A)	Her children arise up, and call her blessed; her husband also, and he praiseth her	2.276	We shall have so saved it [the union], that the succeeding millions of free happy people, the world over, shall rise up, and call us blessed, to the latest generations.	Speech at Peoria, IL	10/16/54
Ecclesiastes	1.4		One generation passeth away, and another generation cometh: but the earth abideth for ever.	5.527	A nation may be said to consist of its territory, its people, and its laws. . . . "One generation passeth away, and another generation cometh, but the earth abideth forever."	Annual Message to Congress	12/1/62
Ecclesiastes	1.9		The thing that hath been, it is that which shall be; and that which is done is that which shall be done: and there is no new thing under the sun.	1.108	In the great journal of things happening under the sun, we, the American People, find our account running, under date of the nineteenth century of the Christian era.	Lyceum Address	1/27/38
Ecclesiastes	3.7		A time to rend, and a time to sew; a time to keep silence, and a time to speak;	4.195	Solomon has said, that there is a time to keep silence. . . . We know certain that they mean the same thing while using the same words now, and it perhaps would be as well if they would keep silence.	Speech at Indianapolis, IN	2/11/61

Ecclesiastes	9.4	For to him that is joined to all the living there is hope: for a living dog is better than a dead lion.	2.467	But "a living dog is better than a dead lion." Judge Douglas, if not a dead lion for this work, is at least a caged and toothless one. How can he oppose the advances of slavery?	A House Divided Speech in Springfield	6/16/58
Isaiah	9.2	The people that walked in darkness have seen a great light: they that dwell in the land of the shadow of death, upon them hath the light shined.	8.182	. . . in showing to the world that your army could be divided, putting the stronger part to an important new service, and yet leaving enough to vanquish the old opposing force of the whole—Hood's army—it brings those who sat in darkness, to see a great light.	Letter to William T. Sherman	12/26/64
Isaiah	11.6	The wolf also shall dwell with the lamb	3.205	Nonsense! Wolves devouring lambs, not because it is good for their own greedy maws, but because it [is] good for the lambs!!!	Proslavery theology	10/1/58
Isaiah	14.24	The Lord of hosts hath sworn, saying, Surely as I have thought, so shall it come to pass; and as I have purposed, so shall it stand.	5.404	I am almost ready to say this is probably true—that God wills this contest, and wills that it shall not end yet.	Meditation on the Divine Will	9/2/62 or 1864?

Book	Verse	See Also S: Supplemental A: Alternative	KJV quote	CW Ref	CW Quote	Who and Where	CW Date
Isaiah	33.21		But there the glorious Lord will be unto us a place of broad rivers and streams; wherein shall go no galley with oars, neither shall gallant ship pass thereby.	2.440	It is not till we reach the book of Isaiah that we meet with the mention of "oars" and "sails." [Lincoln did not mention specific verses]	First Lecture on Discoveries and Inventions	4/6/58
Isaiah	33.23		Thy tacklings are loosed; they could not well strengthen their mast, they could not spread the sail: then is the prey of a great spoil divided; the lame take the prey.	2.440	It is not till we reach the book of Isaiah that we meet with the mention of "oars" and "sails." [Lincoln did not mention specific verses]	First Lecture on Discoveries and Inventions	4/6/58
Isaiah	34.2		For the indignation of the Lord is upon all nations, and his fury upon all their armies: he hath utterly destroyed them, he hath delivered them to the slaughter.	6.156	insomuch as we know that, by His divine law, nations like individuals are subjected to punishments and chastisements in this world.	Proclamation of National Fast Day	3/30/63
Isaiah	34.2		For the indignation of the Lord is upon all nations, and his fury upon all their armies: he hath utterly destroyed them, he hath delivered them to the slaughter.	7.431	to implore Him as the Supreme Ruler of the World, not to destroy us as a people, nor suffer us to be destroyed.	Proclamation of a Day of Prayer	7/7/64

Book	Verse	Bible text	Cross-references	Lincoln's words	Citation	Occasion	Date
Isaiah	41.10	Fear thou not; for I am with thee: be not dismayed; for I am thy God: I will strengthen thee; yea, I will help thee; yea, I will uphold thee with the right hand of my righteousness.	Prov 15.3(S) Luke 1.37(S)	Trusting in Him, who can go with me, and remain with you and be every where for good, let us confidently hope that all will yet be well.	4.190	Farewell Address at Springfield	2/11/61
Isaiah	53.1	Who hath believed our report? and to whom is the arm of the Lord revealed?	Isaiah 51.9 (A) John 12.38(S)	[Jefferson] supposed there was a question of God's eternal justice wrapped up in the enslaving of any race of men, or any man, and that those who did so braved the arm of Jehovah	3.410	Speech at Columbus, OH	9/16/59
Ezekiel	34.26	And I will make them and the places round about my hill a blessing; and I will cause the shower to come down in his season; there shall be showers of blessing.		to the end that the united prayer of the nation may ascend to the Throne of Grace and bring down plentiful blessings upon our Country	4.482	Proclamation of National Fast Day	8/18/61
Ezekiel	37.9	Then said he unto me, Prophesy unto the wind, prophesy, son of man, and say to the wind, Thus saith the Lord God; Come from the four winds, O breath, and breathe upon these slain, that they may live.	Jeremiah 49.36 (A) Daniel 7.2 (A)	"He ever seems to have gone forth, like the Egyptian angel of death... like an exceeding great army" – "Come from the four winds, O breath! and breathe upon these slain, that they may live."	1.278	Temperance Address	2/22/42

Book	Verse	See Also S: Supplemental A: Alternative	KJV quote	CW Ref	CW Quote	Who and Where	CW Date
Jeremiah	3.21	Psalm 44.20 (A) Isaiah 51.13 (A)	A voice was heard upon the high places, weeping and supplications of the children of Israel: for they have perverted their way, and they have forgotten the Lord their God.	6.156	But we have forgotten God.	Proclamation of National Fast Day	3/30/63
Matthew	4.8–9	Luke 4.5–8(A) Matthew 22.39 (S)	Again, the devil taketh him up into an exceeding high mountain, and sheweth him all the kingdoms of the world, and the glory of them; 9 And saith unto him, All these things will I give thee, if thou wilt fall down and worship me.	7.368	... to my thinking, they contemned and insulted God and His church, far more than did Satan when he tempted the Saviour with the Kingdoms of the earth. The devils attempt was no more false, and far less hypocritical.	Letter to Delegation of Baptists: Ide, Doolittle and Hubbell	5/30/64
Matthew	5.42	Luke 6.30(A)	Give to him that asketh thee, and from him that would borrow of thee turn not thou away.	3.204	... is it not the exact reverse justice that the white should, for that reason, take from the negro, any part of the little which has been given him? "Give to him that is needy" is the christian rule of charity; but "Take from him that is needy" is the rule of slavery.	Fragment on proslavery theology	10/1/58

Reference		Verse	No.	Lincoln's quotation	Source	Date
Matthew 5.48		Be ye therefore perfect, even as your Father which is in heaven is perfect.	2,501	My friend has said to me that I am a poor hand to quote Scripture. I will try it again, however. It is said in one of the admonitions of the Lord, "As your Father in Heaven is perfect, be ye also perfect."	Speech at Chicago, IL	7/10/58
Matthew 6.13	Luke 11.4(A)	And lead us not into temptation, but deliver us from evil: For thine is the kingdom, and the power, and the glory, for ever. Amen.	6,501	Agents to execute it, contrary to the great Prayer, were led into temptation. Some might, while others would not resist that temptation.	Letter to Charles D. Drake, et. al.	10/5/63
Matthew 6.11	Luke 11.3(A)	Give us this day our daily bread.	5,374	But if something is started so that you can get your daily bread as soon as you reach there, it is a great advantage.	Address on colonization	8/14/62
Matthew 6.24	Luke 16.13(A)	No man can serve two masters: for either he will hate the one, and love the other; or else he will hold to the one, and despise the other. Ye cannot serve God and mammon.	2,275	we have run down to the other declaration, that for SOME men to enslave OTHERS is a "sacred right of self-government." These principles can not stand together. They are as opposite as God and mammon; and whoever holds to the one, must despise the other.	Speech at Peoria, IL	10/16/54

Book	Verse	See Also S: Supplemental A: Alternative	KJV quote	CW Ref	CW Quote	Who and Where	CW Date
Matthew	6.34		Take therefore no thought for the morrow: for the morrow shall take thought for the things of itself. Sufficient unto the day is the evil thereof.	2.260	As to new acquisitions I said "sufficient unto the day is the evil thereof."	Speech at Peoria, IL	10/16/54
Matthew	7.1	Luke 6.37(A)	Judge not, that ye be not judged.	8.333	Both read the same Bible, and pray to the same God; and each invokes His aid against the other. It may seem strange that any men should dare to ask a just God's assistance in wringing their bread from the sweat of other men's faces; but let us judge not that we be not judged	The Second Inaugural Address	3/4/65
Matthew	7.1	Luke 6.37(A)	Judge not, that ye be not judged	7.368	But let me forbear, remembering it is also written "Judge not, lest ye be judged."	Letter to Delegation of Baptists: Ide, Doolittle and Hubbell	5/30/64
Matthew	7.6	Acts 19.16(A)	Give not that which is holy unto the dogs, neither cast ye your pearls before swine, lest they trample	3.090	And when you have stricken down the principles of the Declaration of Independence, and thereby	Speech at Bloomington, IL	9/4/58

Lincoln's Use of the Bible ✳ 181

Book	Verse	Reference	Biblical Text	Locator	Lincoln's Usage	Source	Date
			them under their feet, and turn again and rend you.		consigned the negro to hopeless and eternal bondage, are you quite sure that the demon will not turn and rend you?		
Matthew	7.6	Acts 19.16(A)	Give not that which is holy unto the dogs, neither cast ye your pearls before swine, lest they trample them under their feet, and turn again and rend you.	3.095	and placed him where the ray of hope is blown out in darkness like that which broods over the spirits of the damned; are you quite sure the demon which you have roused will not turn and rend you?	Speech at Edwardsville, IL	9/11/58
Matthew	7.12	Luke 6.31(A)	Therefore all things whatsoever ye would that men should do to you, do ye even so to them: for this is the law and the prophets.	1.473	Would you venture to so consider them, had they been committed by any nation on earth, against the humblest of our people? I know you would not. Then I ask, is the precept "Whatsoever ye would that men should do to you, do ye even so to them" obsolete?—of no force?—of no application?	Letter to John M. Peck	5/21/48
Matthew	7.12	Luke 6.31(A)	Therefore all things whatsoever ye would that men should do to you, do ye even so to them; for this is the law and the prophets.	7.368	... in the name of Him who said "As ye would all men should do unto you, do ye even so unto them" appealed to the christian world to aid them in doing to a whole race of men, as they would have no man do unto themselves ...	Letter to Delegation of Baptists: Ide, Doolittle and Hubbell	5/30/64

Book	Verse	See Also S: Supplemental A: Alternative	KJV quote	CW Ref	CW Quote	Who and Where	CW Date
Matthew	7.12	Luke 6.31(A)	Therefore all things whatsoever ye would that men should do to you, do ye even so to them: for this is the law and the prophets.	3.376	This is a world of compensations; and he who would be no slave, must consent to have no slave. Those who deny freedom to others, deserve it not for themselves; and, under a just God, can not long retain it.	Letter to Henry L. Pierce	4/6/59
Matthew	7.16–17	Matthew 12.33 (A) Luke 6.43–44 (A)	Ye shall know them by their fruits. Do men gather grapes of thorns, or figs of thistles? Even so every good tree bringeth forth good fruit; but a corrupt tree bringeth forth evil fruit.	1.347	would it not have been good and not evil so to have used your votes, even though it involved the casting of them for a slaveholder? By the fruit the tree is to be known. An evil tree can not bring forth good fruit. If the fruit of electing Mr. Clay would have been to prevent the extension of slavery, could the act of electing have been evil?	Letter to Williamson Durley	10/3/45
Matthew	16.18		And I say also unto thee, That thou art Peter, and upon this rock I will build my church; and the gates of hell shall not prevail against it.	1.115	Upon these] let the proud fabric of freedom r[est, as the] rock of its basis; and as truly as has been said of the only greater institution, "the gates of hell shall not prevail against it."	Lyceum Address	1/27/38

Book	Reference		Scripture	Lincoln's Usage	Source	Date
Matthew	16.18	4.194	And I say also unto thee, That thou art Peter, and upon this rock I will build my church; and the gates of hell shall not prevail against it.	When the people rise in masses in behalf of the Union and the liberties of their country, truly may it be said, "The gates of hell shall not prevail against them."	Reply to Oliver P. Morton in Indianapolis, IN	2/11/61
Matthew	Luke 17.1(A) 18.7	8.333	Woe unto the world because of offences! for it must needs be that offences come; but woe to that man by whom the offence cometh!	"Woe unto the world because of offences! for it must needs be that offences come; but woe to that man by whom the offence cometh!" If we shall suppose that American Slavery…	The Second Inaugural Address	3/4/65
Matthew	Luke 15.4–7(A) 18.13	4.272	And if so be that he find it, verily I say unto you, he rejoiceth more of that sheep, than of the ninety and nine which went not astray.	As towards the disaffected portion of our fellow-citizens, I will say, as every good man throughout the country must feel, that there will be more rejoicing over one sheep that is lost, and is found, than over the ninety-and-nine which have gone not astray.	Reply to a New York Delegation	3/4/61
Matthew	18.22	4.135	Jesus saith unto him, I say not unto thee, Until seventimes: but, until seventy times seven.	If I do finally abstain, it will be because of apprehension that it would do harm. For the good men of the South—and I regard the majority of them as such—I have no objection to repeat seventy and seven times.	Letter to George D. Prentice	10/29/60

Book	Verse	See Also S: Supplemental A: Alternative	KJV quote	CW Ref	CW Quote	Who and Where	CW Date
Matthew	23.12	Luke 14.11(A) Luke 18.14(A)	And whosoever shall exalt himself shall be abased; and he that shall humble himself shall be exalted.	2.090	his name, his memory and example, are all that is left us—his example, verifying the great truth, that "he that humbleth himself, shall be exalted" teaching,	Eulogy of Zachary Taylor	7/25/50
Matthew	24.41	Luke 17.35 (A)	Two women shall be grinding at the mill; the one shall be taken, and the other left.	2.441	The language of the Saviour "Two women shall be grinding at the mill &c" indicates that, even in the populous city of Jerusalem, at that day, mills were operated by hand—having, as yet had no other than human power applied to them. [Lincoln did not give exact verse].	First Lecture on Discoveries and Inventions	4/6/58
Matthew	24.31	Mark 13.27(A)	And he shall send his angels with a great sound of a trumpet, and they shall gather together his elect from the four winds, from one end of heaven to the other.	2.468	Of strange, discordant, and even, hostile elements, we gathered from the four winds, and formed and fought the battle through, under the constant hot fire of a disciplined, proud, and pampered enemy.	A House Divided Speech in Springfield	6/16/58
Matthew	26.72	Mark 14.71(A)	He denied it again, with an oath, I do not know the man!	4.071	Remembering that Peter denied his Lord with an oath, after most solemnly protesting that he never	Letter to Lyman Trumbull	6/5/60

					would, I will not swear that I will make no committals; but I do think I will not.		
Mark	Luke 11.17(A) Matt 12.25(A)	3.25	And If a house be divided against itself, that house cannot stand.	1,315	Aesop, illustrated it by his fable of the bundle of sticks; and he whose wisdom surpasses that of all philosophers, has declared that "a house divided against itself cannot stand."	Campaign Circular from Whig Committee	3/4/43
Mark	Luke 11.17(A) Matt 12.25(A)	3.25	And If a house be divided against itself, that house cannot stand.	2,452	A house divided against itself cannot stand. I believe the government cannot endure permanently half slave and half free. I expressed this belief a year ago; and subsequent developments have but confirmed me. I do not expect the Union to be dissolved. I do not expect the house to fall; but I do expect it will cease to be divided. It will become all one thing or all the other.	Speech at Edwardsville	5/18/58
Mark	Luke 11.17(A) Matt 12.25(A)	3.25	And If a house be divided against itself, that house cannot stand.	2,461	A house divided against itself cannot stand. I believe this government cannot endure, half slave and half free.	A House Divided Speech in Springfield	6/16/58

Book	Verse	See Also S: Supplemental A: Alternative	KJV quote	CW Ref	CW Quote	Who and Where	CW Date
Mark	3.25	Luke 11.17(A) Matt 12.25(A)	And If a house be divided against itself, that house cannot stand.	2.491	I believe it will not cease until a crisis shall have been reached and passed. A house divided against itself cannot stand. I believe this government cannot endure permanently half slave and half free.	Speech at Chicago, IL	7/10/58
Mark	3.25	Luke 11.17(A) Matt 12.25(A)	And If a house be divided against itself, that house cannot stand.	2.513	In my opinion it will not cease till a crisis shall have been reached and passed. "A house divided against itself can not stand."	Speech at Springfield	7/17/58
Mark	3.25	Luke 11.17(A) Matt 12.25(A)	And If a house be divided against itself, that house cannot stand.	3.017	"A house divided against itself can not stand."	Debate at Ottawa, IL	8/21/58
Mark	3.25	Luke 11.17(A) Matt 12.25(A)	And If a house be divided against itself, that house cannot stand.	3.078	"A house divided against itself cannot stand." Does he believe this thing will always stand as it now is—neither expand or diminish?	Speech at Carlinville, IL	8/31/58
Mark	3.25	Luke 11.17(A) Matt 12.25(A)	And If a house be divided against itself, that house cannot stand.	3.082	"A house divided against itself cannot stand." I believe this government cannot endure permanently, half slave and half	Speech at Clinton, IL	9/2/58

Gospel	Ref	Bible text	No.	Parallel refs	Lincoln's quotation	Location	Date
					free. I do not expect the Union to be dissolved—I do not expect the house to fall—but I do expect it will cease to be divided. It will become all one thing, or all the other.		
Mark	3.25	And If a house be divided against itself, that house cannot stand.	3.086	Luke 11.17(A) Matt 12.25(A)	"A house divided against itself cannot stand." I believe this government cannot endure permanently, half slave and half free. I do not expect the Union to be dissolved—I do not expect the house to fall—but I do expect it will cease to be divided. It will become all one thing, or all the other	Speech at Bloomington, IL	9/4/58
Mark	3.25	And If a house be divided against itself, that house cannot stand.	3.120	Luke 11.17(A) Matt 12.25(A)	"A house divided against itself can not stand."	Speech at Jonesboro, IL	9/15/58
Mark	3.25	And If a house be divided against itself, that house cannot stand.	3.305	Luke 11.17(A) Matt 12.25(A)	Judge Douglas has again referred to a Springfield speech in which I said "a house divided against itself cannot stand." The Judge has so often made the entire quotation from that speech that I can make it from memory.	Debate at Alton, IL	10/15/58

Book	Verse	See Also S: Supplemental A: Alternative	KJV quote	CW Ref	CW Quote	Who and Where	CW Date
Mark	3.25	Luke 11.17(A) Matt 12.25(A)	And If a house be divided against itself, that house cannot stand.	3.438	It is my opinion that this government cannot "endure permanently half slave and half free; that a house divided against itself can not stand."	Speech at Cincinnati, OH	9/17/59
Mark	3.25	Luke 11.17(A) Matt 12.25(A)	And If a house be divided against itself, that house cannot stand.	4.147	Aesop, illustrated it by his fable of the bundle of sticks; and he whose wisdom surpasses that of all philosophers, has declared that "a house divided against itself cannot stand."	Certified transcript of passage of the House Divided Speech	12/7/60
Mark	5.4 and 15	Luke 8.29(A)	Because that he had been often bound with fetters and chains, and the chains had been plucked asunder by him, and the fetters broken in pieces: neither could any man tame him.	1.272	But when one, who has long been known as a victim of intemperance, bursts the fetters that have bound him, and appears before his neighbors ...	Temperance Address	2/22/42
Mark	10.8		And the twain shall be one flesh: so then they are no more twain, but one flesh.	1.281	Yours of the 16th Inst announcing that Miss Fanny and you "are no longer twain, but one flesh," reached me this morning.	Letter to Joshua Speed	2/25/42

Book	Verse	Text	References	No.	Context	Speech	Date
Luke	5.32	I came not to call the righteous, but sinners to repentance.	Mark 2.17(A) Matt 9.13(A)	3.550	such as a policy of "don't care" on a question about which all true men do care—such as Union appeals beseeching true Union men to yield to Disunionists, reversing the divine rule, and calling, not the sinners, but the righteous to repentance.	Speech at Cooper Union	2/27/60
Luke	5.32	I came not to call the righteous, but sinners to repentance.	Mark 2.17(A) Matt 9.13(A)	3.554	the "don't care" policy of Douglas—or Union appeals to true Union men to yield to the threats of Disunionists, which was reversing the divine rule, and calling, not the sinners but the righteous to repentance	Speech at Dover, NH	3/2/60
Luke	5.32	I came not to call the righteous, but sinners to repentance.	Mark 2.17(A) Matt 9.13(A)	4.008	This contrivance of a middle ground is such that he who occupies it is neither a dead or a living man. Their "Union" contrivances are not for us, for they reverse the scriptural order and call the righteous, not sinners to repentance.	Speech at Hartford, CT	3/5/60

Book	Verse	See Also S: Supplemental A: Alternative	KJV quote	CW Ref	CW Quote	Who and Where	CW Date
Luke	5.32	Mark 2.17(A) Matt 9.13(A)	I came not to call the righteous, but sinners to repentance.	4.013	The "Union" arrangements are all a humbug—they reverse the scriptural order, calling the righteous and not sinners to repentance.	Speech at Hartford, CT	3/5/60
Luke	6.45	Matt 12.34(A)	A good man out of the good treasure of his heart bringeth forth that which is good; and an evil man out of the evil treasure of his heart bringeth forth that which is evil: for of the abundance of the heart his mouth speaketh.	1.274	Benevolence and charity possess their hearts entirely; and out of the abundance of their hearts, their tongues give utterance.	Temperance Address Springfield	2/22/42
Luke	6.45	Matt 12.34(A)	A good man brings good things out of the good stored up in his heart, and an evil man brings evil things out of the evil stored up in his heart. For the mouth speaks what the heart is full of.	2.271	It still will be the abundance of man's heart, that slavery extension is wrong; and out of the abundance of his heart, his mouth will continue to speak	Speech at Peoria, IL	10/16/54
Luke	8.35	Mark 5.15(A)	Then they went out to see what was done; and came to Jesus, and found the man, out of whom the devils were departed, sitting at the feet of	1.272	and appears before his neighbors "clothed, and in his right mind," a redeemed specimen of long lost humanity, and stands up with tears	Temperance Address	2/22/42

		Jesus, clothed, and in his right mind: and they were afraid.		of joy trembling in eyes, to tell of the miseries once endured,		
Luke	11.23	He that is not with me is against me: and he that gathereth not with me scattereth.	Matt 12.30(A)	3.462	The good old maxims of the Bible are applicable, and truly applicable to human affairs, and in this as in other things, we may say here that he who is not for us is against us; he who gathereth not with us scattereth.	Speech at Cincinnati, OH — 9/17/59
Luke	11.29	And when the people were gathered thick together, he began to say, This is an evil generation: they seek a sign; and there shall no sign be given it, but the sign of Jonas the prophet.	Matt 12.39(A)	4.146	"Party malice" and not "public good" possesses them entirely. "They seek a sign, and no sign shall be given them."	Letter to Henry J. Raymond — 11/28/60
Luke	12.6–7	Are not five sparrows sold for two farthings; and not one of them is forgotten by God. But even, the very hairs of your head are all numbered.	Matt 10.29–30(A)	2.097	He notes the fall of a sparrow, and numbers the hairs of our heads;	Letter to John D. Johnston — 1/12/51

Book	Verse	See Also S: Supplemental A: Alternative	KJV quote	CW Ref	CW Quote	Who and Where	CW Date
Luke	12.10	Mark 3.28–29(A) Matt 12.31–32(A)	And whosoever shall speak a word against the Son of man, it shall be forgiven him: but unto him that blasphemeth against the Holy Ghost shall not be forgiven it.	1.276	By the Washingtonians, this system of consigning the habitual drunkard to hopeless ruin, is repudiated. They adopt a more enlarged philanthropy. They go for present as well as future good. They labor for all now living, as well as all hereafter to live. They teach hope to all—despair to none. As applying to their cause, they deny the doctrine of unpardonable sin. As in Christianity it is taught, so in this they teach…	Temperance Address Springfield	2/22/42
Luke	15.7	Matt 18.12–13(A)	I say unto you, that likewise joy shall be in heaven over one sinner that repenteth, more than over ninety and nine just persons, which need no repentance.	2.510	"Verily, I say unto you, there is more rejoicing in heaven over one sinner that repenteth, than over ninety and nine just persons that need no repentance."	Speech at Springfield	7/17/58
Luke	16.31		And he said unto him, If they hear not Moses and the prophets, neither will they be persuaded, though one rose from the dead.	4.130	"If they hear not Moses and the prophets, neither will they be persuaded though one rose from the dead."	Letter to William Speer	10/30/60

Book	Verse	Cross-ref	Scripture	Vol.Page	Source	Date	Lincoln's Words
Luke	17.3	Colossians 3.13 (A), Matt 18.21–22(A)	Take heed to yourselves: If thy brother trespass against thee, rebuke him; and if he repent, forgive him.	5.343	Letter to Reverdy Johnson	7/26/62	I am a patient man—always willing to forgive on the Christian terms of repentance; and also to give ample time for repentance.
Luke	17.3	Colossians 3.13 (A), Matt 18.21–22(A)	Take heed to yourselves: If thy brother trespass against thee, rebuke him; and if he repent, forgive him.	7.169	Directive to Secretary of War Edwin Stanton	2/5/64	On principle I dislike an oath which requires a man to swear he has not done wrong. It rejects the Christian principle of forgiveness on terms of repentance. I think it is enough if the man does no wrong hereafter
John	1.11		He came unto his own, and his own received him not.	2.282	Speech at Peoria, IL	10/16/54	His old friends have deserted him in such numbers as to leave too few to live by. He came to his own, and his own received him not
John	3.3		Jesus answered and said unto him, Verily, verily, I say unto thee, Except a man be born again, he cannot see the kingdom of God.	7.023	The Gettysburg Address	11/19/63	that this nation, under God, shall have a new birth of freedom—and that government of the people, by the people, for the people, shall not perish from the earth.

Book	Verse	See Also S: Supplemental A: Alternative	KJV quote	CW Ref	CW Quote	Who and Where	CW Date
John	6.26	Matt 14.19–20(A) Mark 6.41–42(A) Luke 12.16–17(A)	Jesus answered them and said, Verily, verily, I say unto you, Ye seek me, not because ye saw the miracles, but because ye did eat of the loaves, and were filled.	3.461	we not only take nothing by our success, but we tacitly admit that we act upon no [other] principle than a desire to have "the loaves and fishes," by which, in the end our apparent success is really an injury to us.	Speech at Cincinnati, OH	9/17/59
John	6.70		Jesus answered them, Have not I chosen you twelve, and one of you is a devil?	1.167	The Saviour of the world chose twelve disciples, and even one of that small number, selected by superhuman wisdom, turned out a traitor and a devil.	Speech on the sub-treasury	12/26/39
John	12.6		This he said, not that he cared for the poor; but because he was a thief, and had the bag, and bare what was put therein.	1.167	And, it may not be improper here to add, that Judas carried the bag—was the Sub-Treasurer of the Saviour and his disciples.	Speech on the sub-treasury	12/26/39
John	13.27		And after the sop Satan entered into him. Then said Jesus unto him, That thou doest, do quickly.	10.01 Suppl2	At last I concluded to take the General Land-Office if I can get it. I have come to this conclusion, more to prevent what would be generally bad for the party here, and particularly bad for me, than	Letter to Moses Hampton	6/1/49

a positive desire for the office. Will you please write old Zach ...as pretty a letter for me as you think the truth will permit? Time is important. What you do, do quickly.

John	15.13	I John 3:16 (A)	7.023	Greater love hath no man than this, that a man lay down his life for his friends.	We have come to dedicate a portion of that field, as a final resting place for those who here gave their lives that that nation might live.	The Gettysburg Address	11/19/63
Acts	13.46		2.282	Then Paul and Barnabas waxed bold, and said, It was necessary that the word of God should first have been spoken to you: but seeing ye put it from you, and judge yourselves unworthy of everlasting life, lo, we turn to the Gentiles.	... and Lo! he turns unto the Gentiles.	Speech at Peoria, IL	10/16/54
Acts	20.32		4.190	And now, brethren, I commend you to God, and to the word of his grace, which is able to build you up, and to give you an inheritance among all them which are sanctified.	To His care commending you, as I hope in your prayers you will commend me, I bid you an affectionate farewell	Farewell Address at Springfield	2/11/61

Book	Verse	See Also S: Supplemental A: Alternative	KJV quote	CW Ref	CW Quote	Who and Where	CW Date
Romans	3.8		And not rather, (as we be slanderously reported, and as some affirm that we say,) Let us do evil, that good may come? whose damnation is just.	1.347	It was this: "We are not to do evil that good may come." This general, proposition is doubtless correct; but did it apply?	Letter to Williamson Durley	10/3/45
Romans	12.18	Romans 14.19 (A) Psalm 34.14 (A)	If it be possible, as much as lieth in you, live peaceably with all men.	8.333	To do all which may achieve and cherish a just, and a lasting peace, among ourselves, and with all nations.	Second Inaugural Address	3/4/65
Romans	14.12		So then every one of us shall give account of himself to God.	7.302	Upon a clear conviction of duty I resolved to turn that element of strength to account; and I am responsible for it to the American people, to the christian world, to history, and on my final account to God.	Address at a Sanity Fair, Baltimore, MD	4/18/64
1 Corinthians	1.20		20 Where is the wise? where is the scribe? where is the disputer of this world? hath not God made foolish the wisdom of this world?	6.039	No one is more deeply than myself aware that without His favor our highest wisdom is but as foolishness and that our most strenuous efforts would avail nothing in the shadow of His displeasure.	Letter to Caleb Russell and Sallie A. Fenton	1/5/63

Book	Verse	Bible text		Lincoln's words	Source	Date
1 Corinthians	15.52	In a moment, in the twinkling of an eye, at the last trump: for the trumpet shall sound, and the dead shall be raised incorruptible, and we shall be changed.	1.115	that we revered his name to the last; [tha]t, during his long sleep, we permitted no hostile foot to pass over or desecrate [his] resting place; shall be that which to le[arn the last] trump shall awaken our WASHINGTON.	Lyceum Address	1/27/38
2 Corinthians	5.10	For we must all appear before the judgment seat of Christ; that every one may receive the things done in his body, according to that he hath done, whether it be good or bad.	7.368	When brought to my final reckoning …	Letter to Ide and Doolittle	5/30/62
Philippians	2.7–8	But made himself of no reputation, and took upon him the form of a servant, and was made in the likeness of men: 8 And being found in fashion as a man, he humbled himself, and became obedient unto death, even the death of the cross.	1.277–278	If they believe, as they profess, that Omnipotence condescended to take on himself the form of sinful man, and, and, as such, to die an ignominious death for their sakes, surely they will not refuse submission to the infinitely lesser condescension, for the temporal, and perhaps eternal salvation, of a large, erring, and unfortunate class of their own fellow creatures.	Temperance Address	2/22/42

Book	Verse	See Also S: Supplemental A: Alternative	KJV quote	CW Ref	CW Quote	Who and Where	CW Date
Colossians	1.16–17	Acts 17.24 (A)	For by him were all things created, that are in heaven, and that are in earth, visible and invisible, whether they be thrones, or dominions, or principalities, or powers: all things were created by him, and for him. 17: And he is before all things, and by him all things consist.	5.478	yet we cannot but believe, that he who made the world still governs it.	Letter to Eliza Gurley	10/26/62
Colossians	3.8 and 14		8: But now ye also put off all these; anger, wrath, malice, blasphemy, filthy communication out of your mouth…. 14 And above all these things put on charity, which is the bond of perfectness.	8.333	With malice toward none; with charity for all;	Second Inaugural Address	3/6/65
2 Thessalonians	3.12	1 Thessalonians 4.11(S) Psalm 128.2 (S)	Now them that are such we command and exhort by our Lord Jesus Christ, that with quietness they work, and eat their own bread	4.003	I think that if anything can be proved by natural theology, it is that slavery is morally wrong. God gave man a mouth to receive bread, hands to feed it, and his hand has a right to carry bread to his mouth without controversy.	Speech at Hartford, CT	3/5/60

2 Thessalonians	3.12	1 Thessalonians 4.11(S) Psalm 128.2 (S)	Now them that are such we command and exhort by our Lord Jesus Christ, that with quietness they work, and eat their own bread	4.009	Every man, black, white or yellow, has a mouth to be fed and two hands with which to feed it—and that bread should be allowed to go to that mouth without controversy.	Speech at Hartford, CT	3/5/60
Hebrews	4.12	Psalms 149.6(A)	For the word of God is quick, and powerful, and sharper than any twoedged sword, piercing even to the dividing asunder of soul and spirit, and of the joints and marrow, and is a discerner of the thoughts and intents of the heart.	2.377	He adverted to the attempt to stigmatize the Republican party as fanatical and disunion on account of the sentiments of particular supporters of that party, and showed, by quoting from the disunion speeches of Toombs, Slidell, Wise and Brooks, that this argument was a two-edged sword.	Speech in State Legislature at Vandalia, IL	9/23/56
Hebrews	4.16		Let us therefore come boldly unto the throne of grace, that we may obtain mercy, and find grace to help in time of need.	4.482	in all humility and with all religious solemnity, to the end that the united prayer of the nation may ascend to the Throne of Grace and bring down plentiful blessings upon our Country.	Proclamation of National Fast Day	8/18/61
Hebrews	9.27		And as it is appointed unto men once to die, but after this the judgment.	2.150	This reminds me of Judge Douglas's so much wanted [vaunted?] confidence in the people. The people had elected Gen. Taylor; and, as is appointed to all men once to do, he died.	Speech to the Springfield Scott Club	8/14/52

Book	Verse	See Also S: Supplemental A: Alternative	KJV quote	CW Ref	CW Quote	Who and Where	CW Date
Hebrews	12.1		...let us run with patience the race that is set before us.	2.459	As to the inclination of some Republicans to favor Douglas, that is one of the chances I have to run, and which I intend to run with patience.	Letter to Ward H. Lamon	6/11/58
Hebrews	12.1		Wherefore seeing we also are compassed about with so great a cloud of witnesses, let us lay aside every weight, and the sin which doth so easily beset us, and let us run with patience the race that is set before us.	6.383	My belief is that the permanent estimate of what a general does in the field, is fixed by the "cloud of witnesses" who have been with him in the field;	Letter to General John A. McClernand	8/12/63
Hebrews	12.2		Looking unto Jesus the author and finisher of our faith; who for the joy that was set before him endured the cross, despising the shame, and is set down at the right hand of the throne of God.	1.109	If destruction be our lot, we must ourselves be its author and finisher.	Lyceum Address	1/27/38
James	1.27	Isaiah 1.17(A)	Pure religion and undefiled before God and the Father is this, To visit the fatherless and widows in their	8.333	to care for him who shall have borne the battle, and for his widow, and his orphan.	Second Inaugural Address	3/4/65

affliction, and to keep himself unspotted from the world.

Book	Ref.	Allusion	Bible Text	Lincoln's Words	Source	Date	CW
1 Peter	4.12	Psalm 50.3 (A)	Beloved, think it not strange concerning the fiery trial which is to try you, as though some strange thing happened unto you.	We are indeed going through a great trial—a fiery trial.	Letter to Eliza P. Guerney	10/26/62	5.478
1 Peter	4.12	Psalm 50.3 (A)	Beloved, think it not strange concerning the fiery trial which is to try you, as though some strange thing happened unto you.	Fellow-citizens, we cannot escape history. We of this Congress and this administration, will be remembered in spite of ourselves. No personal significance, or insignificance, can spare one or another of us. The fiery trial through which we pass, will light us down, in honor or dishonor, to the latest generation.	Annual Message to Congress	12/1/62	5.537
1 John	5.7		For there are three that bear record in heaven, the Father, the Word, and the Holy Ghost: and these three are one.	He a sort of Trinity, three in one, having the right, in his own person, to cast the three votes of Arkansas.	Letter to Mary Lincoln	7/2/48	1.495
Revelation	2.4		Nevertheless I have somewhat against thee, because thou hast left thy first love.	Our policy, then, is to give no offence to others—leave them in a mood to come to us, if they shall be compelled to give up their first love.	Letter to Samuel Galloway	3/24/60	4.034

Book	Verse	See Also S: Supplemental A: Alternative	KJV quote	CW Ref	CW Quote	Who and Where	CW Date
Revelation	6.2		And I saw, and behold a white horse: and he that sat on him had a bow; and a crown was given unto him: and he went forth conquering, and to conquer.	1.271	The list of its friends is daily swelled by the additions of fifties, of hundreds, and of thousands. The cause itself seems suddenly transformed from a cold abstract theory, to a living, breathing, active, and powerful chieftain, going forth "conquering and to conquer."	Temperance Address	2/22/42
Revelation	7.14		14 And I said unto him, Sir, thou knowest. And he said to me, These are they which came out of great tribulation, and have washed their robes, and made them white in the blood of the Lamb.	2.276	Our republican robe is soiled, and trailed in the dust. Let us repurify it. Let us turn and wash it white, in the spirit, if not the blood, of the Revolution. Let us turn slavery from its claims of "moral right," back upon its existing legal rights, and its arguments of "necessity."	Speech at Peoria, IL	10/16/54
Revelation	13.7		it was given unto him to make war with the saints and to overcome them: and power was given him over all kindreds, and tongues, and nations.	7.259	The strongest bond of human sympathy, outside of the family relation, should be one uniting all working people, of all nations, and tongues, and kindreds.	Reply to New York Workingmen's Democratic Republican Association	3/21/64

NOTES

Introduction

1. Bayne, *Tad Lincoln's Father*, 184.
2. Keckley, *Behind the Scenes*, 118–19.
3. See McPherson, *Tried by War*, 7.
4. Transformational leaders motivate followers by making them aware of the importance of accomplishing certain tasks, and by activating their followers' "higher needs," which include moral values such as liberty, justice, and equality. (Bass, *The Handbook of Leadership*, 41). Transformational leaders are "admired, respected, and trusted" and demonstrate "high standards of ethical and moral conduct" (Bass, *Transformational Leadership*, 6). For additional reading on transformational leadership, see Burns, *Leadership*. For a sampling of what scholars have said about Lincoln's transformational leadership skills, see: Bass, *The Ethics of Transformational Leadership*; Leidner, "Measuring the Presidents," 61–76; Leidner, "Lincoln as a Transformational Leader," 111–18; Bowman, "Abraham Lincoln's Transformational Leadership"; and Schrama, "President Abraham Lincoln: Embodiment of Transformational Leadership," at https://www.jagreporter.af.mil/Post/Article-View-Post/Article/2549191 /president-abraham-lincoln accessed 8/29/2022.
5. Bray, "What Abraham Lincoln Read," researches the books that Lincoln read, including those he obtained from the Library of Congress (LOC) while president. He used six books from the LOC that might have provided some limited historical background on past leadership decisions, including a book on the US Constitution, two books on British history, a book on American history, the *Works of Thomas Jefferson*, and General Henry Halleck's book on military art and science. He might have read Plutarch's *Lives* immediately before he became president, but according to Bray in "What Abraham Lincoln Read," this is doubtful (n 164, 70). The same goes for Thomas Carlyle, who wrote about great men and heroes. Bray thinks it unlikely that Lincoln had read Carlyle (43).
6. Miller, *Duty of a Statesman*, 37.
7. Per Donald, *Lincoln*, 29, Lincoln received his education a few weeks at a time. As an adult he estimated that the aggregate of his schooling did not amount to one year.

8. Guelzo, *Redeemer President*, 274. Burlingame, *Hay's Civil War*, xi. Herndon and Weik, *Herndon's Lincoln*, 3:537.

9. Barton, *Soul of Lincoln*, 275. Schwartz, "A Poor Hand to Quote Scripture," 37. Lincoln scholar Louis A. Warren wrote that the Bible was "the single most influential book that Abraham Lincoln read," in *Lincoln Lore*, no. 567. Lincoln scholar Earl Schwartz, in "A Poor Hand to Quote Scripture," said, "Lincoln was clearly well read in the Bible" (n8). Lincoln scholar Elton Trueblood, in *Theologian of American Anguish*, says that "partly in response to the pioneer culture in which he was steeped, Abraham Lincoln's religion was centered far more in the Bible than the Church" (55). Lincoln Scholar William J. Wolf, in *Religion of Abraham Lincoln*, said that "the Bible rather than the Church remained his highroad to the knowledge of God" (75). Lincoln scholar Joseph Fornieri, in *Lincoln's Political Faith*, observes that "Lincoln viewed Scripture as an authoritative, normative standard to be approximated both personally, in his own life, and politically, in the life of the nation" (35).

10. See Ronald C. White, *Lincoln's Greatest Speech*, 103.

11. Basler, *Collected Works of Abraham Lincoln* 1:382. Hereafter, in text, *CW*.

12. Basler, 8:333. For further discussion, see Miller, *Duty of a Statesman*, 407–8. For criticisms that Lincoln didn't use scripture in a manner consistent with its original intent, see Freed, *Lincoln's Political Ambitions*.

13. See, for instance, Schwartz, "A Poor Hand to Quote Scripture," 38–39; and Fornieri, *Lincoln's Political Faith*, 38.

14. The other two-thirds were used for theological illustration, exhibitive, personal faith, and political purposes, in that order.

15. MaCartney, in Lincoln and the Bible, made the first serious effort to list all the scripture used by Lincoln. MaCartney concluded that there were "77 quotations from, or references to, the Bible" in Lincoln's "speeches, state papers, letters, and recorded conversations" (7). Of course, MaCartney's book was published before the *Collected Works of Abraham Lincoln* was published in 1955 and missed a lot of material. Bible scholar Philip L. Ostergard in *Inspired Wisdom* made skillful use of the *Collected Works* and provides a more thorough investigation into this subject. He cites 104 instances in which Lincoln quoted scripture in the *CW* (sixty-nine nonsecular uses in his table on pp. 245–49 and thirty-five (I count thirty-four) instances of secular use in Lincoln's "Discoveries and Inventions" lecture in his tables pp. 251–52). Michael Burlingame has documented many biblical references in his various works, and Michael Burkhimer, in *Lincoln's Christianity*, pointed out at least a half dozen additional scripture not quoted by Ostergard. Other scholars quoted in this book point out a similar number. During my own research of the *CW*, I uncovered over fifty additional scripture references beyond the

cumulative number that MaCartney, Ostergard, and the other scholars found. The appendix lists all 201 of Lincoln's secular and nonsecular uses of scripture in the *CW*.

16. According to Ostergard in *Inspired Wisdom*, Lincoln used forty-five names for "the Deity," (such as Father, Father in Heaven, God, God of Battles, etc.) and invoked those names over four hundred times in the *CW* (257–58).

1. Annals of the Poor

1. Basler, *Collected Works*, 1:1. As mentioned in the introduction, all quoted material in this book will retain original spellings and punctuation, without the addition of *sic* for misspellings.
2. Watts, *Psalms and Hymns*, 354.
3. William Knox, *The Lonely Hearth*, 95–97. According to White, *Lincoln's Greatest Speech*, Lincoln discovered Knox's "Mortality" in 1846 (135). Per Lincoln scholar William Lawrence Miller, *The Early Years*, "The technical construction of . . . Watts hymn—its rhyme and meter—would be the model [Lincoln] used in his own poetry. Indeed, next to this excerpt in his exercise book is the word "meter," suggesting that as a teenager he was analyzing methodology of poetry" (50).
4. Shenk, *Lincoln's Melancholy*, 120. See Wilson's "Spirit of Mortal," 155–70 for an excellent analysis of Lincoln's use of this poem and commentary by scholars.
5. Watts, *Psalms and Hymns*, 354.
6. Wilson and Davis, *Herndon's Informants*, 40. Hereafter, in text, *HI*. Wilson and Davis, 104, 107, 109.
7. Wilson and Davis, 37.
8. Warren, *Lincoln's Youth*, 4. Or Bathsheba, per Tarbell, in *Footsteps of the Lincolns*, 55. Donald, *Lincoln*, 21.
9. Donald, *Lincoln*, 22. Burlingame, *Lincoln: A Life*, 1:5.
10. Herndon and Weik, *Herndon's Lincoln*, 1:3. Warren's *Lincoln's Parentage*, chapter 2, provides an alternate history from Caroline Hanks Hitchcock that Nancy's father was a man named Joseph Hanks, who had married Lucy Shipley Hanks. See Burkhimer, *Essential Lincoln*, 52.
11. For both Nancy Hanks's and Thomas Lincoln's backgrounds I relied largely on Warren's *Lincoln's Youth*, Donald's *Lincoln*, and Warren's *Lincoln's Parentage*.
12. Tarbell, *Footsteps of the Lincolns*, 75.
13. Miller, *The Early Years*, 11–12. An Indiana neighbor, William Wood, referred to Nancy as an intellectual. Wilson and Davis, *Herndon's Informants*, 124. Hertz, *Hidden Lincoln*, 63.
14. Miller, *The Early Years*, 15.

15. Nowlin, *Baptist History*, 189 and KY State Historical Society, v20, no. 59, 214. For discussion of the Lincolns and Little Mount Church see Beveridge, *Abraham Lincoln*, 1:19 and 1:36–37; Warren, *Lincoln's Parentage*, 240–41; Warren, *Lincoln's Youth*, 13; Spencer, *Kentucky Baptists*, 1:164–65; and Cady, "Religious Environment," 17–18. Per nineteenth-century researcher David Benedict, only three hundred of the 17,511 Baptists in Kentucky in 1811 favored emancipation. See Boles, *Antebellum Kentucky*, 116. My thanks to Lincoln scholar Michael Burlingame for bringing Boles to my attention.

16. Per Vicchio, *Abraham Lincoln's Religion*: "The log structure of the Little Mount Meeting House, to which the Lincoln family belonged, stood three miles east of the Lincoln home and now five hundred yards west of current-day Leafdale community, off route 31 East in LaRue County, Kentucky. The structure was destroyed by a windstorm in 1909" (2). My thanks to NPS Lincoln Birthplace historian Gary Ferguson for his advice in researching the Lincoln family's involvement in local church history. See Cady, "Religious Environment," 16–17 and Spencer, *Kentucky Baptists*, 176. Calvinism, also called the Reformed tradition, is a major branch of Protestantism that follows the theological tradition and forms of Christian practice set down by sixteenth-century reformer John Calvin. Modern-day Calvinist churches include Presbyterian, Congregationalist, and Reformed Baptist. Although members of Little Mount did not accept the Philadelphia Calvinistic confession of faith, they did agree with the central tenets of Calvinism, including the position that God has chosen or predestined certain people for heaven. Cady, "Religious Environment," 17–18. Since Thomas and Nancy were Separate Baptists, it is doubtful that they attended the revivals of the greatest religious event of early nineteenth-century America, the Second Great Awakening. See Spencer, *Kentucky Baptists*, 1:536.

17. Shenk, *Lincoln's Melancholy*, 265n82.

18. White, *A. Lincoln*, 7–8.

19. Scripps, *First Published Life*, 10–11.

20. Rankin, *Personal Recollections*, 1:321. Non-CW source.

21. Beveridge, *Abraham Lincoln*, says: "Thomas Lincoln joined the Free will Baptist church in Hardin c[ount]y, Ky., in 1816, and was immersed by a preacher named William Downs in Knob Creek" (1:36n2). Spencer, *Kentucky Baptists*, 1:164. Drunkenness was a common problem among frontier preachers in the nineteenth century.

22. John F. Cady, "Religious Environment," 17. Warren, *Lincoln's Youth*, 114.

23. Warren, *Lincoln's Youth*, 115.

24. Warren, 54–55.

25. Wilson and Davis, *Herndon's Informants*, 40.

26. Wilson and Davis, 40.
27. Miller, *Early Years*, 44. Rankin, *Personal Recollections*, 320. Non-*CW* sources. This Bible was probably the Ostervald King James Bible currently on display at the Lincoln Birthplace in Hodgenville, Kentucky, or might possibly have been a different one owned by Dennis Hanks. See Leidner, "How Many Lincoln Bibles?," 71–72.
28. Miller, *Early Years*, 45.
29. Wilson and Davis, *Herndon's Informants*, 41. Miller, *Early Years*, 46.
30. Barton, *Soul of Lincoln*, 31–32. Wilson and Davis, *Herndon's Informants*, 112.
31. Dilworth, *New Guide*, 56.
32. Wilson and Davis, *Herndon's Informants*, 126. *Kentucky Preceptor*, 1812, 63. Noll, "American Religion, 1809–1865," 87.
33. Wolf, *Religion of Abraham Lincoln*, 37. There were three customary ways of joining a Baptist church, i.e., by baptism, by letter of commendation from one's home church, or by relating a satisfactory Christian experience (testimony). http://media1.razorplanet.com/share/512672-5325/siteDocs/whatwe believe.htm accessed 2/5/21.
34. Wilson and Davis, *Herndon's Informants*, 147, 168.
35. Wilson and Davis, 242. Hanks might have meant Lincoln did not sing hymns outside of church. On another occasion, Wilson and Davis, 105, Hanks mentioned that Lincoln sang hymns. Wilson and Davis, 242.
36. Ford, *History of Illinois*, 38–39.
37. Cady, "Religious Environment," 18–19.
38. Cady, 21–22. Barton, *Life of Lincoln*, 2:460; Guelzo, *Man of Ideas*, 34, and Shenk, *Lincoln's Melancholy*, 82 and 265n. None of these three historians uses this expression in the same way, or elaborates on what they mean by "out-Calvined Calvin." Barton says, "Believing as he [Lincoln] did in the sovereignty of God, and holding it in terms of a Calvinism that would have out-Calvined Calvin," whereas Guelzo uses this expression to describe the "atmosphere" Lincoln lived in, and Shenk uses the expression to describe the Baptist ministers Lincoln was exposed to.
39. Sweet, *American Frontier*, 67. Most Calvinist/Reformed churches have fully supported Christ's Great Commission to preach the gospel to all peoples and nations (Matthew 28:16–20). However, those churches that follow Hyper-Calvinism, which is an aberration of true Calvinism, believe that since God has predestined people to heaven or hell, it is of no use to evangelize.
40. Carroll, *Anti-Missionism*, 87. Carroll also discusses the notorious "Two-Seed Doctrine" supported by preachers like Daniel Parker. Cady, "Religious Environment," 18.
41. Wilson and Davis, *Herndon's Informants*, 107. Cady, "Religious Environment," 26. For more on Parker's obsession with the antimission movement and the

turmoil it caused in Baptist churches, see Mills, *Frontier Baptists*, 311; and nineteenth-century historians Nowlin, *Baptist History*, 105–15, and Stott, *Indiana Baptist History*, 62.

42. Wilson, *Honor's Voice*, 55.

43. Wilson and Davis, *Herndon's Informants*, 41 and 134. This was related by A. H. Chapmann, who married Dennis Hanks's daughter, Harriet.

44. Burlingame, *Lincoln: A Life*, 1:42. Winkle, *Young Eagle*, discusses psychological theories regarding Lincoln's strained relationship with his father, 132. See also Winkle's notes, 340–41.

45. Miller, *Early Years*, 75. A second doctor arrived too late. Both mother and son had already died. Burlingame, *Lincoln: A Life*, 1:45.

46. Wilson and Davis, *Herndon's Informants*, 107.

47. Guelzo, *Redeemer President*, 38. Wilson and Davis, *Herndon's Informants*, 107.

48. Wilson and Davis, *Herndon's Informants*, 226.

49. Herndon and Weik, *Herndon's Lincoln* 1:67–69, Reynolds, *Abe*, 92–93.

2. The Mind Impelled

1. Mearns, *The Lincoln Papers*, 1:151. Wilson and Davis, *Herndon's Informants*, 72.

2. Wilson and Davis, 429.

3. Wilson and Davis, 370, 373.

4. Wilson and Davis, 13, 593.

5. Wilson and Davis, 9, 386. Burlingame, *Lincoln: A Life*, 1:60.

6. Wilson and Davis, 92.

7. Wilson and Davis, 26. Duncan and Nickols, *Mentor Graham*, 128–29.

8. Wilson and Davis, 73.

9. Burlingame, *Lincoln: A Life*, 1:67.

10. Scripps, *First Published Life*, 32. Fehrenbacher, *Recollected Words*, 184.

11. Basler, *Collected Works*, 1:8.

12. Whitney, *Life on the Circuit*, 33.

13. Wilson and Davis, *Herndon's Informants*, 501.

14. Wilson and Davis, 242–43.

15. Burlingame, *Lincoln: A Life*, 1:79.

16. Wilson and Davis, *Herndon's Informants*, 76, 92. Barton, *Soul of Lincoln*, 54, 19.

17. Barton, *Soul of Lincoln*, 152–53. Fornieri, *Political Faith*, 54–55 and Winger, *Lincoln, Religion, and Politics*, 174–75. If Graham is correct on this, it displays considerable depth on Lincoln's part in that he was contemplating the consequences of original sin.

18. Barton, 65–66.

19. Barton, 238–40, 270–72. Winger, *Lincoln, Religion, and Politics*, 175.

20. Wilson, *Lincoln before Washington*, 59.

21. Burlingame, *Lincoln: A Life*, 1:49.

22. Wilson, *Lincoln before Washington*, 64. Non-CW source.

23. Fornieri, *Political Faith*, 49–50.

24. Wilson and Davis, *Herndon's Informants*, 387.

25. Wilson and Davis, 243. Shenk, *Lincoln's Melancholy*, 19.

26. Shenk's *Lincoln's Melancholy* has the most thorough analysis of Lincoln's melancholia.

27. Donald, *Lincoln*, 68. *CW*, 1:55.

28. Basler, *Collected Works*, 1:75.

29. Herndon and Weik, *Herndon's Lincoln*, 1:185.

3. He Will Do for Me Yet

1. Basler, *Collected Works*, 1:78. This quip about staying away from church brings to mind Paul's charge to Timothy in 1 Timothy 3:15, where he told him that he should "know how thou oughtest to behave thyself in the house of God."

2. Basler, *Collected Works*, 1:108. For succinct, yet thorough analyses on the Lyceum Address, see Carwardine, *Life of Purpose*, 48 and Reynolds, *Abe*, 146.

3. Basler, *Collected Works*, 1:109.

4. Simon, *Freedom's Champion*, 49.

5. Basler, *Collected Works*, 1:115.

6. See Fornieri, *Political Faith*, 92 and Wills, *Lincoln at Gettysburg*, 82 for further analysis of these arguments.

7. Basler, *Collected Works*, 1:167.

8. Burlingame, *A Life*, 1:182–84.

9. Burlingame, 187–88.

10. Basler, *Collected Works*, 1:261.

11. Basler, 1:267–68. See Winger, *Lincoln, Religion, and Politics*, 183–86, for a discussion of Lincoln's gain of respect for the Bible and religion in his communications with Speed.

12. Shenk, *Lincoln's Melancholy*, 87.

13. See Fornieri, *Political Faith*, 59–60 and Winger, *Lincoln, Religion, and Politics*, 184 for additional analysis of Lincoln's increasing faith.

14. Winger, *Lincoln, Religion, and Politics*, 187–89. It is possible that his sister's death, due to the incompetence of a drunken doctor, had a long-lasting influence on Lincoln. According to Indiana resident William Wood, Lincoln wrote an "essay" on temperance as early as 1828 (when he would have been nineteen years old, after his sister's death). See Beveridge, *Abraham Lincoln*, 1:82. Burt, in *Lincoln's Tragic Pragmatism*, points out that "historians have

seen in the Temperance speech, ever since Harry Jaffa's commentary on it half a century ago, a foreshadowing of the themes of the Second Inaugural Address" (693).

15. Basler, *Collected Works*, 1:276. Watts, *Psalms and Hymns*, book 1.
16. Basler, *Collected Works*, 1: 271–74.
17. Basler, *Collected Works*, 1: 277–78.
18. Winger, *Lincoln, Religion, and Politics*, 187. Jaffa, *Crisis*, 245–67. See also Briggs, *Lincoln's Speeches Reconsidered*, 65–69 for a searching analysis of the Temperance Address.
19. Basler, *Collected Works*, 1:281.
20. Basler, 1:289.
21. Winger, *Lincoln, Religion, and Politics*, 173. See Winger, 160 for his analysis on why Lincoln described himself as "superstitious."
22. In Morganthau and Hein, 4, *Essays*, Hans J. Morganthau concludes that "Skepticism and fatalism, then, are the dominant moods of Lincoln's religiousity," 15. See further discussion in White, *Lincoln's Greatest Speech*, 133–34 and Guelzo, "Doctrine of Necessity," 57–81. See Fornieri, *Political Faith*, 58–59; White, *Lincoln's Greatest Speech*, 136–37, and Morganthau and Hein, *Essays*, 107.
23. Winger, *Lincoln, Religion, and Politics*, 185.
24. Donald, *Lincoln*, 93.
25. Carwardine, "Lincoln, Evangelical Religion," 31.
26. Basler, *Collected Works*, 1:320. Lincoln appears to speak of deism with some degree of disdain. The difference between deism and theism is that deists believe that one God created the universe, but has not taken an active role in its sustainment since creation, whereas theists believe that one God not only created the universe, but has intervened in human events and answers prayer.
27. According to congressman Henry C. Deming, who knew Lincoln during the war, Lincoln told him "he had never united himself to any church, because he found difficulty in giving his assent, without mental reservation, to the long complicated statements of Christian doctrine, which characterize their Articles of belief and Confessions of Faith. . . . When any church," he continued, "will inscribe over its altar, as its sole qualification for membership the Saviour's condensed statement of the substance of both law and Gospel, 'Thou shalt love the Lord thy God with all thy heart, and with all thy soul and with all thy mind, and thy neighbor as thyself,' that church will I join with all my heart and all my soul." Deming, *Eulogy of Abraham Lincoln*, 42. Non-*CW* source.
28. Basler, 1:347.

29. By saying that it was "held by some Christian denominations," he was speaking of the Calvinist-based faiths.
30. Basler, *Collected Works*, 1:382.
31. Fornieri, *Political Faith*, 56.
32. Basler, *Collected Works*, 1:411. Boritt, "Economics of the American Dream," 94.
33. Basler, *Collected Works*, 1:439.
34. Basler, 1:473.
35. Basler, 2:10–11. These indirect allusions to scripture, where Lincoln is not referring to a specific Bible verse, are not included in the appendix. Basler, *Collected Works*, 2:16. Evidently Lincoln believed in heaven, or he would not have criticized his stepbrother.
36. Basler, *Collected Works*, 3:512. Basler, *Collected Works*, 2d Supplement, 1–2, John 13:27.
37. Wheeler, "Little Eddie," 34. Non-*CW* source.
38. Reed, "The Religious Sentiments of Lincoln," 33–34. Non-*CW* source. Barton, *Soul of Lincoln*, 270–71. For more about Rev. James Smith, see Temple, *From Skeptic to Prophet*, 38–40.
39. Basler, *Collected Works*, 2:90.
40. Basler., 2:97.
41. Barton, *Soul of Lincoln*, 77–78. Herndon could never quite make up his mind when it came to what he thought about Lincoln's religious beliefs. Randall and Current, in *Last Full Measure*, explain that if Lincoln was no professing Christian, neither was he in any sense an atheist. Indeed, even Herndon did not really think he was. Herndon was driven to overstatement by his zeal against the cant of pious moralizers, yet he sometimes qualified his statements and contradicted himself. "I affirm that Mr. Lincoln died an unbeliever—was not an evangelical Christian," he said in a rebuttal against the Rev. James A. Reed. On another occasion Herndon declared that Lincoln "was in short an infidel—was a universalist—was a Unitarian—a Theist. He did not believe that Jesus was God nor the son of God, etc." Of course, a theist is not an atheist and, except by fundamentalist standards, a universalist or unitarian is hardly an infidel. Nor is a person necessarily an unbeliever simply because he is not an "evangelical" Christian. (373–74).
42. Freed, *Political Ambitions*, 62. Noll, *America's God*, 434; White, "Abraham Lincoln and Christianity," 82; Talbot, "The Place of the Bible," 217.
43. Wilson, *Honor's Voice*, 90. Gienapp, *Civil War America*, 48.
44. Basler, *Collected Works*, 1:261.
45. Basler, *Collected Works*, 1:289, 2:97.

4. Drawing the Sword

1. Egerton, *Year of Meteors*, 21–23.
2. Egerton, 21.
3. Egerton, 256.
4. Newton, *Lincoln and Herndon*, 57.
5. Johannsen, *Stephen A. Douglas*, 451–54 and Newton, *Lincoln and Herndon*, 56.
6. Waugh, *One Man Great Enough*, 212.
7. Basler, *Collected Works*, 2:255.
8. Fornieri, *Abraham Lincoln Philosopher Statesman*, 34.
9. Fornieri, see 41–42 for further discussion by Fornieri of the Declaration and its biblical foundations.
10. Basler, *Collected Works*, 2:255–60.
11. Basler, 2:265–66. See Huhn, "A Higher Law," 234–40 for an insightful analysis of Lincoln's Peoria address from the viewpoint of both legal and biblical argument.
12. Basler, *Collected Works*, 2:266–67, 270.
13. Basler, 2:271.
14. Basler, 2:275.
15. Basler, 2:276.
16. Basler, 2:278.
17. Basler, 2:282
18. White, "Abraham Lincoln in 1854," 10.
19. Direct election of United States senators was not allowed until passage of the 17th amendment in 1913. Prior to that, state legislatures elected senators.
20. He refused to associate with the Know-Nothing party. The Know-Nothing political party was a xenophobic nativist party that was popular in the mid-1850s. They were primarily opposed to Roman Catholics and the immigration of Irish people.
21. Basler, *Collected Works*, 2:322–23.
22. Herndon and Weik, *Herndon's Lincoln*, 2:384. Wilson, *Intimate Memories of Lincoln*, 154.
23. Basler, *Collected Works*, 2:385.
24. Waugh, *One Man Great Enough*, 240–41.
25. Noll, *Theological Crisis*, 34.
26. Noll, 31 and 39.
27. Noll, 40–42. See also Noll, *America's God*, chapter 19 for a thorough analysis of the use of the Bible in the antebellum slavery argument.
28. Schwartz, "A Poor Hand to Quote Scripture" (41), says that, regarding Genesis 3:19, "[Gabor] Boritt contends that 'Whatever ideal he held to, whatever

America stood for in his eyes, in the most basic sense was embodied for him in this faith.'" In "Economics of the American Dream," Boritt concludes that this was, to use Lincoln's own expression, the "central idea" of his political outlook throughout his public life" (94).

29. Basler, *Collected Works*, 2:405.
30. Preamble of the US Declaration of Independence. Wilson, *Intimate Memories of Lincoln*, 205.
31. Donald, *Lincoln*, 214–15.
32. Lincoln's began his Discoveries and Inventions speech by saying "All creation is a mine, and every man, a miner." This is an indirect allusion to Job chapter 28, the search for wisdom. The second part of Lincoln's Discoveries and Inventions speech was later presented on February 11, 1859, in the Congregational Church of Jacksonville, Illinois. It did not directly quote scripture.
33. Lincoln was evidently familiar with biblical tools such as a concordance. Alexander Williamson, tutor for the Lincoln boys in the White House, said that "Mr. Lincoln very frequently studied the Bible with the aid of [G]ruden's Concordance, which lay on his table." From Samuel Trevena Jackson, *Lincoln's Use of the Bible* (New York: Eaton & Mains, 1909), 8.

5. A House Divided

1. *Illinois State Journal*, 17 June 1858.
2. Herndon and Weik, *Herndon's Lincoln*, 2:398. House divided is from Mark 3:25, where Jesus uses the parable of a divided kingdom and a divided house to show that if He is using Satan's power to cast out demons, Satan's kingdom won't survive. The full text of Habakkuk 2:2 reads, "And the Lord answered me, and said, Write the vision, and make it plain upon tables, that he may run that readeth it." God commanded Habakkuk to write down the prophetic vision so that it would not be misunderstood. Non-CW source.
3. Herndon and Weik, *Herndon's Lincoln*, 2:399.
4. *Herndon's Lincoln*, 2:398–400.
5. Basler, *Collected Works*, 2:461.
6. Huhn, "A Higher Law," 241–42.
7. Basler, *Collected Works*, 2:501. For an analysis of the logical argument in the House Divided Speech, see Kaplan, *Writer*, 270–73.
8. Basler, *Collected Works*, 2:510–11.
9. Basler, 2:520.
10. Johnson, *Stephen A. Douglas*, 352.
11. Basler, *Collected Works*, 2:546.
12. See Wolf, *Religion of Abraham Lincoln*, 96–97 and Freed, *Political Ambitions* 102–3 for further discussion.

13. Burlingame, *Lincoln: A Life*, 1:485.
14. Basler, *Collected Works*, 3:16.
15. Basler, 3:29.
16. Basler, 3:43. For a full discussion, see Guelzo, *Lincoln and Douglas*, 162–63.
17. Basler, *Collected Works*, 3:51.
18. Basler, 3:90.
19. Basler, 3:120–21.
20. Basler, 3:204–5.
21. Basler, 2:532. Morel, *Lincoln's Sacred Effort*, 208.
22. Basler, *Collected Works*, 3:226.
23. Basler, 3:249.
24. Basler, 3:305.
25. Carwardine, *Life of Purpose*, 87.
26. Basler, *Collected Works*, 3:308.
27. Basler, 3:312–13, 315.
28. Basler, 3:376. See also Fornieri, *Political Faith*, 42–43.
29. Basler, 3:410.
30. Basler, 1st Supplement, 44–45.
31. Basler, 3:461.
32. Basler, 3:462.
33. Basler, 3:480.
34. Wilson, *Intimate Memories of Lincoln*, 175.
35. Wilson and Davis, *Herndon's Informants*, 716. Non-CW source.

6. A Humbled Instrument

1. Holzer, *Lincoln at Cooper Union*, 10. Freeman, *Lincoln Goes to New York*, 51.
2. Basler, *Collected Works*, 3:550.
3. *New-York Tribune*, February 28, 1860. Wills, *Lincoln at Gettysburg*, 188.
4. Basler, *Collected Works*, 4:34.
5. For a detailed account of the 1860 Republican National Convention activities, see Burlingame, *Lincoln: A Life*, vi, chapter 15.
6. Basler, *Collected Works*, 4:71.
7. Basler, 4:130.
8. Basler, 4:135.
9. Basler, 4:146.
10. See Harris, *Rise to the Presidency*, 248–78 for a review of Lincoln's cabinet building.
11. Basler, *Collected Works*, 4:169 and 161.
12. Wilson and Davis, *Herndon's Informants*, 137. Non-CW source.
13. Basler, *Collected Works*, 4:190.

14. Basler, 188–90.
15. Burlingame, ed., *Oral History of Abraham Lincoln by John Nicolay*, 110. Widmar, *Lincoln on the Verge*, 188.
16. Basler, *Collected Works*, 4:192–94, 199, 207. On July 4, 1842, Lincoln had described himself as an instrument of God when he wrote to Joshua Speed about bringing Speed and his future wife Fanny Henning together. See also Winger, *Lincoln, Religion, and Politics*, 160 and Shenk, *Lincoln's Melancholy*, 197.
17. Basler, *Collected Works*, 4:236.
18. See, for example, Fornieri's *Political Faith*, 28–29 and Shenk's *Lincoln's Melancholy*, 198.
19. Basler, *Collected Works*, 4:239 and 240. His reference to assassination was pertinent. He had recently been informed of an assassination plot that awaited him in Baltimore.
20. Basler, 4:271.
21. Basler, 4:271.
22. Basler, 4:271.
23. McPherson, *Tried by War*, 20.
24. For the Fort Sumter crisis, I relied largely on Doris Kearns Goodwin's *Team of Rivals*, 340–46.
25. Miller, *Duty of a Statesman*, 87. In *Lincoln's Sacred Effort*, Lucas Morel agrees, saying, "Lincoln was too careful a writer, especially when it came to religious matters, to approve public statements . . . unless he agreed wholeheartedly with their sentiments" (92).
26. See White, *Lincoln's Greatest Speech*, 146–49 for in-depth discussion of Old School vs. New School Presbyterianism, as well as Lincoln's transition away from fatalism. O'Brien, "Lincoln and Rev. Dr. Gurley," 55. O'Brien presents an in-depth study of Lincoln's relationship with his pastor. Non-*CW* source.
27. White, *Lincoln's Greatest Speech*, 139.
28. Goodwin, *Team of Rivals*, 348.
29. Gienapp, *Civil War America*, 84.
30. US Constitution Article One, Section 9, clause 2. Basler, *Collected Works*, 4:430.
31. Basler, 4:426.
32. Basler, 4:441.
33. Sherman, *Memoirs*, 1:190.
34. Burlingame, ed., *Oral History of Abraham Lincoln*, 5; and Wilson, *Lincoln's Sword*, 252. Non-*CW* source.
35. Bayne, *Tad Lincoln's Father*, 183–84 and 33.
36. Bayne, *Tad Lincoln's Father*, 184–855. Non-CW source.

37. Basler, *Collected Works*, 4:482. In his review of this proclamation, Parrillo, "Lincoln's Calvinist Transformation," says that this was the "first time" Lincoln added "the dynamic of sin and chastisement" to the equation (239). Slavery, however, is not mentioned.
38. Burkhimer, *Lincoln's Christianity*, 130. Morel, *Lincoln's Sacred Effort*, 92.
39. In "Lincoln's Calvinist Transformation" Parrillo says,

> No one is sure to what degree Lincoln shared with Seward the authorship of the other proclamations [all but the October 3, 1863 Thanksgiving Proclamation—which Seward authored] ... I assume that Lincoln wrote all the documents and that the stronger religious sense of those from the latter half of the war (e.g., "Proclamation Appointing a National Fast Day," Mar. 30, 1863) indicates Lincoln's deepening apprehension of God's sovereignty; it is just as much in keeping with this interpretation to assume that Lincoln allowed others to write the early proclamations (resulting in the perfunctory and impersonal tone of "Proclamation of National Fast Day," Aug. 12, 1861) and then took greater part in the authorship when he was ready. Even without taking such factors into account, one thing is certain: we risk distorting Lincoln's religion just as much by rejecting the documents as by accepting them, since, in the vacuum of conclusive documentary evidence, it is just as possible that Lincoln wrote the proclamations as he did not (239n47).

See also Hein, "Lincoln's Theology and Political Ethics," 110–11, 119–23 regarding the authorship debate.
40. Nicolay, *Personal Traits*, 32–33.

7. The Fiery Trial

1. Burlingame, *A Life*, 2:220.
2. For military events in early 1862 I relied principally on McPherson, *Tried by War*, 67–74.
3. Keckley, *Behind the Scenes*, 103. Non-CW source.
4. Basler, *Collected Works*, 5:326
5. Boyden, *Pomroy's Experience in War Times*, 55–56. Szasz, *Lincoln and Religion*, 39. Non-CW sources.
6. Boyden, 56, 62–63. See also Fehrenbacher, *Recollected Words*, 362. Non-CW sources.
7. Shenk, *Lincoln's Melancholy*, 197. Donald, *Lincoln*, 337.
8. Chapman, "Latest Light on Abraham Lincoln," 2:504–5.
9. Shenk, *Lincoln's Melancholy*, 197. White, *Lincoln's Greatest Speech*, 140–41.

10. For a thorough review of Lincoln's effort to strike a blow against slavery in the spring and summer of 1862, see Burlingame, *Lincoln: A Life*, 2: chapter 27.

11. See Parrillo, "Lincoln's Calvinist Transformation" 240–44.

12. Wolf, *The Religion of Abraham Lincoln*, 124. Testimony about Lincoln's habit of prayer and Bible reading abound. John Nicolay said, "Mr. Lincoln was a praying man. I know that to be a fact and I have heard him request other people to pray" (Wolf, 124). Before leaving Springfield, Lincoln had asked Rev. James Smith to pray for him, and asked the congregation of the First Presbyterian Church in Springfield to pray for him also (Wolf, 114). In Turner and Turner, *Mary Todd Lincoln*, Mary said her husband "always read his Bible diligently," 567. According to Leidner, "How Many Lincoln Bibles," 75, n90, there are numerous testimonies about Lincoln's frequent reading of the Bible. Among them: the Lincoln boys' babysitter Julia Taft spoke of his midday reading; his secretaries Nicolay and Hay talk about the president reaching "for the Bible which commonly lay on his desk" to look up scripture; Captain James B. Mix, a member of Lincoln's bodyguard, said Lincoln, with his arm around Tad, "read the Bible each morning"; presidential bodyguard William Henry Cook said "the daily life of Mr. and Mrs. Lincoln usually commenced at eight o'clock, and immediately upon dressing the President would go into the library, where he would sit in his favorite chair in the middle of the room and read a chapter or two of his Bible"; Alexander Williamson, tutor for the Lincoln boys said that "Mr. Lincoln very frequently studied the Bible"; Nurse Rebecca Pomroy spoke about how Lincoln frequently read the Bible and liked the Psalms the best; and Mary Lincoln's seamstress Elizabeth Keckley spoke of Lincoln's use of a small Bible.

13. Basler, *Collected Works*, 5:212–13.

14. Basler, 5:215–16.

15. Basler, 5:279.

16. Basler, 5:327.

17. Welles, "The History of Emancipation," 838–51.

18. Basler, *Collected Works*, 5:343, 346, and 356.

19. Basler, 5:388.

20. McPherson, *Battle Cry of Freedom*, 529–33.

21. McPherson, 537.

22. Basler, *Collected Works*, 5:419–20, 425.

23. Nicolay and Hay, *Lincoln: A History*, 6:159.

24. Fragments written by Lincoln in the *CW* often preceded public statements he made shortly afterward. Taking this into consideration, he probably would

have written his "Meditation on the Divine Will" much later in the war, possibly as late as early 1864. Wilson, *Lincoln's Sword*, 255–56.

25. McPherson, *Tried by War*, 125.

26. Although Lincoln's reference to God as "my Maker" is here from a non-*CW* source (and not included in the appendix), it is nevertheless a reliable one. Fehrenbacher rates it "A," in Fehrenbacher and Fehrenbacher, *Recollected Words*, 96. Job is the only book in the Bible in which the term "my Maker" is employed, and is stated three times in Job. This is yet another testimony to Lincoln's deep acquaintance with Job, which many Bible scholars believe is the oldest book of the Bible. Nicolay and Hay, *Lincoln: A History*, 5:159.

27. For an interesting comparison and analysis of the Chase and Welles accounts, see Hein's "Lincoln's Theology and Political Ethics," in *Essays*, 150.

28. Gienapp, *Diary of Gideon Welles*.

29. Basler, *Collected Works*, 5:434. The Emancipation Proclamation was the first blow, the Thirteenth Amendment, which Lincoln would later initiate, was the second. Claims that Lincoln had little to do with freeing the slaves are untenable. Lincoln was the driving force behind both the enactment for the Emancipation Proclamation and passage of the Thirteenth Amendment.

30. Basler, 5:438. In fact there was significant push-back on the Emancipation Proclamation, primarily by Democrats but also some Republicans. See McPherson, *Battle Cry of Freedom*, 557–62, 594–95.

31. There is some confusion as to the exact date of the interview, and the date of Lincoln's reply. Various dates are suggested by the editors of the *Collected Works*.

32. Basler, *Collected Works*, 5:478.

33. Basler, 5:518.

34. Basler, 5:527.

35. Basler, 5:537.

36. Burlingame, *Inner Life*, 105. Burlingame, *A Life*, 2:446. Non-*CW* source.

37. Donald, *Lincoln*, 394–95. Basler, *Collected Works*, 5:537–38, 543.

38. For analysis of this theme, see Parrillo, "Lincoln's Calvinist Transformation," 230.

39. From Brown and Downes, "A Conference," 61. Non-*CW* source.

8. To Highly Resolve

1. Carpenter, *Six Months in the White House*, 269–70.

2. Basler, *Collected Works*, 6:29. Guelzo, *Emancipation Proclamation*, 214 and 352n13. Since the Emancipation Proclamation was a war measure and not a constitutional amendment, it had authority only in the ten states still in rebellion as of January 1, 1863. It could not free slaves in the neutral states of

Kentucky, Missouri, Maryland, and Delaware. Tennessee was also exempt, since by 1863 it was under a recognized Union government. This is one of the reasons why Lincoln pushed for the passage of the Thirteenth Amendment before the war was over.

3. Basler, *Collected Works*, 6:39–40.

4. "Father Abraham" was a popular nickname for Lincoln used by both Black and White soldiers. Davis, *Lincoln's Men*, 197. Also popular were "Uncle Abe," "Honest Abe," and "Old Abe," 135.

5. McPherson, *Battle Cry of Freedom*, 639. Wert, *Sword of Lincoln*, 227.

6. Basler, *Collected Works*, 6:155–56.

7. Parrillo, "Lincoln's Calvinist Transformation," 246.

8. Basler, *Collected Works*, 6:266.

9. Hertz, *Hidden Lincoln*, 327. Non-*CW* source.

10. Burlingame, *Lincoln: A Life*, 2:493. Non-*CW* source. Nicolay, *Personal Traits of Abraham Lincoln*, 283. Non-*CW* source.

11. Brooks, *Washington, D.C., in Lincoln's Time*, 61.

12. See https://archive.spurgeon.org/sermons/2457.php accessed 12/18/20.

13. McPherson, *Battle Cry of Freedom*, 629–37.

14. Basler, *Collected Works*, 6:332.

15. Parrillo, "Lincoln's Calvinist Transformation," 248.

16. Burlingame, *At Lincoln's Side*, 49.

17. Basler, *Collected Works*, 6:410.

18. Douglass, *The Life and Times of Frederick Douglass*, 422–23.

19. Douglass, 302–4. Later, when it became politically feasible, Lincoln was able to increase the Black soldiers' pay.

20. Basler, *Collected Works*, 6:497 note. Although a "permanent" holiday, it required an annual proclamation by the president.

21. Basler, 6:496–97. Per *CW* note on 497, this pronouncement was written by Seward. It had a number of themes previously used by the administration and was probably read and approved by Lincoln.

22. Basler, 6:535–36.

23. Wilson, "William H. Herndon and Mary Todd Lincoln," 18.

24. Boritt, *Gettysburg Gospel*, 168. See also Jaffa, *Crisis*, 228. Jaffa calls birth and rebirth the "central metaphor" of the Gettysburg Address.

25. See Fornieri, *Political Faith* (47) and Wills, *Lincoln at Gettysburg* (62). Wills quotes literary critic James Hurt and others who observe the birth-death-rebirth theme. Wills also points out that "the Gettysburg Address, . . . fails to express the whole of Lincoln's mind. It must be supplemented with his other significant address, the Second Inaugural, where sin is added to the picture" (177). Basler, *Collected Works*, 7:23.

26. Wills, *Lincoln at Gettysburg*, 62–63, Fornieri, *Political Faith*, 47, and Boritt, *Gettysburg Gospel*, 120. Boritt and others such as poet Robert Lowell point out the various allusions to birth in the address. See also E. A. Elmore's in-depth analysis in *Lincoln's Gettysburg Address*.

27. Gienapp, *Civil War America*, 146. Great Britain's Palmerston administration had hoped to recognize the Confederacy during the Civil War, but Lincoln's judicious policies, and hard-earned military victories, prevented this. McPherson, in *Battle Cry of Freedom*, explains how Lincoln's timely announcement of the Emancipation Proclamation was a significant factor in dissuading Britain from interposing on behalf of the South, 567.

9. *The Will of God*

1. Basler, *Collected Works*, 7:169.
2. Stevenson, *Proceedings*, vi. Non-*CW* source.
3. Stevenson, viii. Non-*CW* source.
4. Basler, *Collected Works*, 7:254.
5. Basler, 7:259.
6. Wilson, *Lincoln's Sword*, 244.
7. Basler, *Collected Works*, 7:281–82.
8. Basler, 7:282, 8:333.
9. Basler, 7:287.
10. Basler, 7:301–2. This speech is significant in that it also employs biblical language that Lincoln was fond of, including reference to wolves and sheep and the use of King James language such as the words "wrought," "ere," and "blessings." It also includes Lincoln's unique definition of the word "liberty."
11. Basler, 7:333. This proclamation came out as a press release that was printed in the papers on May 10, 1864. Seward's name does not appear on it.
12. Basler, 7:368.
13. Burlingame, *A Life*, 2:636. Non-*CW* source.
14. Basler, *Collected Works*, 7:431–32.
15. Davis, *Lincoln's Men*, 199.
16. Basler, *Collected Works*, 7:512.
17. Basler, 7:514.
18. Basler, 7:507.
19. Basler, 8:152. Lincoln's statement recalls Jeremiah 34:11–22, where the Lord was angered toward those that forced previously freed people back into slavery.
20. McPherson, *Battle Cry of Freedom*, 774.
21. Basler, *Collected Works*, 7:533.
22. See Parrillo, "Lincoln's Calvinist Transformation," 250 for further discussion.

23. Nicolay and Hay, *Lincoln: A History* 6:159.

24. Basler, *Collected Works*, 5:403–4. Evidently Lincoln's lifelong belief was that God's modus operandi for influencing human events was through the human mind. In the days when he believed in the doctrine of necessity, he mentioned the influence on the human mind by "some power," and now over twenty years later he speaks of God's ability to influence the mind of the human "contestants." See Calhoun and Morel, "Lincoln's Religion," 4, for additional insight on this theme.

25. Miller, *Duty of a Statesman*, agreed that Wilson's analysis on the timing of the Meditation on the Divine Will in *Lincoln's Sword* (255–56, 329–30n255) is "persuasively argued" (406). Burlingame in *Lincoln: A Life*, also agrees, saying that the meditation was "probably written in the summer of 1864" (2:711).

26. White, *Lincoln's Greatest Speech*, 127.

27. Guelzo, *Redeemer President*, 327. Noll, *America's God*, 430–32.

28. Basler, *Collected Works*, 7:535.

29. Basler, 7:542.

30. Basler, 8:55–56.

31. For 1864 election results, see Gienapp, *Civil War America*, 174.

32. Basler, *Collected Works*, 8:154–55.

33. McPherson, *Tried by War*, 254.

34. McPherson, 254.

10. The Judgements of the Lord

1. Shakespeare, *Dramatic Works*, *Macbeth*, 3:243. Donald, *Lincoln*, 396. Basler, *Collected Works*, 8:254.

2. For Lincoln's political maneuvers to pass the Thirteenth Amendment see Burlingame, *Lincoln: A Life*, 2:745–50.

3. Brooks, *Washington, DC in Lincoln's Time*, 213. Non-*CW* Source.

4. There are also several biblical terms and phrases such as "finish the work" (John 4:34, Romans 9:28), "scourge" (Isaiah 28:15–18, Hebrews 12:6), "bondman" (Deuteronomy 15:15, Genesis 44:33), and "requited" (Judges 1:7, 1 Samuel 25:21). See White, *Greatest Speech*, 153–55; and Freed, *Political Ambitions*, 139–43.

5. Basler, *Collected Works*, 8:332. Noll, *Theological Crisis*, 89.

6. Basler, 8:333.

7. See Miller, *Duty of a Statesman*, 410–11; and White, *Lincoln's Greatest Speech*, 158 and 179.

8. Basler, *Collected Works*, 8:333.

9. Quoted in Noll, *America's God*, 428; and Shenk, *Lincoln's Melancholy*, 208.

10. Noll, *America's God*, 434–35. In "The Religion of Abraham Lincoln," theologian Reinhold Niebuhr concurs, saying, "Lincoln's religious convictions were superior in depth and purity to those, not only of the political leaders of his day, but of the religious leaders of the era." (72–73).

11. White, *Lincoln's Greatest Speech*, 182–84.

12. White, 199.

13. Basler, *Collected Works*, 8:356.

14. See Winger, *Lincoln, Religion, and Politics*, 205; and Wills, *Lincoln at Gettysburg*, 189, for further discussion.

15. McPherson, *Battle Cry of Freedom*, 849.

16. Basler, *Collected Works*, 8:399–400. "From Whom All Blessings Flow" was an allusion to a popular hymn by Thomas Ken.

17. Burlingame, *Lincoln: A Life*, 2:803.

18. For example, see the testimony of Lincoln's reaching out to Black people, see Sojourner Truth in Holzer, *Lincoln as I Knew Him*, 198–201. White, *House Built by Slaves*, Epilogue. Douglass, *Life and Times of Frederick Douglass*, 357. For "educating tendency" see supra note 8:19.

19. *Diary of Gideon Welles*, April 14, 1865, 2:282. Shenk, *Lincoln's Melancholy*, 209.

20. Leidner, *Conversations with Lincoln*, 143–48. Shenk, *Lincoln's Melancholy*, 209; and Miers, *Lincoln Day by Day*, 3:329–30.

Conclusion

1. Lincoln undoubtedly enjoyed the Bible not only for the Bible stories and principles, but also for its language. The King James Bible had been translated from previous texts into an Early Modern English style often called Elizabethan English. This style was similar to that of the works of William Shakespeare. The King James Bible was published in 1611, about the time Shakespeare's *The Tempest* saw its first performance.

2. Born Again," *Encyclopedia of Christian Civilization*, v1, 301–302. Even though Jesus was the first to talk of the necessity of being "born again" (John 3:3, 7), it was not a popular phrase in the nineteenth century. A review of late nineteenth and early twentieth century resources used in this book (Carroll, Spencer, Stott) reveals the use of the term "born again" only three times in their cumulative twelve hundred pages. A review of an additional nineteenth-century work not quoted herein, Redford's *A History of Methodism in Kentucky*, reveals only one use in fourteen hundred pages.

3. Barton, *Soul of Lincoln*, 271. Per Barton, Lincoln was "reared a Predestinarian Baptist; and while he never became a Baptist he never ceased to be a Predestinarian." Barton, 271.

4. Barton, *Soul of Lincoln*, 142, 321.

5. Donald, *Lincoln's Herndon*, 359; and Fornieri, *Political Faith*, 53. Barton, *Soul of Lincoln*, 328. According to Guelzo in *Redeemer President*, [Herndon] "realized by 1866 that the spiritual life of the man he had worked with for over a decade really had been a closed book . . . there were wild fluctuations in what even Lincoln's closest friends thought his religion, if any, had been like" (443). Scholars have concluded that although Herndon knew Lincoln well, and had probably heard him critique the Bible, Herndon went beyond reasonable argument in his passionate attempt to disprove the claims of persons like Newton Bateman who said Lincoln was a conventional Christian. Herndon, who had a reasonable case to make about Lincoln's religious doubts when he was a lawyer in Illinois, vividly demonstrated his bias when he claimed, after perfunctory investigation, that Lincoln never changed from his New Salem position as a skeptic while he was in the White House. Lincoln scholar Richard Current said in *The Lincoln Nobody Knows*, "Herndon had little evidence of arguing [that Lincoln's faith didn't change when president], and the evidence he had is far from convincing" (61).

6. White, *Lincoln's Greatest Speech*, 111–12.

7. Speed, *Reminiscences of Abraham Lincoln*, 32–33. "The balance on faith" is an allusion to Habakkuk 2:4. Non-*CW* source. This was about the time President Lincoln called the Bible "the best gift God has given to man." Gillespie, in *Lincoln Memorial Album*, says that Lincoln could never reconcile the "prescience of Deity with the uncertainty of events" (457). Shenk, in *Lincoln's Melancholy* says, "Although Lincoln's doubts have often been mistaken for lack of interest in religious matters, the reverse is probably true. Many of history's greatest believers have also been the fiercest doubters" (195).

8. Basler, *Collected Works*, 6:535.

9. Speed, *Reminiscences of Abraham Lincoln*, 27–28. Non-*CW* source.

10. Bruce, "The Riddle of Death," 130–45. In partial support of his conclusion that Lincoln did not believe in heaven, he says that in the *Collected Works*, "the word 'Heaven' shows up on a few occasions . . . But it does so in a figurative or casual way" (139). But in my own research of the *CW*, Lincoln uses the word "heaven" two dozen times. How many of these references to heaven are merely "figurative or casual" is, of course, debatable. Basler, *Collected Works*, 2:97. Wheeler, "Little Eddie," 34. Keckley, *Behind the Scenes*, 103. Herndon quoted in Lamon, *Life of Abraham Lincoln*, 495.

11. Per Kermit White's PhD dissertation, "Abraham Lincoln and Christianity," "There is no proof that Lincoln disbelieved the existence of God. Herndon always portrayed his unorthodoxy in comparison with orthodox Christianity, but he did not depict him as an atheist. Herndon implied that Lincoln, during his moments of melancholy, did border between theism and atheism;

however, he affirmed that Lincoln "was a deeply-religious man at all times and places, in spite of his transient doubts" (82). See also Hein, *Historian's Lincoln*, 144. Trueblood, *Lessons in Spiritual Leadership*, quotes John Nicolay as saying, "Mr. Lincoln was a praying man. I know that to be a fact and I have heard him request people to pray for him, which he would never have done had he not believed that prayer is answered," 86.

12. Herndon and Weik, *Herndon's Lincoln*, 3:445–46. Herndon's allusion to eternal punishment and unorthodox faith is primarily a reference to Lincoln's conversations with friends in the New Salem and early Springfield years, where he doubted the punishment in hell was "endless." Per Barton, Lincoln believed "in future punishment, but not in endless punishment" and that "whatever right the human race had possessed to immortality and lost through sin, had been restored in Christ. . . . [Lincoln was] not an infidel, nor even a deist, but essentially a Universalist." Barton, *Soul of Abraham Lincoln*, 287, 136–37. Lincoln's doubt about endless punishment in hell might be comparable to belief in what is today called "annihilationism."

BIBLIOGRAPHY

Barton, William E. *Life of Abraham Lincoln.* 2 vols. New York: Bobbs, 1925.

———. *The Soul of Abraham Lincoln.* New York: George H. Doran, 1920.

Basler, Roy P., ed. *The Collected Works of Abraham Lincoln.* 9 vols. New Brunswick, N.J.: Rutgers University Press, 1953–55, and Supplement, 1832–1865. 2 vols. Westport, CT: Greenwood Press, 1974.

Bass, Bernard M. *The Ethics of Transformational Leadership.* New York: State University of New York Center for Leadership Studies, 1996.

———. *Transformational Leadership,* New York: Psychology Press, 2006.

———. *The Bass Handbook of Leadership,* New York: Free Press, 2008.

Bayne, Julia Taft. *Tad Lincoln's Father.* New York: Little, Brown, and Company, 1931.

Beveridge, Albert J. *Abraham Lincoln 1809–1858.* 2 vols. Boston and New York: Houghton Mifflin Company, 1928.

Boles, John B. *Religion in Antebellum Kentucky.* Boston and Lexington: University Press of Kentucky, 1976.

Boritt, Gabor S. "Lincoln and the Economics of the American Dream." In *The Historian's Lincoln: Pseudohistory, Psychohistory, and History,* edited by Gabor S. Boritt, 87–106. Urbana: University of Illinois Press, 1988.

———. *The Gettysburg Gospel: The Lincoln Speech That Nobody Knows.* New York: Simon and Schuster, 2006.

Bowman, Cindy H. "Abraham Lincoln's Transformational Leadership." PhD diss. Lincoln Memorial University, 2011.

Boyden, Anna. *Echoes from Hospital and White House, A Record of Mrs. Rebecca R. Pomroy's Experience in War Times.* Boston: D. Lothrop and Co., 1884.

Bray, Robert. *Reading with Lincoln.* Carbondale: Southern Illinois University Press, 2010.

———. "What Abraham Lincoln Read—An Evaluative and Annotated List." *Journal of the Abraham Lincoln Association* 28, no. 2 (Summer 2007): 28–81.

Briggs, John Channing. *Lincoln's Speeches Reconsidered.* Baltimore, MD: Johns Hopkins University Press, 2005.

———. *Washington in Lincoln's Time.* New York: The Century Company, 1894.

Brown, W. North, and Randolf C. Downes, eds. "A Conference with AL: From the Diary of Rev. Nathan Brown." *Northwest Ohio Quarterly* 22 (1949–1959).

Bruce, Robert V. "The Riddle of Death." In *The Lincoln Enigma: The Changing Faces of an American Icon*, edited by Gabor Boritt, 130–45. New York: Oxford University Press, 2001.

Burkhimer, Michael. *100 Essential Lincoln Books*. Nashville, TN: Cumberland House Publishing, 2003.

———. *Lincoln's Christianity*. Yardley, PA: Westholme Publishing, 2007.

Burlingame, Michael. *Abraham Lincoln: A Life*. 2 volumes. Baltimore: Johns Hopkins University Press, 2008.

———, ed. *At Lincoln's Side: John Hay's Civil War Correspondence and Selected Writings*. Carbondale: Southern Illinois University Press, 2000.

———. *Lincoln Observed: Civil War Dispatches of Noah Brooks*. Baltimore: Johns Hopkins University Press, 1998.

———. *An Oral History of Abraham Lincoln: John G. Nicolay's Interviews and Essays*. Carbondale: Southern Illinois University Press, 1996.

Burns, James MacGregor. *Leadership*. New York: Harper and Row, 1978.

Burt, John. *Lincoln's Tragic Pragmatism: Lincoln, Douglas, and Moral Conflict*. Cambridge, MA: Harvard University Press, 2013.

Cady, John F. "The Religious Environment of Lincoln's Youth." *Indiana Magazine of History* 37, no. 1 (March 1941).

Calhoun, Samuel, and Lucas Morel. "Abraham Lincoln's Religion: The Case for His Ultimate Belief in a Personal, Sovereign God." *Journal of the Abraham Lincoln Association* 33, no. 1 (Winter 2012): 38–74.

Carpenter, F. B. *The Inner Life of Abraham Lincoln: Six Months at the White House*. Boston: Hurd and Houghton, 1874.

Carroll, B. H. *The Genesis of American Anti-Missionism*. Louisville, KY: Baptist Book Concern, 1902.

Carwardine, Richard. *Lincoln: A Life of Purpose and Power*. New York: Alfred A. Knopf, 2007.

———. "Lincoln, Evangelical Religion, and American Political Culture in the Era of the Civil War." *Journal of the Abraham Lincoln Association* 18, no. 1 (Winter 1997).

Daily Pantagraph (Bloomington, IL). April 9, 1858.

Davis, William C. *Lincoln's Men: How President Lincoln Became Father to an Army and a Nation*. New York: Free Press, 1999.

Deming, Henry C. *Eulogy of Abraham Lincoln before the General Assembly of Connecticut*. Hartford, CT: A. N. Clark and Co., 1865.

Dennett, Tyler. *Lincoln and the Civil War Diaries of John Hay*. Dodd Meade and Company, 1939.

Dilworth, Thomas. *A New Guide to the English Tongue*. Philadelphia: John McCulloch, 1796.

Donald, David Herbert. *Lincoln*. New York: Simon and Schuster, 1995.

———. *Lincoln's Herndon: A Biography*. New York: Alfred A. Knopf, 1948.

Douglass, Frederick. *The Life and Times of Frederick Douglass*. Hartford, CT.: Park Publishing Company, 1882.

Egerton, Douglas R. *Year of Meteors: Stephen A. Douglas, Abraham Lincoln, and the Election That Brought on the Civil War*. Bloomsbury Press, 2010.

E. A. Elmore. *Lincoln's Gettysburg Address: Echoes of the Bible and the Book of Common Prayer*. Carbondale: Southern Illinois University Press, 2009.

Fehrenbacher, Don E., and Virginia Fehrenbacher, eds. *Recollected Words of Abraham Lincoln*. Stanford, CA: Stanford University Press, 1996.

Ford, Thomas. *A History of Illinois: From Its Commencement as a State in 1818 to 1847*. Chicago: S. C. Griggs and Company, 1854.

Fornieri, Joseph. *Abraham Lincoln's Political Faith*. Dekalb: Northern Illinois University Press, 2005.

———. *Abraham Lincoln: Philosopher Statesman*. Carbondale: Southern Illinois University Press, 2014.

Freed, Edwin D. *Lincoln's Political Ambitions, Slavery, and the Bible*. Eugene, OR: Pickwick Publications, 2012.

Gienapp, William E. *Abraham Lincoln and Civil War America*. New York: Oxford University Press, 2002.

———. *The Civil War Diaries of Gideon Welles*. Champaign: University of Illinois Press, 2014.

Goodwin, Doris Kearns. *Team of Rivals: The Political Genius of Abraham Lincoln*. New York: Simon and Schuster, 2005.

Guelzo Allen C. *Abraham Lincoln: A Man of Ideas*. Carbondale: Southern Illinois University Press, 2009.

———. *Abraham Lincoln: Redeemer President*. Grand Rapids, MI: William B. Eerdmans, 1999.

———. *Lincoln and Douglas: The Debates That Defined America*. New York: Simon and Schuster, 2008.

———. *Lincoln's Emancipation Proclamation*. New York: Simon and Schuster, reissue edition, 2006.

———. "Abraham Lincoln and the Doctrine of Necessity." *Journal of the Abraham Lincoln Association* 18, no. 1 (Winter 1997): 57–81.

Harris, William C. *Lincoln and the Border States: Preserving the Union*. Lawrence: University Press of Kansas, 2011.

———. *Lincoln's Rise to the Presidency*. Lawrence: University Press of Kansas, 2007.

Hein, David. "Commentary on Thurow's 'Abraham Lincoln and American Political Religion.'" In *The Historian's Lincoln: Pseudohistory, Psychohistory, and*

History, edited by Gabor S. Boritt, 144–48. Champaign: University of Illinois Press, 1988.

———. "Lincoln's Theology and Political Ethics." In *Essays on Lincoln's Faith and Politics,* ed. by Kenneth W. Thompson, 105–56. Vol. 4. Lanham, MD: University Press of America, 1983.

———. "The Calvinistic Tenor of Abraham Lincoln's Religious Thought." *Lincoln Herald* 85, (Winter 1983) 212–20.

Herndon, William H., and Jesse W. Weik. *Herndon's Lincoln: The True Story of a Great Life.* 3 vols. Springfield, IL: Herndon's Lincoln Publishing Company, 1921.

Holland, Josiah G. *Life of Abraham Lincoln.* Springfield, MA: Gurdon Bill, 1866.

Holy Bible, Containing the Old and New Testaments, With Arguments Prefixed to the Different Books and Moral and Theological Observations Composed by the Reverend Mr. Ostervald. London: Society for Propagating Christian Knowledge, 1799.

Holzer, Harold. *Lincoln as I Knew Him.* Chapel Hill, NC: Algonquin Books, 1999.

———. *Lincoln at Cooper Union: The Speech That Made Abraham Lincoln President.* New York: Simon and Schuster, 2004.

Hubbard, Charles M. *Lincoln Reshapes the Presidency.* Macon, GA: Mercer University Press, 2003.

Huhn, Wilson. "A Higher Law: Abraham Lincoln's Use of Biblical Imagery." *Rutgers Journal of Law and Religion* 13 (2011): 227–79. https://ideaexchange .uakron.edu/ua_law_publications/83/ accessed 2/8/2021.

Jackson, Samuel Trevena. *Lincoln's Use of the Bible.* New York: Eaton and Mains, 1909.

Jaffa, Harry V. *Crisis of the House Divided: An Interpretation of the Issues in the Lincoln-Douglas Debates.* Chicago: University of Chicago Press, 1959.

Johannsen, Robert W. *Stephen A. Douglas.* Champaign: University of Illinois Press, 1997.

Johnson, Allen. *Stephen A. Douglas: A Study in American Politics.* New York: MacMillan Company, 1908.

Johnson, William Jackson. *Abraham Lincoln, the Christian.* New York: Abingdon Press, 1913.

Jones, Edgar D. *Lincoln and the Preachers.* New York: Harper and Brothers, 1948.

Kaplan, Fred. *Lincoln: A Biography of a Writer.* New York: Harper Perennial, reprint edition, 2010.

Keckley, Elizabeth. *Behind the Scenes, Or, Thirty Years a Slave and Four Years in the White House.* New York: G. W. Carlton, 1868.

Kentucky Preceptor, by A Teacher. Lexington, KY: Maccoun, Tilford and Co., 1812.

Knox, William. *The Lonely Hearth, the Songs of Israel, Harp of Zion and Other Poems.* London: John Johnstone, Edinburgh, 1847.

Kurian, George Thomas, ed. *Encyclopedia of Christian Civilization,* Vol. 1. Hoboken, NJ: Wiley-Blackwell, 2012.

Lamon, Ward Hill. *The Life of Abraham Lincoln: From His Birth to His Inauguration as President.* Boston: James R. Osgood and Company, 1872.

Leidner, Gordon. *Conversations with Lincoln: Little-Known Stories from Those Who Met America's 16th President.* Naperville, IL: Cumberland House.

———. "How Many Lincoln Bibles?" *Journal of the Abraham Lincoln Association* 41, no. 1 (Winter 2020): 47–79.

———. "Lincoln as a Transformational Leader." *Lincoln Herald* 104, no. 3 (Fall 2002): 111–18.

———. "Measuring the Presidents: Modern Leadership Theory Provides a Framework for Comparing the Presidential Skills of Lincoln and Davis." *Columbiad: A Quarterly Review of the War between the States* 2, no. 1 (Spring 1998): 61–76.

MaCartney, Clarence E. *Lincoln and the Bible.* New York: Abingdon-Cokesbury Press, 1949.

McPherson, James. *Battle Cry of Freedom.* Oxford: Oxford University Press, 1988.

———. *For Cause and Comrades: Why Men Fought in the Civil War.* New York: Oxford University Press, 1997.

———. *Tried by War: Abraham Lincoln as Commander in Chief.* London: Penguin, 2008.

Mearns, David C., ed. *The Lincoln Papers.* 2 vols. Garden City: Doubleday, 1948.

Miers, Earl Schenk, ed. *Lincoln Day by Day: A Chronology, 1809–1865.* Washington, DC: Lincoln Sesquicentennial Commission, 1960.

Miller, William Lawrence. *Lincoln and His World: The Early Years, Birth to Illinois Legislature.* Stackpole Books, 2006.

Miller, William Lee. *President Lincoln: The Duty of a Statesman.* New York: Vintage Books, 2009.

Mills, Randy K. "The Struggle for the Soul of Frontier Baptists: The Anti-Mission Controversy in the Lower Wabash Valley." *Indiana Magazine of History* 94 (1998): 303–22.

Morel, Lucas E. *Lincoln's Sacred Effort: Defining Religion's Role in American Self-Government.* Lanham, MD: Lexington Books, 2000.

———. *Lincoln and Liberty: Wisdom for the Ages.* Lexington: University Press of Kentucky, 2014.

Morganthau, Hans J., and David Hein. Edited by Kenneth W. Thompson. *Essays on Lincoln's Faith and Politics.* Vol. 4. Lanham, MD: University Press of America, 1983.

Mott, Richard F., ed. *Memoir and Correspondence of Eliza P. Gurney*. Philadelphia: J. B. Lippincott and Co. 1884.

New-York Tribune, February 28, 1860.

Newton, Joseph Fort. *Lincoln and Herndon*. Cedar Rapids, IA: Torch Press, 1910.

Nicolay, John, and John Hay. *Abraham Lincoln: A History*. New York: Century Company, 1890.

Nicolay, Helen. *Personal Traits of Abraham Lincoln*. New York: Century Company, 1912.

Niebuhr, Reinhold. "The Religion of Abraham Lincoln." In *Lincoln and the Gettysburg Address*, edited by Allan Nevins, 72–87. Urbana: University of Illinois Press, 1964.

Mark Noll. *America's God: From Jonathan Edwards to Abraham Lincoln*. Oxford University Press, 2005.

———. "American Religion, 1809–1865." In *Lincoln's America: 1809–1865*, edited by Joseph R. Fornieri and Sara Vaughn Gabbard, 72–93. Carbondale: Southern Illinois University Press, 2008.

———. *The Civil War as a Theological Crisis*. Chapel Hill: University of North Carolina Press, 2015.

Nowlin, William Dudley. *Kentucky Baptist History: 1770–1922*. Louisville, KY: Baptist Book Concern, 1922.

O'Brien, John. "Seeking God's Will: President Lincoln and Rev. Dr. Gurley." *Journal of the Abraham Lincoln Association* 39, no. 2 (Summer 2018): 29–54.

Oldroyd, Osborn H. *The Lincoln Memorial: Album-Immortelles*. New York: G. W. Carleton and Company Publishers, 1883.

Ostergard, Philip L. *The Inspired Wisdom of Abraham Lincoln*. Carol Stream, IL: Tyndale House, 2008.

Parrillo, Nicholas. "Lincoln's Calvinist Transformation: Emancipation and War." *Civil War History* 46, no. 3. (2000):227–53.

Randall J. G., and Richard Nelson Current. *Lincoln the President: Midstream to the Last Full Measure*. Boston: Da Capo Press, 1997.

Rankin, Henry B. *Personal Recollections of Abraham Lincoln*. 2 vols. New York: G. P. Putnam, 1916.

Reed, James. "The Religious Sentiments of Abraham Lincoln." *Scribner's Monthly* (July 1873).

Register of the Kentucky State Historical Society 20, no. 59.

Reynolds, David S. *Abe: Abraham Lincoln and His Times*. New York: Penguin Press, 2020.

Schrama, Major Michael A. "President Abraham Lincoln: Embodiment of Transformational Leadership." *The Reporter: The Judge Advocate General's School (AFJAGS) for the Office of the Judge Advocate General, United States Air Force.*

10 October 2018. https://www.jagreporter.af.mil/Post/Article-View-Post/Article/2549191/president-abraham-lincoln/.

Schwartz, Earl. "'A Poor Hand to Quote Scripture': Lincoln and Genesis 3:19." *Journal of the Abraham Lincoln Association* 23, no. 2 (Summer, 2002): 37–49.

Scripps, John Locke. *The First Published Life of Abraham Lincoln.* 1860. Detroit: Cranbrook Press, 1900. Reprint.

Shakespeare, William. *The Dramatic Works of William Shakespeare.* 3 vols. Boston: Phillips, Samson, and Co. 1850.

Shenk, Joshua Wolf. *Lincoln's Melancholy: How Depression Challenged a President and Fueled His Greatness.* New York: Houghton Mifflin, 2005.

Sherman, William Tecumseh. *Memoirs.* 2 vols. New York: D. Appleton and Company, 1889.

Simon, Paul. *Freedom's Champion: Elijah Lovejoy.* Carbondale: Southern Illinois University Press, 1994.

———. *Lincoln's Preparation for Greatness: The Illinois Legislative Years.* Norman: University of Oklahoma Press, 1965.

Speed, Joshua. *Reminiscences of Abraham Lincoln and Notes of a Visit to California.* Louisville, KY: John P. Morgan and Company, 1884.

Spencer, J. H. *A History of Kentucky Baptists from 1789 to 1885.* 2 vols. Privately printed, 1886.

Stevenson, T. P. *Proceedings of the National Convention to Secure the Religious Amendment of the Constitution of the United States.* Philadelphia: James B. Rodgers and Co., 1872.

Stott, William T. *Indiana Baptist History: 1798–1908.* Franklin: Indiana, 1908.

Sweet, William. *Religion on the American Frontier: The Baptists, 1783–1830.* New York: Henry Holt and Company, 1931.

Szasz, Ferenc Morton with Margaret Connell Szasz. *Lincoln and Religion.* Carbondale: Southern Illinois University Press, 2014.

Talbot, Derek W. "*The Place of the Bible in Abraham Lincoln's Career.*" PhD diss. University of Bangor, 2014.

Tarbell, Ida. *In the Footsteps of the Lincolns.* New York: Harper and Brothers, 1924.

Temple, Wayne C. *Abraham Lincoln: From Skeptic to Prophet.* Mahomet, IL: Mayhaven, 1995.

Thomas, Benjamin P. *Lincoln's New Salem.* Springfield, IL: Abraham Lincoln Association, 1934.

Trueblood, Elton. *Abraham Lincoln: Lessons in Spiritual Leadership.* New York: HarperOne, 2012.

———. *Abraham Lincoln: Theologian of American Anguish.* New York: Harper and Row, 1973.

Turner, J. G., and L. L. Turner. *Mary Todd Lincoln: Her Life and Letters.* New York: Fromm Publishing Corporation, 1987.

Vicchio, Stephen J. *Abraham Lincoln's Religion: An Essay on One Man's Faith.* Eugene, OR: Wipf and Stock, 2018.

Warren, Louis A. *Lincoln Lore* 567 (February 19, 1940). Lincoln Financial Foundation Collection: Allen County Public Library.

———. *Lincoln's Parentage and Childhood.* Century Company, 1926.

———. *Lincoln's Youth: Indiana Years 1816–1830.* New York: Appleton-Century-Crofts, 1959.

Waugh, John C. *One Man Great Enough.* New York: Houghton Mifflin Harcourt, 2007.

Watts, Isaac. *Psalms and Hymns.* London: C. Whittingham, 1806.

Welles, Gideon. *Diary.* Edited by Howard K. Beale. New York: Norton, 1960.

———. "The History of Emancipation," *Galaxy* 14, December 1872.

Wert, Jeffrey D. *The Sword of Lincoln.* New York: Simon and Schuster, 2005.

Wheeler, Samuel P. "Solving a Literary Mystery, Little Eddie." *Journal of the Abraham Lincoln Association* 33, no. 2, (Summer 2012): 34–46.

White, Horace. "Abraham Lincoln in 1854." Address before Illinois State Historical Society, January 1908.

White, Jonathan W. *A House Built by Slaves.* Lanham, MD: Rowman and Littlefield, 2022.

White, Kermit. "Abraham Lincoln and Christianity." PhD diss. Boston University, 1954.

White, Ronald C. *A. Lincoln: A Biography.* New York: Random House, 2009.

———. *The Eloquent President: A Portrait of Lincoln through His Words.* New York: Random House, 2006.

———. *Lincoln's Greatest Speech: The Second Inaugural.* New York: Simon and Schuster, 2002.

Whitney, Henry C. *Life on the Circuit with Lincoln.* Boston: Estes and Lauriat, 1892.

Wills, Garry. *Lincoln at Gettysburg.* New York: Simon and Schuster, 2006.

Wilson, Douglas L., and Rodney O. Davis, eds. *Herndon's Informants: Letters, Interviews, and Statements about Abraham Lincoln.* Champaign: University of Illinois Press, 1998.

Wilson, Douglas L. "Abraham Lincoln's Indiana and the Spirit of Mortal." *Indiana Magazine of History* 87, no. 2 (1991): 155–70.

———. *Herndon on Lincoln: Letters.* Urbana, IL: Knox College Lincoln Studies Center and University of Illinois Press, 2016.

———. *Honor's Voice: The Transformation of Abraham Lincoln.* New York: Alfred A. Knopf, 1998.

———. *Lincoln before Washington: New Perspectives on the Illinois Years.* Champaign: University of Illinois Press, 1997.

———. *Lincoln's Sword.* New York: Vintage, 2007.

———. "William H. Herndon on Lincoln's Fatalism." *Journal of the Abraham Lincoln Association* 35, no. 2 (2014): 1–18.

———. "William H. Herndon and Mary Todd Lincoln." *Journal of the Abraham Lincoln Association* 22, no. 2 (2001): 1–26.

Wilson, Rufus Rockwell, ed. *Intimate Memories of Lincoln.* Elmira, NY: Primavera Press, 1945.

Winger, Stewart. *Lincoln, Religion, and Romantic Cultural Politics.* Northern Illinois University Press, 2002.

Winkle, Kenneth J. *The Young Eagle: The Life of Abraham Lincoln.* New York: Taylor Trade Publishing, 2001.

Wolf, William J. *The Religion of Abraham Lincoln.* New York: Seabury Press, 1963.

INDEX

Page locators in italics refer to the appendix,
figures, photographs, and tables

abolitionists, 28, 30, 46, 50, 60, 107; Douglass, *78*, 113

Adams, Charles Francis, 3, 117

Age of Reason (Paine), 24, 25

"almost chosen" people, Americans as, 86

Anderson, Robert, 87–88

antimissionism, 18–20, 26, 207–8n41

apologetic, Christian, 40

Army of Northern Virginia, 102, 130, 137

Army of the Potomac, 1, 98–99, 101–2, 105, 109, 111–12, 121–23

atheism, 25, 144, 211n41223–224n11

Baker, Edward, 36, 37

Baltimore Presbyterian Synod, 115, 142, *173*

Baptists, 13–15, 17–18, 25, 206n15, 207n33

Baptized Licking Locust Association of Regular Baptists, 12–13, 18

Barrow, David, 12–13

Barton, William E., 4, 25, 40, 140–41

Bateman, Newton, 141, 223n5

Bates, Edward, 84

Beardstown Chronicle, 26

Beecher, Henry Ward, 81, 135

Berry, Polly Ewing, 12

Berry, Richard, Jr., 12

Bible, 204–5n15; exhibitive uses of, 34; Garrison's rejection of, 52; and Lincoln's decisionmaking process, 4; moral authority of accepted by Lincoln, 144–45; Northern ministers' use of, 52–53; as personal driving force for Lincoln, 67, 204n9; presentation of to Lincoln by Loyal Colored People of Baltimore, 129; as schoolbook, 16–17; used to justify and oppose slavery, 46, 52–53. *See also* Christ, Lincoln's references to; New Testament, Lincoln's references to; Old Testament, Lincoln's references to; Psalms, Lincoln's references to

Bible, King James, 5, *80*, 207n27, 222n1; Gettysburg Address reminiscent of, 116; Oxford edition presented to Lincoln, 32

Black Hawk, Chief, 22

Black Hawk War, 22–23

Blackstone, William, 27, 29

Blair, Montgomery, 84

Book of Common Prayer, 116

Booth, John Wilkes, 138

Boritt, Gabor, 38

born again conversion experiences, 140, 222n2

Bragg, Braxton, 107, 114, 117

Breckenridge, John C., 83

Brooks, Noah, 79, 98, 130, 133, *152*

Browning, Orville H., 91

Bruce, Robert, 143–44

Buchanan, James, 52, 54

Burkhimer, Michael, 93

Burnside, Ambrose E., 105, 106, 110

Bushnell, Horace, 118

Bushrod, Nancy (former enslaved person), 139

Butler, William, 21

Cabinet, 3, 83–84; April 14, 1865 meeting, 138; and Emancipation Proclamation, 100, 102–3

Cady, John F., 18–19

Calhoun, John, 46

Calvinism, 7, 121, 206n16, 207n38; antimissionism, 18–19, 20; and Book of Job, 111–12; Lincoln's, 34, 35, 37, 128, 134, 140–41, 216n37; Philadelphia Confession of Faith, 13; Predestinarianism, 140–41, 206n16; ultra-Calvinistic (Hyper-Calvinistic), 18, 35, 207n39. *See also* Baptists; Presbyterianism

Cameron, Simon, 84, 94

Carmen, Caleb, 21

Carroll, B. H., 18

Cartwright, Peter, 25–27, 37, 73

Carwardine, Richard, 36

Chase, Salmon P., 84, 102–3

Chicago Tribune, 51

Christ, Lincoln's references to, 31, 33, 46–47; Golden Rule, 39; Sermon on the Mount, 62; Sermon on the Plain, 48

Christian's Defense, The (Smith), 40, 75

Civil War: border states, 89, 90, 97, 117; Fort Sumter, 87–88, 97; habeas corpus, suspension of, 89–90; Kentucky, troops in, 94; Lee's surrender at Appomattox Court House, 137, 138; Lincoln's views of God's plans

for, 98–99, 110, 115, 126; measures taken by Lincoln, 89–90; objectives of, 2–3; peace talks, 124–25; theological aspects of, 135; war in the West, 1

Civil War battles: Battle of the Wilderness (1863), 121; Chancellorsville, Virginia (1863), 1, 111, 127; Chattanooga (1863), 119; Chickamauga Creek (1863), 114; Cold Harbor (1863), 122; Five Forks (April 1–2, 1865), 137; Fredericksburg, Virginia (1862), 106, 109, 111; Gettysburg, Pennsylvania (1863), 112, 115; Grant's advance on Atlanta (1863), 116–17; Hampton Roads, Virginia (1862), 96; Kentucky and Tennessee, 94; Manassas (Second Manassas, August 28–30, 1862), 101, 127; Manassas, Virginia (Battle of Bull Run, 1861), 90–91; Petersburg (1863), 123; Sharpsburg (Antietam, 1862), 102, 105; Sherman's advance on Atlanta (1863), 123, 125; Sherman's march from Atlanta to Savannah, 130; Shiloh (April 6–7, 1861), 98; Spotsylvania Court House (1863), 122; Stones River, Tennessee (1862), 106–7; summer of 1864, 127; Vicksburg, Mississippi (1863), 112

Clary, Royal A., 21

Clay, Henry C., 49, 61; Lincoln's eulogy for, 41–42, *160*

Collected Works of Abraham Lincoln (Basler, ed.), 4, 5, 70, 102; 199 biblical allusions or quotes in, 7, 8; communications from 1861, 93; memoranda ("fragments"), 38, 63–64, 102, 217–18n24

Commentaries on the Laws of England (Blackstone), 27, 29

Commonwealth (Frankfort, Kentucky), 120

Compromise of 1850, 43

Congress: 30th (1848–1849), 38–39; 38th, 132; 39th, 132–33; annual message to (1862), 106, 125, *167, 174, 201,* 220n19; First Confiscation Act (1861), 97; second annual message to (1862), 105–6, 107; Second Confiscation Act (July 17, 1862), 99, 100; Senate committee on the territories, 43; senatorial campaign, 1854, 44–46; special session (July 4, 1861), 90

Conkling, James C., 113

Constitution, US, 51; abolition amendment, 130, 132; "covert language" about slavery in, 65; habeas corpus, suspension of, 89–90; Lincoln's pledge of dedication to, 86–87; proposal to change preamble, 118–19; signers of, 81; Thirteenth Amendment, 130, 132–33, 218n29

conversion experience, language of, 34

covenant, concept of, 125

CSS *Virginia,* 96

Curtin, Andrew, 106

Dakota warriors, execution of, 106

Davis, David, 3, 78, 141

Davis, Jefferson, 87, 88, 117, 125, 138

Dayton, William L., 51

Declaration of Independence, 130; equated with creation of man in divine image, 59–60; in Gettysburg Address, 115; invoked by Lincoln to oppose slavery, 45–49, 51–54, 58, 59–60, 62; Lincoln's 1861 notes on, 84; Lincoln's pledge of dedication to, 86–87

deism, 36, 144, 210n26, 224n12

Deming, Henry C., 210n27

Democratic National Convention (1860), 82–83

Democratic Party: and 1864 election, 124; Freeport Doctrine and split in, 62, 82–83; and Missouri Compromise, 43–44; "State equality" position, 51

Dickey, Theophilus Lyle, 44

Dix, Dorothea, 95

Donald, David, 141

Douglas, Stephen A., 6, 31, 74; and 1854 senatorial campaign, 44–50; claims of indifference to slavery, 46, 60–61, 67; *Dred Scott* decision attributed to by Lincoln, 52; Freeport Doctrine, 62, 82–83; on House Divided metaphor, 58; on inequality of races, 53; and Kansas-Nebraska Act, 43–45, 47, 54; lack of Bible knowledge, 44; and Missouri Compromise, 43–44; popular sovereignty stance, 44, 47, 54, 60; as presidential candidate (1860), 82–83; State Constitution question, 62. *See also* Lincoln-Douglas debates

Douglass, Frederick, 78, 113–14, 135–36, 138

Downs, Thomas, 14

Downs, William, 1314

Dred Scott decision, 51–52, 53, 61, 65, 69–70

E. Barton, William, 24

Edwards, Elizabeth, 31

Edwards, Jonathan, 89

Edwards, Ninian, 31, 40

Elmore, E. A., 116

"emancipationist" churches, 13

Emancipation Proclamation, 125, 218–19n2, 218n30; draft (1862), 100,

Emancipation Proclamation (*continued*) 102; limits of, 132; preliminary, 103–4; signing of, 108

equality of man, 46, 51, 53, 58, 60–61, 63–64, 64–65, 67, 114–15, 137–38; Black suffrage proposal, 137–38; Lincoln's progress toward idea of, 114

Euclid, 39–40

Everett, Edward, 115

fatalism, 38, 42, 210n22, 215n26; necessity, doctrine of, 35, 37–38, 221n24

First Confiscation Act (1861), 97

First Presbyterian Church (Springfield, Illinois), 6, 40

Ford, Thomas, 17–18

Ford's Theatre, 139

Fornieri, Joseph, 25, 27, 35

Fort Sumter (South Carolina), 87–88, 97

Founders, 46, 48, 65–66, 81

Freed, Edwin D., 41

Freeport Doctrine, 62, 82–83

Frémont, John C., 51, 122

Garrison, William Lloyd, 52

General Land Office of Illinois, 39

Gettysburg Address (November 19, 1863), 124, 136–37, 155, 161, 193, 195; birth, death, and rebirth theme in, 115–16, 219nn24, 25, 220n26

Godey's Lady's Book, 114, 129

Golden Rule, 52, 53, 64, 67

Graham, Mentor, 21–22, 24, 25, 27, 208n17

Grant, Ulysses S., 1, 94, 98, 112, 114, 116–17, 137, 138

Great Britain, 117, 220n27

Greeley, Horace, 54, 82, 100

Green, Bowling, 24

Grigsby, Aaron, 19

Guelzo, Allen C., 127, 223n5

Gurley, Phineas D., 6, 76, 88–89, 111, 112, 115; funeral sermon for Willie, 96–97

Gurney, Mrs. Eliza P., 103–4, 127–28

Hale, Sara Josepha, 114, 129

Hamlin, Hannibal, 84

Hanks, Dennis, 11, 15, 17, 19

Hanks, John, 20

Hanks, Lucy, 11–12, 205n10

Hay, John, 3, 102, 113, 126, 217n12

Head, Jesse, 12

Hein, David, 35

Henning, Fanny, 32–33, 34–35

Herndon, J. Rowan, 21, 22, 24

Herndon, William H., 11–12, 24, 37, 41, 75; on "house divided" statement, 56; on Lincoln's faith, 141, 144, 211n41, 223–24n11, 223n5, 224n12; on Lincoln's fervor, 50–51, 55

Hill, Samuel, 24–26, 37

Hitt, Walter, 65

Hood, John Bell, 125, 130

Hooker, Joseph, 1, 109, 111

"house divided" scripture (Mark 3:25), 7–8, 56–57, 59, 61, 63, 65, 68–69, 83, 213n2

House Divided Speech (Republican Party of Illinois convention, June 16, 1858), 56–58, 60–64, 69, 175, 184, 185; certified transcript of, 188; Douglas's view of as call for war, 58, 61, 69

Howells, William Dean, 86

Huhn, Wilson, 57

hymn books, 17, 34

Ide, George B., 121–22

Illinois Eighth Judicial Circuit, 39, 44

*Inspired Wisdom of Abraham Lincoln,
The* (Ostergard), 7–8

Jacksonian politics, 37
Jefferson, Thomas, 67–68
Johnson, Andrew, 138–39
Johnson, Joseph, 99, 125, 137
Johnston, Daniel, 16
Johnston, John D, 19, 40–41
Johnston, Joseph E., 117, 123, 133, 138
Jones, John, 27
Journal (Louisville, Kentucky), 83

Kansas-Nebraska Act (1853), 6, 44–45,
   47, 54
Keckley, Elizabeth, 1, 77, 95, 111
Kentucky, 89, 90, 94, 97
Kentucky Preceptor (textbook), 17
Knob Creek farm (Lincoln family
   home), 13–14
Know-Nothings, 50, 212n20
Knox, William, 9, *10*, 40, 205n3

Lecompton Constitution (Kansas),
   54, 58
Lee, Robert E., 1, 99, 101, 105, 106,
   111–12, 119, 130; surrender at Appomattox Court House, 137, 138
Lincoln, Abraham: assassination
   plots against, 87, 215n19; as assistant
   surveyor, 24; belief in himself as
   "instrument" of God, 35, 86, 103–4,
   107, 120, 141, 215n16; as biblical
   monotheist, 144; in Black Hawk
   War, 22–23; books accessible to,
   13, 16, 27, 203n5; Calvinism of, 34,
   35, 37, 128, 134, 140–41, 216n37;
   decision-making process, 3–4, 103;
   democracy, definition of, 64; early
   years, 5–7, 12–20; effect of Willie's
   death on, 95–96; forgiving nature

of, 59, 110, 135, 137, 138; heaven, not
often referenced by, 41, 143–44,
223n10; as "Honest Abe," 22; Inauguration Day, March 4, 1865, 133;
increasing faith of, 33; as "infidel,"
4, 25, 37, 211n41, 224n12; jocoseness
of, 11, 21; journey from Springfield
to Washington (1861), 84–86; as
junior partner in Stuart's law firm,
28; lack of religious affiliation, 29,
36, 37, 40, 204n9, 209n1, 210n27;
law, study of, 23–24; law practice
of, 37, 39, 42; marriage, 35–36;
melancholia of, 9–11, 27, 31–32, 35,
42, 223–24n11; ministers, meetings
with, 101–2, 104; photograph of, 71;
as private about personal beliefs,
141; providence, conception of, 17,
33, 35, 89, 96, 98–99, 101–2, 104–5,
107, 134; reading habits of, 2, 5, 19,
22, 39–40, 91–92, 111, 213n33; "reflections" of, 4; school attendance, 16,
203n7; second inaugural ceremony,
79; as skeptic, 24, 32, 142, 210n22; as
transformational leader, 3, 70, 123,
135, 203n4; war measures taken by,
89–90. *See also* biblical language
used by Lincoln; Christ, Lincoln's
references to; Lincoln, Abraham:
campaigns; Lincoln, Abraham: letters; Lincoln, Abraham: speeches;
Lincoln, Abraham: writings; New
Testament, Lincoln's references to;
Old Testament, Lincoln's references
to; providence, Lincoln's conception of
Lincoln, Abraham: campaigns: presidential (1860), 82–84; presidential
(1864), 130; senatorial campaign,
1854, 44–50; state legislature, 1832,
22–23; state legislature, 1834, 24–25;

Lincoln, Abraham: campaigns (*continued*)
state legislature, 1836, 28; state legislature, 1840, 31; state legislature, 1846, 37–38

Lincoln, Abraham: letters: to delegation of Quakers, 99, *167*; to Drake, Charles D., *179*; to Durley, Williamson, 37, *182, 196*; Evangelical Lutherans, response to, 99, *166*; to Galloway, Samuel, *201*; to Gurney, Eliza P., 103–4, 127–28, *128, 167, 198, 201*; to Hall, Amanda H., *168*; to Hampton, Moses, 39, *194–95*; to Herndon, William H., 39, *165*; to Hodges, Albert G., 120, 127, *128, 169*; to Ide, George B., 121–22, *152, 163, 178, 180, 181, 197*; to Johnson, Reverdy, 100, *193*; to Johnston, John D., 40–41, *165, 173, 191*; to Lamon, Ward A., *200*; to Lincoln, Mary, *201*; to McClernand, John A., *200*; to Morton, Oliver P., *183*; to a Mrs. Mann, 120–21; to New York Delegation, *183*; to Owen, Mary, 28, 29; to Peck, John M., 39, *181*; to Pierce, Henry L., 66–67, *182*; to Prentice, George D., 83–84, *183*; to Raymond, Henry J., 84, *191*; to religious groups (1862), 99; to Russell, Caleb, *196*; to Sherman, William T., *175*; to Speed, Joshua, 32–33, 50, *165, 188*, 215n16; to Speer, William S., 83, *192*; to Trumbull, Lyman, 83, *184–85*; to Victoria, Queen, *163*; to Weed, Thurlow, 136, *168*

Lincoln, Abraham: speeches: address on colonization (August 14, 1862), *179*; annual message to Congress (1862), 106, 125, *167, 174, 201*, 220n19; Bloomington, Illinois (1856, "lost speech"), 50–51, 55; Bloomington, Illinois (April 6, 1858), 55; Bloomington, Illinois (September 4, 1858), 62, *180, 187*; Carlinville, Illinois (August 31, 1858), 62, *186*; Chicago (July 10, 1858), 58, *170, 179, 186*; Cincinnati, Ohio (September 17, 1859), 68–69, *153, 171, 188, 191, 194*; Clinton, Illinois (September 2, 1858), 62, *186–87*; Columbus, Ohio (September 16, 1859), 67–68, *164, 171, 177*; to Congress (July 4, 1861), 90; Cooper Union (February 27, 1860), 81–82, *189*; December 1839 speech to the state legislature, 31; December 1856 speech to the state legislature, *199*; Dover, NH (March 2, 1860), *189*; Edwardsville, Illinois (September 11, 1858), 62, *181, 185*; eulogy for Clay (1852), 41–42, *160*; eulogy for Zachary Taylor (1850), 40, *184*; Farewell Address at Springfield (February 11, 1861), 85, *177, 195*; first inaugural address (March 4, 1861), 87; "First Lecture on Discoveries and Inventions" (1858), 7, 55, *149, 150, 151, 153–63 passim, 166, 173, 176, 184*, 213n32; Gettysburg Address (November 19, 1863), 115–16, 124, 136–37, *155, 161, 193, 195*, 219nn24, 25; Hartford, Connecticut (1860), 82, *189, 190, 198, 199*; House Divided Speech (Republican Party of Illinois convention, June 16, 1858), 56–58, 60–64, 69, *175, 184, 185*; to House of Representative (January, 1848), 39, *153*; Independence Hall, Philadelphia (1861), 86–87, *172*; Lewistown, Illinois (August 17, 1858), 59–60, *150*; Lyceum Address ("The Perpetuation of our Political Institutions,"

1838), 29–30, 42, *174*, *182*, *197*, *200*; National Fast Day proclamation (August 12, 1861), 92–93, *164*, *169*, *177*, *199*; New Jersey Senate address (February 21, 1861), 86, *162*; New York Workingmen's Democratic Republican Association, 119, *202*; Peoria speech against slavery (October 16, 1854), 45–50, *150*, *174*, *179*, *190*, *193*, *195*, *202*; reply to Chicago Christians, 101, *158*; Republican banquet, Chicago (December 10, 1856), 51; Republican Party, 1856 ("lost speech"), 50–51, 55; at Sanitary Fairs, 119, 121, *165*, *173*, *196*, 220n10; second annual message to Congress (1862), 105–6, 107; second inaugural address, 6, 8, 17, 33, 120, 127, *128*, 133–38, *153*, *167*, *168*, *172*, *180*, *183*, *196*, *198*, *200–201*; soldiers, talks to, 91, 123–24; Springfield (July 17, 1858), 53, *170*, *186*, *192*; Springfield (June 26, 1857), 53, *170*; Springfield Scott club (1852), 42, *154*, *199*; stump speeches (1858), 62; to the sub-treasury (December 26, 1839), *194*; Washington Temperance Society address (1842), 33–34, 42, *157*, *177*, *188*, *190–92*, *197*, *202*, 209–10n14; White House lawn, April 11, 1865, 137; Wisconsin State Agricultural Society, 69. *See also* Lincoln-Douglas debates (1858)

Lincoln, Abraham: writings: campaign circular (1846), 37–38; campaign circular from Whig Committee (1843), *185*; Constitution, fragment on, 84, *173*; directive to Stanton, *193*; Emancipation Proclamation draft (1862), 100, 102–4; fragment on proslavery theology, *166*, *172*, *175*, *178*; "ghost written" political jab at Cartwright, 26, 37; *Handbill Replying to Religious Infidelity*, 4; letter to Union supporters in Springfield (August, 1863), 113; "Meditation on the Divine Will" (undated), 101, 126–28, *128*, *166*, *175*, 217–18n24, 221n25; memoranda ("fragments"), 38, 63–64, 102; national proclamations of thanksgiving, fasting, and prayer, 93, 97, 109–10, *164*; political handbill (March 9, 1832), 23; "The President's Last, Shortest, and Best Speech," 130–31, *152*; Proclamation for a Day of Prayer (August 4, 1863), 123; proclamation for Thanksgiving and prayer (May 9, 1863), 121, 220n11; Proclamation of a Day or Prayer (July 7, 1864), *176*; "Proclamation of Appointing a National Fast Day" (March 30, 1863), 109–10, *169*, *176*, *178*; Proclamation of Thanksgiving (July 15, 1862), 112–13; Proclamation of Thanksgiving and Prayer (September 3, 1864), 125–26, *168*; proclamation revoking Hunter's military order of emancipation (1862), *156*; religious essays (on infidelity or universal salvation), 4, 24–25; *Sangamo Journal* announcement (1836), 28; on slavery (March 3, 1837), 28; Thanksgiving national holiday proclamation (October 3, 1863), 114–15, *169*, 216n39; Thanksgiving national holiday proclamation (October 20, 1864), 129–30, *168*; verses written in copy book at age fifteen, 9–11

Lincoln, Abraham (Sr.), 11
Lincoln, Edward Baker "Eddy," 37, 40, 42, 144

Lincoln, Josiah, 11
Lincoln, Mary, 1–2, 31, 40, 95, 138–39, 217n12; photograph of, 72; wedding, 35–36
Lincoln, Mordecai, 11
Lincoln, Nancy Hanks, 11–12, 15–165, 20
Lincoln, Robert Todd, 36
Lincoln, Sarah, 12–15, 19, 209n14
Lincoln, Sarah Bush "Sally" Johnston, 16, 19–20, 85
Lincoln, Thomas, 11–15, 19–20, 40–41, 206n21; family Bible, 80
Lincoln, Thomas, Jr., 14
Lincoln, Thomas "Tad," 42, 92, 95, 111
Lincoln, William Wallace "Willie," 40, 77, 95–97, 111, 144
Lincoln-Douglas debates (1858): Alton (October 15), 65–66, 69, 70, 187; Charleston (September 18), 63; Freeport, 61–62; Galesburg (October 7), 64; Jonesboro (September 15), 62–63, 187; Ottawa (August 21), 60, 157, 170, 186; Quincy (October 13), 64, 170. See also Lincoln, Abraham: speeches
Little Mount Separate Baptist Church, 13, 14, 206n16
Little Pigeon Association, 18, 26
Little Pigeon Creek Baptist Church, 11, 14–15
Little Pigeon Creek Church Community, 17
Little Pigeon Creek region (Indiana), 14–15
Louisiana, 137
Louisiana Purchase territory, 43
Lovejoy, Elijah Parish, 30, 65
Loyal Colored People of Baltimore, 129
Lyceum forums, 29

Manifest Destiny, 43
Maryland, 89–90, 97
Matheny, Judge, 23
McClellan. George B., 91, 94, 98, 99, 101, 105, 124; presidential campaign (1864), 130
McDowell, Irwin, 90–91
McIntosh, Frank, 30
McPike, Henry G., 69
Meade, George Gordon, 111, 112
Medill, Joseph, 51
Methodism, 33, 34, 89, 140
Mexican American War, 39, 43
Miegs, Montgomery, 94
Miles, James, 70
"milk sickness (tremetol vomiting), 15, 20
Miller, William Lee, 88
Minnesota territory, 106
Missouri, 89, 90, 97
Missouri Compromise of 1820, 43, 45–47
Morel, Lucas, 64, 215n25
"Mortality" (Knox), 9, 10, 40, 205n3

natural law interpretation of morality, 27
necessity, doctrine of, 35, 37–38, 221n24
New Salem, Illinois, 20
New School Presbyterianism, 33, 34, 89
New Testament, Lincoln's references to: 1 Corinthians 1:20, 196; 1 Corinthians 1:20–21, 109; 1 Corinthians 9:24, 124; 1 Corinthians 13:8, 36; 1 Corinthians 15:22, 25; 1 Corinthians 15:52, 197; 1 John 5:7, 201; 1 Peter 4:12, 104, 106, 201; 2 Corinthians 5:10, 122, 197; Acts 1:8, 124; Acts 13:46, 49, 195; Acts 19:15–16, 62; Acts 20:32, 85, 195;

Colossians 1:16–17, 105, *198*; Colossians 3:8 and 14, 135, *198*; Colossians 3:12, *198*; Colossians 3:13, 100, 118; Ephesians 1:4–5, 144; Hebrews 4:12, *199*; Hebrews 4:16, *199*; Hebrews 9:27, *199*; Hebrews 12:1, *200*; Hebrews 12:2, *200*; James 1:27, 135, *200–201*; John, Gospel of, 116; John 1:11, 49, *193*; John 3:3, 116, *193*, 222n2; John 6:26, 68–69, *194*; John 6:70, 31, *194*; John 12:6, 31, *194*; John 13:27, 39, *194*; John 15:13, 116, *195*; John 15:16, 144; Luke 1:57, 116; Luke 5:32, 82, *189*, *190*; Luke 6:44–45, 37; Luke 6:45, 34, 48, *190*; Luke 8:35, 34, *190*; Luke 11:23, 69, *191*; Luke 11:29, 84, *191*; Luke 12:6–7, 41, *191*; Luke 12:10, 34, *192*; Luke 15:7, 58–59, *192*; Luke 16:31, 83, *192*; Luke 17:3, *193*; Luke 17:3–4, 100, 118; Mark 3:25, 7, 56–57, 59, 61, 63, 65, 68, 83, *185–88*, 213n2; Mark 5:4, 34, *188*; Mark 5:15, *188*; Mark 10:8, 35, *188*; Matthew, Mark, Luke, and John, 5; Matthew 4:8–9, *178*; Matthew 4:8–10, 122; Matthew 5:39, 135; Matthew 5:42, 63, *178*; Matthew 5:48, 58, *179*; Matthew 6:11, *179*; Matthew 6:13, *179*; Matthew 6:24, 48, *179*; Matthew 6:34, *180*; Matthew 7:1, 122, 134, 135, *180*; Matthew 7:6, 62, *180*, *181*; Matthew 7:12, 28, 39, 67, 122, 135, *181*, *182*; Matthew 7:16–17, *183*; Matthew 16:18, 30, 86, *182*, *183*; Matthew 18:7, 6, 134, *183*; Matthew 18:13, *183*; Matthew 18:22, 83, 135, *183*; Matthew 19:14, 40; Matthew 23:12, 40, *184*; Matthew 24:31, *184*; Matthew 24:35, 7; Matthew 24:41, *184*; Matthew 26:72, 83, *184*; Philippians 2:7–8, 34, *197*; Revelation 2:4, 82, *201*; Revelation 6:2, 34; Revelation 7:14, 48; Revelation 13:7, 119; Romans 3:8, 37, *196*; Romans 12:18, 135; Romans 14:12, 121, *196*; Thessalonians 3:12, *198*, *199*

New York Avenue Presbyterian Church (Washington, D. C.), 6, 88–89, 97
New York Times, 84
New York Tribune, 54, 82
New York Workingmen's Democratic Republican Association, 119
Niagara Falls, 39
Nicolay, John, 86, 98, 102, 126, 144, 217n12
Niebuhr, Reinhold, 222n10
Noll, Mark, 52, 53, 127, 135
Northwest Ordinance of 1787, 45

"offences," 6
Offutt, Denton, 21, 22
Old Testament, Lincoln's references to: 1 Samuel 12:3, 122, *163*; 2 Chronicles 7:14, 110, *164*, *168*; 2 Chronicles 20:17, 35; 2 Chronicles 20:29, 68; 2 Chronicles 30:9, 41, *165*; 2 Kings 22:13, 68, *164*; 2 Samuel 22:2, 122; 2 Samuel 22:29, 7; Deuteronomy 3:11, *161*; Deuteronomy 4:20, *162*; Deuteronomy 7:6, 86, *162*; Deuteronomy 8:9, *162*; Deuteronomy 19:5, *162*; Deuteronomy 22:10, *163*; Deuteronomy 27:5, *163*; Deuteronomy 32:39, *163*; Ecclesiastes 1:4, 105, *174*; Ecclesiastes 1:9, 29, *174*; Ecclesiastes 3:7, *174*; Ecclesiastes 3:13, 29; Ecclesiastes 9:14, *175*; Esther 7:10, *165*; Exodus 4:22, 61, *157*; Exodus 12:29–30, *157*; Exodus 12:37, *158*; Exodus 13:21, *158*; Exodus 14:9, *158*; Exodus 14:13, 35, *158*; Exodus 14:23, *159*; Exodus 14:25, *159*; Exodus 14:28, *160*;

Old Testament (*continued*)
  Exodus 15:1, *160*; Exodus 28:42, *160*;
  Exodus 35:25, *160*; Exodus 35:26,
  161; Exodus 35:35, *161*; Ezekiel 34:26,
  92, *177*; Ezekiel 37:9, *177*; Genesis
  1:26–27, 59–60, *150*; Genesis 2:15,
  150; Genesis 3:1–3, 49, *150*; Genesis
  3:7, *151*; Genesis 3:17–19, *151*; Genesis
  3:19, 7, 26, 38, 53–54, 68, 69, 130,
  152–53, 212–13n28; Genesis 3:21, *153*;
  Genesis 4:10, 39, *153*; Genesis 4:22,
  154; Genesis 5:24, *154*; Genesis 6:14,
  154; Genesis 9:23, *154*; Genesis 14:23,
  155; Genesis 16:16, 116, *155*; Genesis
  22:3, *155*; Genesis 24:61, *155*; Genesis 27:28, *156*; Genesis 27:36, 124;
  Genesis 41:43, *156*; Genesis 42:26,
  156; Genesis 46:29, *156*; Genesis
  49:13, *157*; Habakkuk 2:2, 56, 213n2;
  Hebrews 4:16, 92; Hebrews 9:22, 111;
  Hebrews 12:2, 29; Isaiah 2:4, 126;
  Isaiah 9:2, 130, *175*; Isaiah 11:6, 64, *175*;
  Isaiah 14:24, 127, *175*; Isaiah 33:21, *176*;
  Isaiah 33:23, *176*; Isaiah 34: 2, 109;
  Isaiah 34:2, 123, *176*; Isaiah 41:10, 85;
  Isaiah 53:1, 67–68, *177*; Jeremiah 3:21,
  110, *178*; Job, 218n26; Job 1:21, 111;
  Job 2:4, *165*; Job 7:6, *166*; Job 12:23,
  99, *166*; Job 18:17, *166*; Job 23:13,
  63–64, 126, 128, 129, 134, *166*, *167*;
  Job 28:28, 92; Job 29:3, 7, 99, 104, 105,
  129, *167*; Job 36:3, 103; Job 40:15, *167*;
  Job 42:6, 130, *168*; Leviticus 25:38, 116;
  Numbers 35:16, *161*; Pentateuch, 5;
  Proverbs 3:5–6, 85, 115, *173*; Proverbs
  6:6, *173*; Proverbs 9:10, 92; Proverbs
  15:3, 85; Proverbs 16:9, *173*; Proverbs
  19:21, 121; Proverbs 25:11, 84, *173*;
  Proverbs 30:5, 41, *173*; Proverbs 31:28,
  48, *174*. *See also* Psalms, Lincoln's
  references to

Oregon boundary question, 39
Ostergard, Philip, 7–8
Owens, Mary, 24, 28, 29

Paine, Thomas, 24, 25, 129
Parker, Daniel, 18–19, 26, 207–8n41
Parrillo, Nicholas R., 93, 110, 113
Pemberton, John, 112
Pettit, John, 46
Philadelphia Confession of Faith, 13
Pierce, Franklin, 44, 52
Pillow, Gideon J., 94
Pomroy, Rebecca, 77, 95–96
Pope, John, 101
popular sovereignty, 44, 47, 48–49, 60
"Prayer of Twenty Millions, The"
  (Greeley), 100
Presbyterianism: New School, 33, 34,
  89; Old School, 88–89, 107, 141. *See
  also* Calvinism
providence, Lincoln's conception of,
  17, 35, 89, 96, 98–99, 101–2, 107; and
  letter to Gurney, 104–5; in letter to
  supporters (August, 1863), 113; in
  Proclamation of Thanksgiving and
  Prayer (September 3, 1863), 125–26,
  168
Psalms, Lincoln's references to: Psalm
  19:9, 17, 120, 134, *168*; Psalm 22:28,
  126, 136, *168*; Psalm 32:8, 8; Psalm
  33:12, 109, *169*; Psalm 52:1, 120, *169*;
  Psalm 78, 38, 56, *169*; Psalm 78:38,
  56, 114; Psalm 90:10, 116; Psalm
  111:10, 92, *169*; Psalm 119:105, 7, 129;
  Psalm 128:2, 7, 53–54, 59, 60, 62,
  64, 66, 68–69, 82, 83, *170–72*; Psalm
  137:5–6, 87, *172*; Psalm 147:3, 135, *172*.
  See also Old Testament, Lincoln's
  references to

Quakers, 99, 104, 108, 128, *167*

Radical Republicans, 122
Regular Baptists, 13–14
Republican National Convention
(1860), 82
Republican Party, 54; as "Black
Republican Party," 60, 63; first na-
tional convention, 51; Founders, po-
sition on, 81; Illinois, 50–51; Radical
Republicans, 122; and Thirteenth
Amendment, 132
Republican Party of Illinois, 50, 55,
56. *See also* House Divided Speech
(Republican Party of Illinois con-
vention, June 16, 1858)
revivalism, 89
Richmond, Virginia, 87, 117, 122–23
Robinson, Robert, 17
Rosecrans, William, 106–7, 114
Ruins (Volney), 24, 25
rule of law, 30
Rutledge, Ann, 24, 27
Rutledge, James, 24
Rutledge, Robert B., 22

Sanitary Fairs, 119, 121, *165, 173*
Schwartz, Earl, 4
Scripps, John Locke, 13–14
Second Presbyterian Church (Spring-
field, Illinois), 33
Separate Baptists, 13–15
Seward, William H., 82, 84, 88, 93, 100,
125, 216n39, 219n21
Shakespeare, William, 132
Shenk, Joshua Wolf, 13
Sheridan, Philip, 137
Sherman, William Tecumseh, 91, 112,
123, 125, 130, 132–33
Short, James, 21, 22
"Shortness of Life and the Goodness
of God, The" (Watts), 9–11, *10*, 205n3
Simon, Paul, 30

slavery: differences between biblical
times and nineteenth century,
52–53; Douglas's claims of indifference to, 46, 60–61, 67; enslaved
people, attempts to free, 97, 98, 99;
goal of abolishing, 2–3; Jefferson's
view, 67–68; Lincoln's attempts
to undermine, 97–98; Lincoln's
early antislavery statements, 28;
Lincoln seeks God's will for, 98–99;
Lincoln's moral arguments against,
6, 45–46, 45–47, 49, 51–52, 55, 58–63,
66–67, 81, 130; Lincoln's Peoria
speech against, 45–50, *150, 174, 179,
190, 193, 195, 202*; as national sin,
67, 70, 107, 110, 120, 123, 133; and
territories, 43–44; in Washington,
D. C., 28. *See also* Emancipation
Proclamation
Smith, Abraham, 60
Smith, James, 6, 40, 75, 217n12
Soul of Abraham Lincoln, The (Bar-
ton), 141
South Fork Baptist Church (Eliza-
bethtown, Kentucky), 13
Sparrow, Elizabeth, 12, 15
Sparrow, Thomas, 12, 15
Speed, Fanny, 73
Speed, Joshua F., 5, 29, 31–33, 42,
73; "balance on faith" statement
attributed to Lincoln, 142–43,
223n7; last visit with Lincoln, 143;
Lincoln's letters to, 32–33, 50, *158,
188*, 215n16; on Lincoln's religious
beliefs, 141–43; marriage of, 34–35
Speed, Lucy, 32, 33
Spencer, J. H., 13, 14
Spurgeon, Charles, 111–12
Stanton, Edwin, 94, 118, *193*
State of the Union addresses, 105–6
Stephens, Alexander, 84

Stoddard, William O., 98

Strong, George Templeton, 120

Stuart, John Todd, 27, 28

Supreme Court: *Dred Scott* decision, 51–52, 53, 61, 65, 69–70

Sweet, William Warren, 18

Swett, Leonard, 3–4

Taft, Julia (Bayne), 2, 76, 91–92, 217n12

Taney, Roger, 51–52, 89–90

Taylor, Zachary, 40

temperance, 33–34

Tennessee, 94, 98

territories, 43; Founders' views on expansion of slavery into, 81; free-state supporters, 54; State Constitution question, 61–62

Thanksgiving, 114–15, 129–30

theism, 210n26, 223n11

Thirteenth Amendment (abolition amendment), 130, 132–33, 218n29

Thomas, George H., 130

transformational leadership, 3, 70, 123, 135, 203n4

Trumbull, Lyman, 50, 83, *184*

Truth, Sojourner, 138

Tucker, J. W., 52

Union Army: 166th Ohio Regiment, 123–24; Black troops, 109, 113–14, 117, 121, 124–25, 139; death sentences for soldiers, 110–11. *See also* Army of the Potomac

universalism, 25

USS *Monitor*, 96

Vallandigham, Clement L., 110

Vicksburg, Mississippi, campaign of, 1

Volney, C. F., 24, 25

War Department, 1–2, 94

Washington, George, 82, 85

Washington Temperance Society, 33–34

Watts, Isaac, 9–11, *10*, 17, 34, 205n3

Webster, Daniel, 49

Weed, Thurlow, 136

Welles, Gideon, 84, 88, 103, 125

West Virginia, 117

Whig Party, 36, 41; Clay and Webster, 49; senatorial campaign, 1854, 44–45

White, Ronald C., 4, 35, 127, 141

Wills, Gary, 82

Wilson, Douglas, 24–25, 102, 119–20, 126

Winger, Stewart, 25, 33, 34

working class people, 54

Young Men's Association (Bloomington, Illinois), 55

GORDON LEIDNER is an author of numerous articles and books about Abraham Lincoln and America's founding fathers. He has researched and analyzed the transformational leadership skills of Abraham Lincoln and Alexander Hamilton, the results of which have been published in academic journals and trade magazines. A past president of the Lincoln Group of the District of Columbia, he is currently on the board of directors of the Abraham Lincoln Institute and is the author of www.great americanhistory.net.